China's Energy Security

ANALYSIS, ASSESSMENT AND IMPROVEMENT

China's Energy Security

ANALYSIS, ASSESSMENT AND IMPROVEMENT

EDITOR

JINGZHENG REN

The Hong Kong Polytechnic University, Hong Kong

World Scientific

EW JERSEY • LONDON • SINGAPORE • BEIJING • SHANGHAI • HONG KONG • TAIPEI • CHENNAI • TOKYO

Published by

World Scientific Publishing Europe Ltd.

57 Shelton Street, Covent Garden, London WC2H 9HE

Head office: 5 Toh Tuck Link, Singapore 596224

USA office: 27 Warren Street, Suite 401-402, Hackensack, NJ 07601

Library of Congress Cataloging-in-Publication Data
Names: Ren, Jingzheng, editor.
Title: China's energy security : analysis, assessment and improvement /
Jingzheng Ren, The Hong Kong Polytechnic University, Hong Kong.
Description: USA : World Scientific, 2020. | Includes bibliographical references and index.
Identifiers: LCCN 2020029666 | ISBN 9781786349217 (hardcover) |
ISBN 9781786349224 (ebook) | ISBN 9781786349231 (ebook other)
Subjects: LCSH: Energy policy--China. | Energy security--China. |
Energy development--China. | Energy industries--China.
Classification: LCC HD9502.C62 R456 2020 | DDC 333.790951--dc23
LC record available at https://lccn.loc.gov/2020029666

British Library Cataloguing-in-Publication Data
A catalogue record for this book is available from the British Library.

For any available supplementary material, please visit
https://www.worldscientific.com/worldscibooks/10.1142/Q0270#t=suppl

Desk Editors: Aanand Jayaraman/Michael Beale/Shi Ying Koe

Typeset by Stallion Press
Email: enquiries@stallionpress.com

https://doi.org/10.1142/9781786349224_fmatter

Dedication

This book is dedicated to all the people who worked/are working in the energy field of China and brought/are bringing a sustainable future for us.

Also, to my teachers for their instruction and support.

https://doi.org/10.1142/9781786349224_fmatter

Preface

I was born and raised in a small town with a large coal mine (it was not actually large at all, but "large" in the mind of a little boy) that happened to be the most critical source of income for this small town. Since the age of seven, I had seen the long queue of trains transporting coal from our town to other cities almost every day. This is my first memory of the word "energy," and back then I only knew that energy is coal and coal is energy. I understood that energy was important to our town (especially for the quality of life and residential income) as well as other cities (industrial development and economic growth). As I was only a little boy, however, I did not understand the idea of energy security. Time is fleeting! I eventually visited the University of Aarhus and worked as a PhD researcher in 2014 under the supervision of Prof. Benjamin K. Sovacool, one of the top-tier experts on energy policy and energy security in the world. We worked together on papers focusing on the measurement and improvement of China's energy security, and the more I have worked on energy security, the more complicated it is becoming to me. My past work reveals that energy security is a multi-dimensional, multi-scale, and multi-perspective concept—dozens of factors can influence energy security. Moreover, these influential factors are not independent but usually interdependent and interactive. Energy security in China is further complicated by China's special requirements. China is a country that is home to about 1.4 billion people and more than 30 provinces, autonomous regions, direct-controlled municipalities, and special administrative regions; it has been one of the fastest-growing countries since 1978, and its GDP increased from $150 billion in 1978 to $12.24 trillion by 2017 according to the World Bank. Energy as the food of industry and society plays a significantly important role in China's industrialization, modernization, and civilization. Various kinds of countermeasures, actions, and policies have been implemented in China to solve the energy security crisis. Nevertheless, energy security remains a great challenge to China.

The coal mine near my hometown reduced its production capacity gradually with the development of new energy plans in China, and it is no longer the main source of income for our small town. I do not see the trains for coal transportation every day when I return to my hometown for summer vacation these days. However, this old coal mine reminded me of days gone past, but the scene is still fresh in my memory. Therefore, I decided to edit a book specially for China to rethink and redefine energy security. This book aims to present the methods of analysis, assessment, and improvement of energy security while investigating China's energy security based on the methods presented in this book. The methods and the implications contained within can be popularized to other countries as well.

This book is organized as follows: Chapter 1 analyzes the status quo, policies, and pathways of China's energy supply. Chapter 2 provides a comprehensive summary of the concept of energy security by conceptualizing and redefining it. Chapter 3 measures China's energy security performance using a bilevel approach including both national- and provincial-level analysis. Chapter 4 develops a multi-dimensional comprehensive and quantifiable energy security index for measuring China's energy security. Chapter 5 develops a quantitative energy security analysis method for measuring China's energy security from a subnational perspective. Chapter 6 develops a composite energy security index for measuring China's integrated energy security performances. Chapter 7 measures China's oil imports from the perspective of external suppliers. And Chapter 8 examines China's contributions and challenges on energy security from the perspective of multi-energy transition from fossil fuels to renewable energy.

Last but not least, I appreciate the work of the contributors of each chapter in this book as well as the assistance and help from World Scientific Publishing, especially from Natalie Watson, Shi Ying Koe, and Michael Beale during this whole journey.

Jingzheng Ren
Hong Kong SAR, China
May 2020

https://doi.org/10.1142/9781786349224_fmatter

About the Editor

Jingzheng Ren is an Assistant Professor of The Hong Kong Polytechnic University (PolyU), and he was also appointed as Honorary/Adjunct Associate Professor of University of Southern Denmark (Denmark) and Associated Senior Research Fellow of Institute for Security & Development Policy (Stockholm, Sweden). His research focuses on Engineering Operations Research for Energy, Environment and Sustainability. He has also authored/co-authored more than 150 peer-reviewed journal papers in the leading refereed SCI journals, authored 1 book published in Springer, edited 7 books published by Elsevier and Springer, and contributed more than 40 book chapters. Many of his papers have been selected as the Essential Science Indicators (ESI) top 1% highly cited papers or identified and highlighted as the key scientific article contributing to the excellence in energy research. He serves as the Editor of *Sustainable Production and Consumption* (Elsevier), Editor of the Book Series *Industrial Ecology and Environmental Management* (Springer), Associate Editor of *Environment, Development and Sustainability* (Springer), Specialty Chief Editor of *Frontier in Sustainability/Multi-criteria Decision Making*, Editor of *Journal of Environmental Engineering and Landscape Management*, previous

Associate Editor of *Journal of Renewable and Sustainable Energy* (AIP, 2016–2019), Associate Editor of *Renewable Energy & Sustainable Development*, Section Chief Editor of *Journal of Renewable Energy Research* and Guest Editor of several leading SCI indexed international journals.

https://doi.org/10.1142/9781786349224_fmatter

About the Contributors

Wuliyasu Bai is currently working as a Teaching Assistant in Xinyang Normal University, China. Her research fields include the management of resources and the environment, green mining, and green marketing. She has published several academic papers related to the evaluation of green mining and mineral security in China, financing models for hydrogen infrastructure, and China's energy consumption and economic growth.

John V. Bowlus is a researcher and Lecturer at the Center for Energy and Sustainable Development (CESD) at Kadir Has University in Istanbul. He received his PhD in History from Georgetown University, where he wrote his dissertation on the politics and economics of oil transportation in the Middle East. His research interests include oil, geopolitics, energy transitions, U.S. foreign policy, and the Middle East, and he has published academic articles in *The Historical Journal*, *Diplomatic History*, *Middle Eastern Studies*, and *Energy Research & Social Science*. Dr. Bowlus is also Editor-in-Chief of *Energy Reporters*, where he writes about historical and contemporary energy-related topics.

Nguyen Phuc Canh is a Senior Lecturer at School of Banking, University of Economics Ho Chi Minh City (UEH) and a Research Fellow at Leicester Institute of Advanced Studies, University of Leicester (UoL), the UK. He teaches several courses in Investment, Financial Statement Analysis, Macroeconomics, Institutions, and Macroeconomics. His research areas include Institutional Economics, Banking and Financial Economics, Tourism Economics, and Environmental Economics.

Dr. Nguyen has published in several peer-reviewed journals such as *Energy Policy*, *Climate and Development*, *Resources Policy*, *Economic Analysis and Policy*, *Finance Research Letters*, and *Research in International Business and Finance*. His current research interests are Energy Security, Shadow Economy, and Financial Economics in the Cryptocurrency Market.

Lichun Dong is Associate Head, School of Chemistry and Chemical Engineering, Chongqing University, China. His areas of specialization include optimization of sustainable industrial systems, energy management, resource conservation via process integration techniques, and synthesis and analysis of chemical processing and integration. Dr. Dong is well published, with over 100 papers with an h-index of 26. He has established international collaboration with researchers from various countries in Asia, Europe, and America.

Ahmet Faruk Dursun is a Master's candidate in the Energy and Sustainable Development Program at Kadir Has University in Istanbul, Turkey. His current research areas include energy mercantilism, the role of national oil companies in energy geopolitics, and transformations in the oil and gas industry.

Volkan Ş. Ediger's professional career has been shaped by research, teaching, and consultancy simultaneously carried out at the Research Center of the Turkish Petroleum Corporation, the Middle East Technical University, the Pennsylvania State University, and the Office of the President of the Republic of Turkey. Between 1998 and 2010, he was the first person to hold the position of the Energy Advisor to the President, where he had the chance to work with three successive presidents. Prof. Ediger is currently the Founding Director of Center for Energy and Sustainable Development (CESD) at the Kadir Has University, Istanbul, Turkey. His current research interests include all aspects of multi-energy transition, including energy security, geopolitics, and sustainable energy development.

Wei Hao is a Lecturer at the School of Economics and Finance, Massey University, New Zealand. Dr. Hao received her PhD from Massey University in 2016 and joined the university in 2017. One of her PhD thesis papers has been published in *Journal of Banking and*

Finance. Her current research interests lie in the areas of stock price informativeness, asset pricing, and corporate finance.

Yuzhuo Huang is a PhD student at the Graduate School of Fisheries and Environmental Sciences, Nagasaki University, Japan. He majors in Environmental Science. He received his MSc degree from Nagasaki University in 2020. His Master's thesis was titled "Urbanization's impacts on changes in CO_2 emissions in 30 provinces in China". He has also published one paper in the journal *Energies.*

Thai-Ha Le is the Director of Research and a Senior Faculty Member at Fulbright School of Public Policy and Management, Fulbright University, Vietnam. She holds a Bachelor of Arts (Hons) and PhD in Economics from Nanyang Technological University, Singapore, where she completed the requirements for her PhD in two years. Her primary fields of research include Energy Economics, Environmental Economics, and Applied Economics. Dr. Le is an active researcher who has published more than 30 scholarly research articles in international, peer-reviewed journals such as *Energy Economics*, *The Energy Journal*, *Energy Policy*, *Renewable Energy*, *Resources Policy*, *Economic Modelling*, *International Review of Financial Analysis*, *Empirical Economics*, *Applied Economics*, and *Emerging Markets Finance and Trade.*

She has consulted for Asian Development Bank (ADB) Headquarters and Economic Research Institute for ASEAN and East Asia (ERIA). Besides, Dr. Le is an affiliated research fellow at IPAG Business School in Paris, the third best French business school. She is also a recipient of multiple competitive research grants and fellowships such as the Pacific Trade and Development (PAFTAD) Fellowship for Young Scholars in 2013, the Public Diplomacy Federal Assistance Award by the U.S. Consulate General in Ho Chi Minh City, Vietnam's Public Affairs Section, in 2018, and the National Foundation for Science and Technology Development (NAFOSTED) funds for research in social sciences and humanities in 2019 as the principal investigator.

Caixia Li is a PhD student at the Graduate School of Fisheries and Environmental Sciences, Nagasaki University, Japan. She majors in Environmental Marine Science. During her undergraduate study at Shandong University of Technology and Industrial Economics, her majors were International Economics and Trade. She is now interested in agricultural economics, particularly focusing on agricultural development in Japan, which includes the impact of climate change on agricultural products, technical efficiency, and agricultural security.

Weichen Li is a PhD candidate in Chemical Engineering, Chongqing University, China. His current research areas include sustainability evaluation of process systems engineering, sustainability optimization of energy and chemical systems, and life cycle evaluation of industrial systems. His academic publications include several papers and a book chapter related to the energy systems.

Ken'ichi Matsumoto, born in 1982, is an Associate Professor at the Graduate School of Fisheries and Environmental Sciences, Nagasaki University, Japan. Before the current position, he was working at the University of Shiga Prefecture as an Assistant Professor and at the National Institute for Environmental Studies as a Research Associate. Also, he was a JSPS Research Fellow. He specializes in environmental/energy economics and policy. Particularly, he has worked on climate change and energy issues and the related policy analyses using computable general equilibrium models, agent-based models, and econometric methods. He has also contributed to developing the Representative Concentration Pathways for the Fifth IPCC Assessment Report. He has publications in high-impact journals including *Renewable and Sustainable Energy Reviews*, *Applied Energy*, *Energy Policy*, and *Climatic Change*. He has also co-edited a book titled *Economic Instruments to Combat Climate Change in Asian Countries*, published in 2015. He received his PhD in Policy Studies from Kwansei Gakuin University, Japan (2007) and MSc in Engineering from Waseda University, Japan (2004). Further details can be found on his website (https://www.matsumoto-lab.net/en).

Aliaksandr Novikau, PhD is currently working at the International University of Sarajevo, Bosnia and Herzegovina. His research interests include environmental policy and politics, nuclear and energy policy, environmental and risk communication, and environmental values. Dr. Novikau examines both enduring questions of regulatory politics as well as new topics that emerge because of the recent political, social, economic, and environmental transformations in a comparative perspective. His research efforts to date have resulted in several research articles and chapters in edited volumes.

Anting Wang is an undergraduate student at the Hong Kong Polytechnic University. She majors in Industrial and Systems Engineering and minors in Applied Mathematics. In terms of professional courses, she has taken subjects including Systems Modelling and Simulation, Industrial Engineering Techniques and Methods, Operations Research, etc. Apart from the courses, she also has a great interest in data analysis. She has participated in a project to analyze the sales situation of milk tea shops on the e-business platform Meituan-Dianping. Also, she was a participant in the Hong Kong mini competition for student competition of Global Grand Challenges Summit (GGCS 2019–2020).

Huijuan Xiao is a PhD student at the Hong Kong Polytechnic University. She specializes in China's energy and CO_2 emissions, focusing primarily on the accounting and evaluation of energy and CO_2 emissions performance at the city level.

Di Xu, PhD, is currently working at Chongqing University of Science & Technology, China. His research interests include sustainability in the context of process systems engineering, sustainable energy systems, and engineering operations research for industrial systems. Dr. Xu has worked on sustainability assessment/enhancement of hydrogen, ammonia, biofuels, and coal-to-chemical systems. He has also been actively involved in the development of decision-making tools and metrics/indicators in energy-related researches with the perspective of sustainability. His academic publications include dozens of papers related to the energy systems, two book chapters, "Introduction of Hydrogen Routines" by Academic Press (2017), and "A Composite Life Cycle Sustainability Index for Sustainability Prioritization of Industrial Systems" by Elsevier (2019).

Yingkui Yang received his PhD in Business Administration with an emphasis on green power marketing and is an Associate Professor in the Department of Sociology, Environmental and Business Economics, University of Southern Denmark. His current research areas focus on sustainable energy market integration and energy consumption. His research has been published in international academic journals, books, and conference proceedings. He has participated in EU energy projects such as "Energy at Sea" and projects financed by Danish energy authorities. He has also worked in close collaboration with large utility companies.

Mengqin Yu is currently a Master's student at the School of Business, Xinyang Normal University. His current research mainly focuses on energy strategy and policy and cooperative financial strategy.

Long Zhang, Assistant Professor in Xinyang Normal University, China, specializes in the management of resources and the environment, energy security and policy, sustainability evaluation and transition, as well as Multi-Criteria Decision-Making methods. Currently, Dr. Zhang focuses on the research area of economic and environmental sustainability. He has published dozens of academic papers in international academic journals including *Energy Policy, Energy, International Journal of Hydrogen Energy, Transportation Research Part A: Policy and Practice, Sustainable Energy,* etc.

Zhengnan Zhang, undergraduate, is an Industrial Systems engineering student at the Hong Kong Polytechnic University. In terms of professional courses, Systems Modelling and Simulation, Operation Research, and Electricity and Electronics have been taken.

https://doi.org/10.1142/9781786349224_fmatter

Contents

https://doi.org/10.1142/9781786349224_0001

Chapter 1

China's Energy Supply: Status Quo, Policies, and Pathways

Long Zhang[*,‡], Wuliyasu Bai[*,§], Mengqin Yu[*], and Jingzheng Ren[†,¶]

[*]School of Business, Xinyang Normal University, No. 237 Nanhu Road, Xinyang, 464000, China

[†]Department of Industrial and Systems Engineering, The Hong Kong Polytechnic University, Hong Kong SAR, China

[‡]hbzhanglong876@163.com

[§]wuliyasu666@163.com

[¶]jzhren@polyu.edu.hk

Abstract

China has been the largest energy consumer in the world for almost a decade and faces increasing pressure in terms of energy supply. By reviewing China's historical energy data since the reform and opening up, we analyzed the status quo of China from five aspects including growing external energy dependence, coal-dominated energy mix, regional imbalance between supply and demand, rapid development of renewable energy, and structural overcapacity. Then, we analyzed the evolution of China's energy strategy and policy since the reform and opening up, dividing it into three stages: diversification strategy focused on electricity (1981–2005), energy security strategy focused on energy conservation and efficiency (2005–2015), and transition strategy focused on low-carbon and clean energy (2015–Present). Over this history of near forty years, China's energy production and consumption has grown at a surprising speed, as did their dependence on external energy supplies. Energy intensity exhibited early fluctuations and a subsequent gradual decrease after the turbulence phase, and a diverse trend has been witnessed with the increasing growth of gas consumption and renewable energy capacity. Finally, this chapter proposes the future path for China's energy transition: diversification, low-carbonization, intellectualization, integration, and international cooperation, which offers some policy implications for shaping China's energy future.

Keywords: China; Energy supply; Energy strategy; Energy transition.

1. Introduction

Energy has been an increasingly important input for economic development with the deepening of industrialization and urbanization around the world, especially in emerging economies. In order to ensure sustainable energy supply, countries around the world have formulated national, regional, and even sectoral energy strategies one after another since the 1970s (Lovins, 1974; Franklin, 1991; Ishida, 2009; Schott and Campbell, 2013).

As the largest developing country worldwide, China has been faced with continuously increasing pressure in terms of energy supply for a few decades due to the explosive growth of its economy. Since the reform and opening up of China in the late 1970s, great changes have taken place in this country. Faced with the continuous and rapid growth of China's economy, the Gross Domestic Product in 2018 rose to 36 times its value in 1978 (National Bureau of Statistics of China, 2019), which stimulated the ever-growing demand for energy, especially primary energy. As a result, a series of problems have arisen: unplanned and crude exploitation of coal resources, coal-dominated energy consumption structure, stagnation in the development of unconventional fossil fuel, increasing dependence on foreign energy products and services, low efficiency of energy utilization, and large amounts of harmful and greenhouse gas emissions (Chen *et al.*, 2014; Wang *et al.*, 2016; Sun *et al.*, 2017; Tang *et al.*, 2018). Nowadays, China is the biggest energy consumer in the world, and has been so for more than a decade, overtaking the European Union in 2006 and the United States in 2009 (British Petroleum, 2019).

In order to acquire the necessary energy sources to maintain rapid economic growth, energy supply security has become one of the most important topics of interest to high-level policymakers. In fact, the energy industry has never been out of the purview of the Chinese central government since the establishment of the People's Republic of

China, and the focus of the energy policies in China has also undergone several changes (Leung, 2011; Zhang *et al.*, 2017a). In recent years, the supply-side reform of the economy has been implemented, and this has gradually penetrated into many sectors including the energy industry (Zhang *et al.*, 2018). As the basic and most strategic sector in Chinese economy, the supply-side reform of the energy industry is imperative. More importantly, the energy sector has fallen into a state of slow growth and intense pollution when China's economy entered the new normal stage (Wu *et al.*, 2017). What is more, a series of problems have built up during the long-term development of the energy industry, e.g., excess capacity, low efficiency of resource allocation, and outdated technology, all of which not just drag down the overall productivity of the energy sector but also affect the effectiveness and efficiency of the supply and demand system of the industry (Zhang *et al.*, 2017a, 2017b, 2018; Liu and Wang, 2015). Therefore, the future of China's energy security is still worth discussing.

Besides this Introduction section, the remainder of this chapter has been organized as follows: we will first analyze the status quo of China's energy supply and summarize the dilemma of China's energy security in Section 2. Then, we will investigate the evolution of China's energy policies since the reform and opening up in Section 3. Finally, in Section 4, the future pathways for ensuring China's energy supply security and energy transition are discussed.

2. Status Quo of China's Energy Supply

On the basis of the relationship between energy consumption and economic growth (as shown in Figure 1), China's historical energy consumption growth since the reform and opening up in 1978 can be divided into three phases. (1) The phase of steady growth from 1978 to 2000 saw a slow and almost synchronous increase in energy consumption and GDP. During this period, the energy consumption in China grew from 571 million tons of coal equivalent (TCE) to 1470 million TCE, at an annual growth rate of 4–5%, with slight stagnation and even slight decrease of energy consumption being observed at the end of this phase. (2) The second phase, from 2001 to 2014, was characterized by rapid growth of energy consumption as well as GDP, and the energy consumption increased about 10% annually.

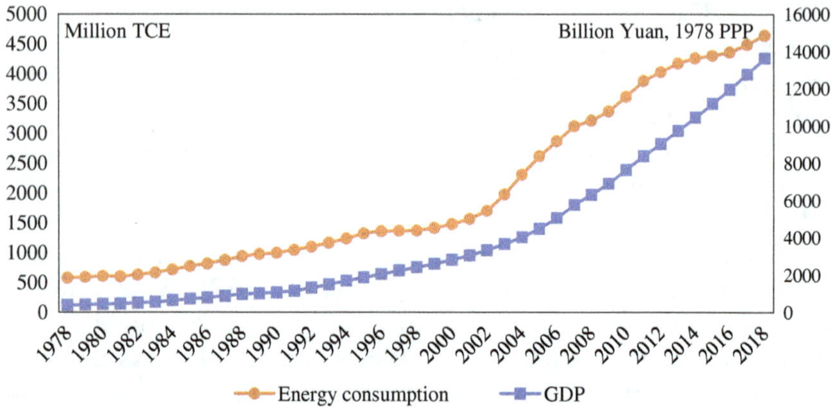

Figure 1: China's energy consumption and economic growth from 1978 to 2018. *Source*: China Statistical Yearbook; China Energy Statistical Yearbook.

(3) The latest phase of energy transition, which started in 2015, is still expected to continue for a few years. We noticed that energy consumption increase has slowed down significantly, with an annual growth rate of $2 \sim 3\%$. Although the economy has gradually stabilized in recent years, this still occurred faster than energy consumption did.

Owing to the dynamic growth of China's energy consumption, the energy supply in this country has also been significantly influenced. Thus, we have tried to analyze the features of China's energy supply during the past decades with the following five aspects.

2.1. *Growing external energy dependence*

As the third largest country by territory, China is richly endowed with energy resources. However, due to the large population, energy resource per capita seems to be in serious shortage. Although energy production in China has shown an obvious increase during the past several decades, the explosive growth of the national economy in recent decades has pushed the rapid increase in energy demand. As a result, the domestic energy supply can hardly meet the surging demand for energy. In order to plug the gap between energy demand and domestic production, the country has to increasingly depend on import of energy products from overseas.

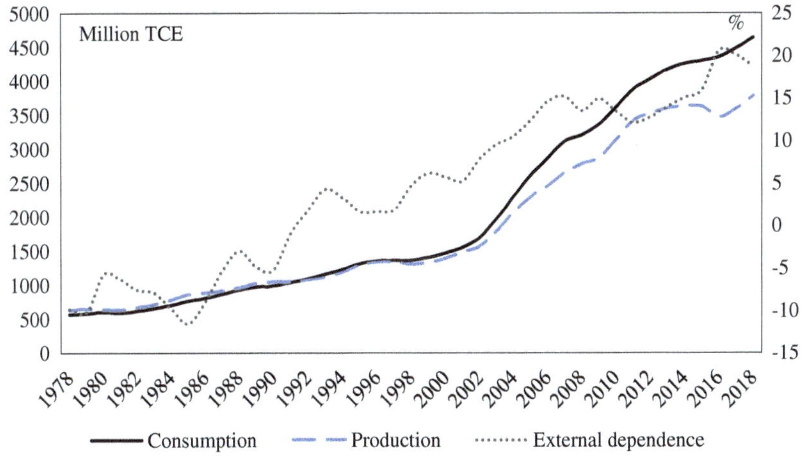

Figure 2: China's energy production, consumption, and dependence from 1978 to 2018.

Source: China Energy Statistical Yearbook.

Figure 2 presents a comparison between energy consumption and production in China, which was characterized by complete energy independence before 1992. After 1992, China has tried its best to meet its energy demand independently; however, five years later, all these efforts proved to be in vain as the gap between energy supply and demand kept expanding. From 1998 to 2018, China's dependence on external energy supply increased from less than 5% to 18.75%, even reaching the highest level of 20.6% and 20.1% in 2016 and 2017, respectively.

Nowadays, the increasing dependence on external energy supply has been a critical threat to China's energy security. Figure 3 shows China's dependence on external supplies of oil, natural gas and coal. As can be seen in the figure, before the 1990s, China could fully achieve energy independence. However, the turning point came in 1992, and since then, China's external energy dependence has kept rising. To be specific, oil has experienced the greatest growth in external dependence during the past decades. With the continuous discovery and of oil fields in northern and western China since the late 1950s, oil production in this country has experienced rapid and stable growth in the following decades. However, as energy consumption grew much faster than production, China gradually changed from

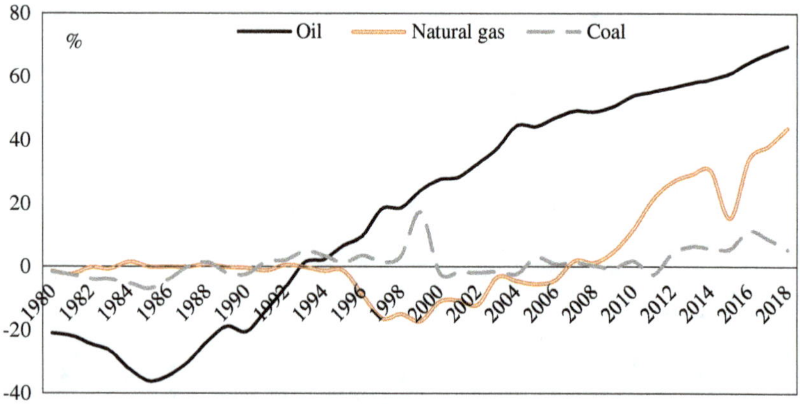

Figure 3: External dependence of China's fossil fuels from 1980 to 2018. *Source*:China Energy Statistical Yearbook.

being a net oil exporter to an being an importer in early 1990s. Since then, China's oil external dependence has grown sharply to the historically high level of more than 70% in less than 30 years. Natural gas, traditionally, played an dispensable role in China's energy structure before 2000, with a share of less than 2%, mainly due to scarce gas reserves and backward exploitation technology. Stepping into the 21st century, considering the sharp increase in energy demand, China gradually took on natural gas as a regular energy source and began to increase its share in the energy mix. Since then, however, domestic production is far from meeting the soaring demand. By the end of 2018, dependence on external gas sources even reached 45%—this was within a decade. As a leading energy source, coal used to be one of China's major export in terms of industrial products. However, the situation has permanently changed since 2012, when China became a regular net coal importer, and the external dependence is still rising in the following years.

2.2. *Coal-dominated energy mix*

A distinguishing feature of China's energy endowment is its rich sources of coal, but it has less reserves of oil and scarce sources of gas. According to the data from British Petroleum, by the end of 2018, China was home to 13.2% of world proved coal reserves, just

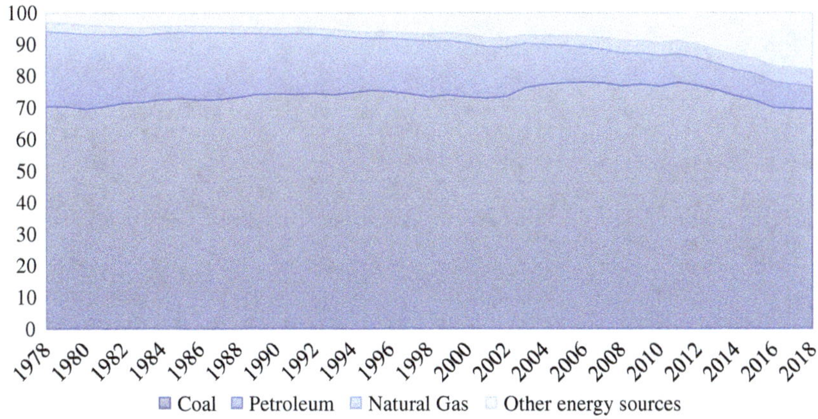

Figure 4: Share of different energy sources in China's energy production, 1978–2018.

Source: China Energy Statistical Yearbook.

behind the United States, Russia, and Australia (British Petroleum, 2019). However, it only accounts for 3.1% and 1.5% of oil and gas in the world total, ranking seventh and thirteenth in the world, respectively. This unbalanced energy endowment in China led to the energy mix being dominated by coal. Despite that, China is trying hard to diversify its energy mix by reducing the share of coal and increasing the share of natural gas and renewable energy.

The dynamic changes in different energy sources in China's energy production mix during the period of 1978–2018 are presented in Figure 4. From this figure, we can see that China's energy production is mainly supported by coal, the share of which in the energy production mix has never been less than 70%. In fact, coal saw a continuously increasing presence in China's energy production before 2011, by increasing its share from 70% to the highest level of 78% around 2010. However, this trend has changed since 2012, and the share dropped back to 70% in five years. Oil, an energy source for which China is highly dependent on imports, has seen a reduction of its share in total energy production from 24% to 7% during this period. By contrast, natural gas and other energy sources, like primary electricity from nuclear, hydro, wind, and solar power and biofuels, have penetrated China's energy market rapidly. Before 2005, the share of natural gas in China's total energy production had never

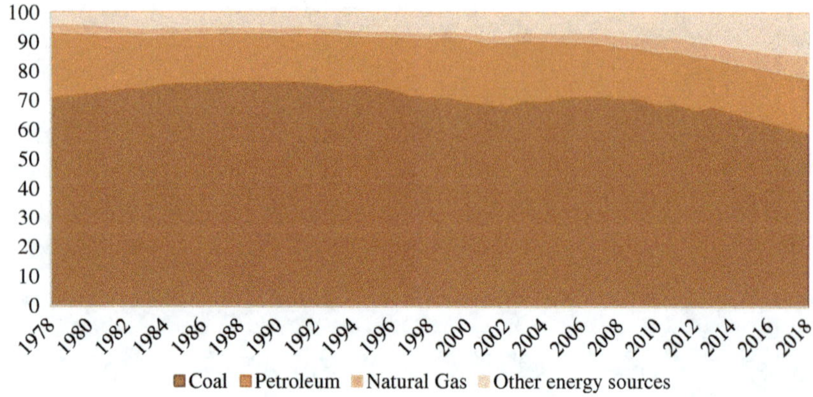

Figure 5: Share of different energy sources in China's energy consumption, 1978–2018.

Source: China Energy Statistical Yearbook.

exceeded 3%. After that, the national energy strategy was to expand gas production; thus, we witnessed the gradually increase of the share of natural gas in China's energy production after 2005. However, the share of natural gas has grown very slowly, only about 5% at present, mainly due to restrictions from limited economic recoverable reserves and significant difficulty in mining. On the other hand, we observe that primary electricity production from nuclear and renewable energy has presented an encouraging and dramatic rise, especially in the 2010s, with the share even reaching 18%.

In contrast, the share of different energy sources in China's energy consumption with respect to this period is been shown in Figure 5. The dominant position of coal in this energy mix can be clearly seen. We noticed that more than 70% of China's energy consumption was provided by coal before 2010; even as much as 76% in the late 1980s and early 1990s. After 2010, a decreasing trend has appeared, and this decreased rate has even been accelerating since 2015, when the Chinese government decided to reduce the capacity of coal production on a large scale (Wang *et al.*, 2019). Surprisingly, China has maintained a stable share of around 20% for oil use in the energy consumption mix during the past four decades of dramatic energy consumption growth. The share of natural gas in China's energy consumption has shown a similar trend, but the growing share in total energy consumption has been accelerating since 2010, and it finally accounted for 18% of the total energy consumption. Other energy sources, mainly primary electricity from nuclear sources and renewables, also followed the same path as did the ones early in China's energy production before it entered the new century. After that, their share gradually expanded from 6.4% in 2000 to 14.3% in 2018.

Both the energy production and consumption mix have revealed that China has always been highly dependent on coal to ensure energy supply, with a share of no less than 60% of the total primary energy supply, which is much higher than the global average, while oil and natural gas occupy 18.9% and 7.8%, respectively. By contrast, the world energy consumption mix is led by oil, with a share of 32%, followed by coal and natural gas at 27% and 22%, respectively (International Energy Agency, 2019). We can see that the world energy mix is more diversified and balanced than that in China. The good news is that China has put great efforts into diversifying its energy mix through a series of measures. For instance, the government has reduced 500 million tons of overcapacity in coal production during the 12th Five-Year Plan (FYP) (Zhang *et al.*, 2017a), constructed a series of cross-border natural gas pipelines and LNG terminals to increase the consumption of natural gas (Yong, 2017), and continued increasing investment in renewable energy on a large scale to stimulate the development of renewable energy (REN21, 2019). As a result of these policy actions, very good effects have been seen in the diversification of China's energy mix in recent years, as shown in Figure 5.

2.3. *Regional imbalance between energy supply and demand*

Imbalance between energy supply and demand is not only a problem in the world energy market but also exists within China. Energy resources on land in China are mainly located in the western and northern regions and are highly concentrated in some specific types of terrain. In fact, more than 75% of China's fossil fuel reserves are located the following six provinces in west and north China: Shanxi, Inner Mongolia, Xinjiang, Shannxi, Guizhou, and Henan, with Shanxi and Inner Mongolia being home to more than half of China's fossil fuel reserves (NBSC, 2019b). All of the top ten provincial energy producers in China are from the west or north part of the

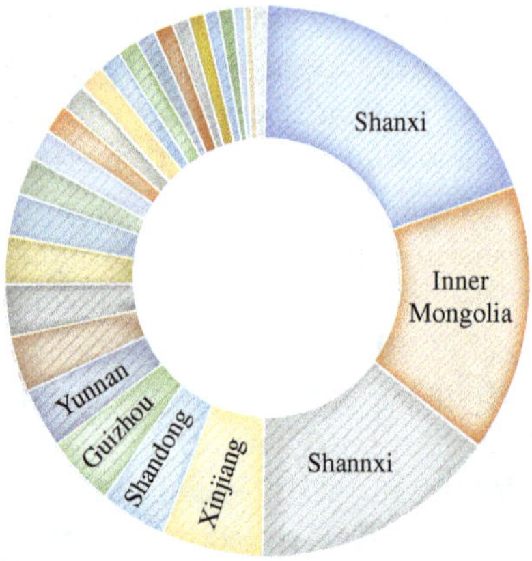

(a)

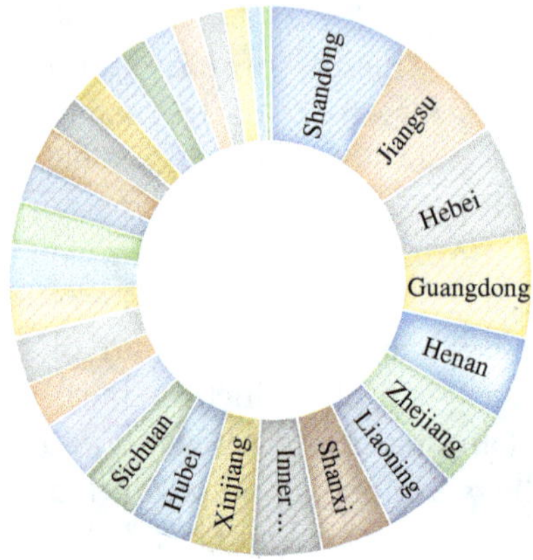

(b)

Figure 6: Provincial energy production (a) and consumption (b) in China in 2017.

Source: China Energy Statistical Yearbook; Provincial Statistical Yearbook.

country, and the top three provinces, Shanxi, Inner Mongolia, and Shannxi, account for 55% of China's energy production, as presented in Figure 6(a). By contrast, China's provincial energy consumers are not as disparate as the producers. The top five provincial consumers make up nearly 55% of China's total energy consumption, and there are six coastal provinces in the east as well, as shown in Figure 6(b). While Shanxi, Inner Mongolia, and Xinjiang are also among the top ten consumers, they mainly transform primary energy into secondaries, which are then sent to the eastern and southern provinces.

In fact, renewable energy also faces the same dilemma. Due to the specificities in geographical location and climatic conditions, northwest China also enjoys more sunshine and wind than other regions of this country, which gives it significant potential in developing solar photovoltaic (PV) and wind power. In 2019, the accumulated installed capacity of wind power in China reached 210 GW, and about 75% was contributed by fifteen northern provinces. Among the fifteen provinces with the most accumulated wind capacity, thirteen were from the north, except for Jiangsu and Yunnan. Although the situation with respect to the accumulated installed PV power capacity is a little different with more eastern coastal provinces ranking higher, more than 60% of the capacity came from the north and west

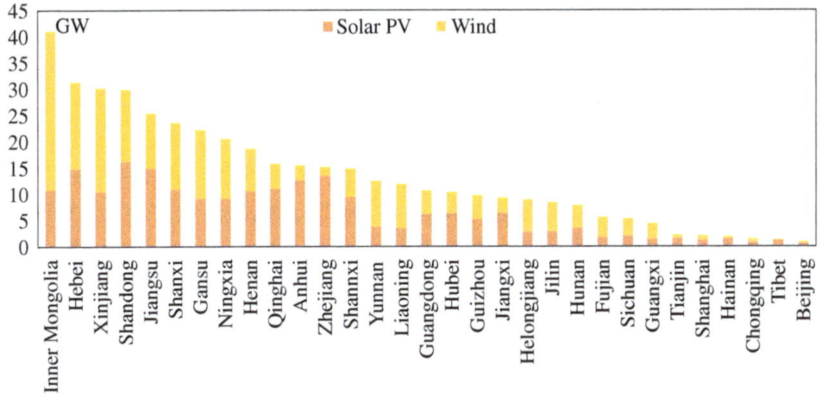

Figure 7: The accumulated wind and solar PV capacity of 31 provinces in China in 2019.

Source: China Energy Statistical Yearbook; Provincial Statistical Yearbook.

provinces. The accumulated installed wind and PV power capacity has been presented in Figure 7, from which we find that the top ten provinces have provided more than 60% of accumulated capacity. What is more, nine provinces of the top ten are located in the north, except Jiangsu, and this situation has intensified the regional disparity of China's energy resources.

In order to tackle the regional differences in energy resources, China has to transport energy products from western and northern China to the eastern and southern regions. However, the long transport distance has brought about several challenges. First, the capacity for shipping energy products is insufficient to meet the massive transportation demand. The largest energy exporters in China are Shanxi, Shannxi, Inner Mongolia, and Xinjiang, which are hundreds, even thousands, of kilometers away from the importers in eastern and northern China. In order to transfer energy products, special railways and pipelines have to be established. However, with the increase of the distance between the energy supply center and demand center, the problem of large-scale and long-distance coal transportation becomes more and more prominent (Liu, 2010). Railways carry more than 60% of China's coal transportation, and the average coal transport distance has increased to more than hundreds of kilometers (Zhang, 2018). Besides, the capacity for coal transportation has gradually saturated in recent years, and the contradiction between limited transportation capacity and expanding transportation demand is increasingly magnified (Mou and Li, 2012). What is more, long-distance transportation has caused high economic costs. For example, the cheapest way to move coal products from Datong in Shanxi Province to Guangzhou in Guangdong Province is through the coal transport-specific railway to Qinhuangdao Port in Hebei Province, followed by transfer to Guangzhou by sea. Even so, transportation costs and taxes account for 55–60% of the delivered price (Zhang, 2018). In addition, unreasonable transportation modes also lead to low transportation efficiency and large energy loss. China mainly uses railways for energy transportation; however, most trains in China are used for passenger and freight transport, as are the port terminals, thus leading to reduced capacity for energy transportation. In addition, the railway stations and ports face shortage of specialized handling equipment, thus leading to frequent energy loss and inefficiency in transit.

2.4. *Fast growing renewable energy*

Due to its cleanliness and inexhaustibility, renewable energy has been seen as the most promising energy source for the future (Panwar *et al.*, 2011). During the past decades, renewable energy has made great progress. The annual investment in renewable energy has increased from 39.5 billion USD in 2004 to 326 billion USD in 2018. During this period, the installed capacity of renewable energy power generation nearly tripled, increasing from 800 GW to 2378 GW, as shown in Figure 8 (REN 21, 2019). By the end of 2018, renewable energy occupies more than 11% of the world's total primary energy supply, and the electricity from renewables even accounts for 22.1% of the world's total electricity output (International Energy Agency, 2019).

Renewable energy development in China also shows tremendous growth. Stepping into the 2000s, China had already introduced a series of policies to support the development of renewable energy. Marked by the "Renewable Energy Law of the People's Republic of China" issued in 2005, China entered a new stage of vigorous development in renewable energy. Before that, renewable energy was mainly contributed by hydropower, while other renewables, including wind, solar, and bioenergy, did not receive enough attention due to

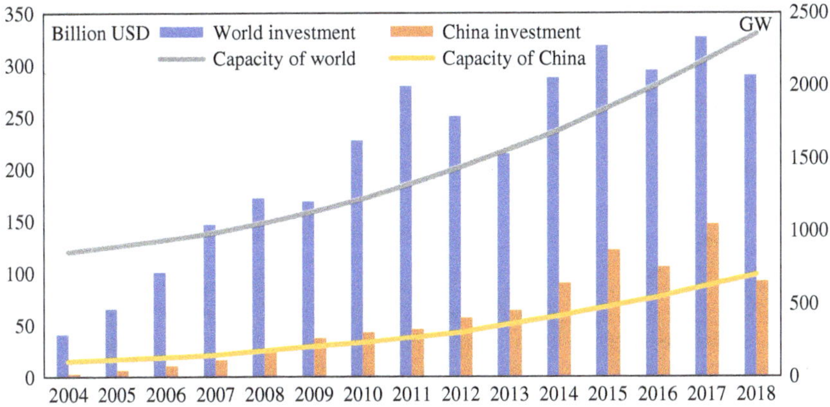

Figure 8: Renewable energy investment and accumulated capacity of the world and China, 2004–2018.
Source: Renewables: Global Status Report (REN21).

technical and economic infeasibility. Figure 8 shows the contribution of China in pushing renewable energy development at the world level. According to the data from International Renewable Agency, China has contributed about 1/3 of the world's total renewable energy investment per year and owns nearly 30% of the world's total accumulated installed renewable energy capacity. Also, more than 25% of electricity generated by renewables all over the world comes from China. In recent years, China has led the development of renewable energy on a global scale with its investment in renewable energy and installed capacity as well as electricity generation, both ranking first among all countries in worldwide rankings. The proportion of installed renewable energy capacity as a proportion of China's total energy generation capacity exceeds 25%. In a word, China has set a good example in enhancing energy sustainability.

2.5. *Structural overcapacity*

For a long time, China invested a great deal in fixed assets to support the fast-growing national economy, and the energy sector is an important field that has received significant attention from policymakers. As demonstrated in Figure 9, China's investment in fixed assets has been growing at an amazing speed since the reform and opening-up, especially in the 21st century. We note that fixed assets

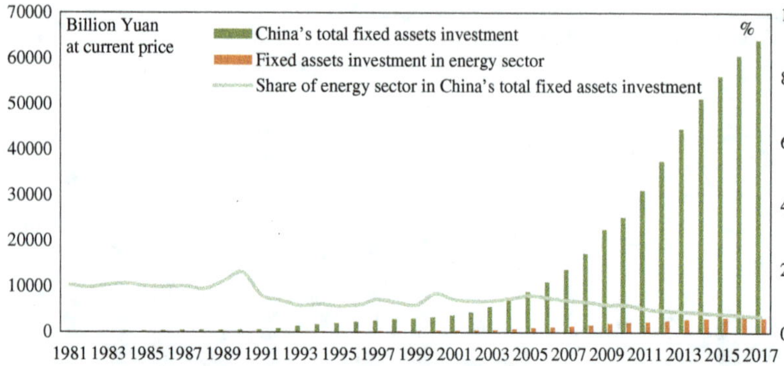

Figure 9: China's total investment in fixed assets from 1981 to 2017.
Source: China Statistical Yearbook.

investment in the energy sector also increased rapidly, while always maintaining a share of no less than 10% of China's total fixed assets investment before 2005, even hitting the historical record of nearly 19% in 1990. After that, although we have witnessed a decreasing share of added fixed assets investment in the energy sector, absolute investment still increased, which means the capacity for energy production has continued expanding.

Plenty of studies have been carried out to investigate China's overcapacity or capacity utilization in the energy sector, especially in the coal industry. For instance, Qiao and Song (2019) measured the overcapacity of China's coal enterprises during the period 1998–2013 by introducing productivity heterogeneity of coal enterprises into the traditional estimation framework of capacity utilization. Luo (2019) analyzed the national and provincial coal capacity of China from 2003 to 2016 using Data Envelopment Analysis. Feng *et al.* (2015) estimated the capacity utilization in China's coal sector during 1980 to 2013 with the help of the Data Envelopment Analysis. Wang *et al.* (2018) calculated capacity utilization in China from 1989 to 2016 by considering three different types of coal capacity usage types. Yang *et al.* (2019) summarized the excess capacity rate of China's coal industry during the period from 1995–2015. Ju & Wang (2019) also estimated capacity utilization in 24 coal-producing provinces and regions in China from 2001 to 2016 by using heterogeneous stochastic frontier analysis. The estimates of capacity utilization from these researches are shown in Figure 10.

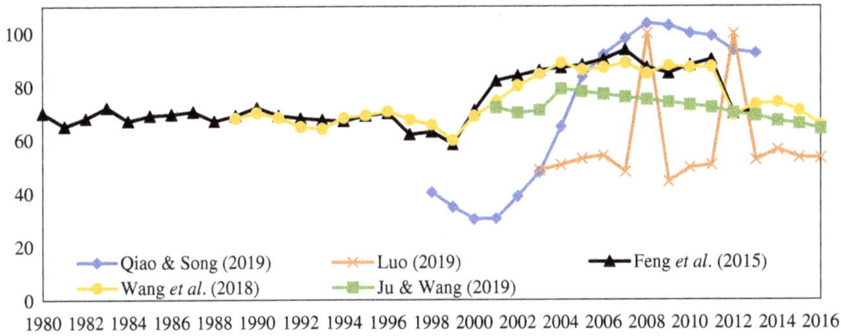

Figure 10: Capacity utilization of China's coal industry in some representative studies.

As can be seen from Figure 10, the curve of capacity utilization derived by Wang *et al.* (2018) almost coincides with the results of Feng *et al.* (2015), despite the fact that they have used different estimation methods. Although other scholars (Qiao and Song, 2019; Luo, 2019; Ju and Wang, 2019) have derived various specific values of coal capacity utilization in their studies from different perspectives and with different methods, we can still conclude some periodic characteristics of coal capacity in China over the past several decades. From 1980 to 1996, China maintained a capacity utilization around 70%, mainly due to the stable and moderate growth of the national economy (Feng *et al.*, 2015; Wang *et al.*, 2018). During the 1990s, the government encouraged the development of small coal mines in villages and towns, which led to the sharp increase of small coal mines. However, actual production from these small mines was far below their actual capacity due to their extensive exploitation and outdated technologies, which resulted in a decrease of capacity utilization and stagnation of coal enterprises in the late 1990s (Feng *et al.*, 2015; Wang *et al.*, 2018; Qiao and Song, 2019). From 2000, the Chinese government began to rectify the unreasonable operation in the coal industry by liberalizing the management of large state-owned coal mines, shutting down small coal mines and reducing coal productions, which dragged the energy industry gradually out of the trough. On the other hand, the Chinese economy entered the golden age of rapid development, and so the demand for coal products rose significantly, necessitating the quick increase of capacity utilization in China's coal industry (Qiao and Song, 2019; Luo, 2019;

Feng *et al.*, 2015; Wang *et al.*, 2018; Juan and Wang, 2019). From the early 2010s, the growth of demand for coal products declined due to the slowdown of economic growth and continuous deterioration of air quality, and so the capacity utilization dropped down again (Qiao and Song, 2019; Luo, 2019; Feng *et al.*, 2015; Wang *et al.*, 2018; Juan and Wang, 2019). This trend has also been proven by Yang *et al.* (2019), who believed that China has experienced undercapacity from 2000 to 2012, and overcapacity after 2014.

In fact, overcapacity has also existed in the oil industry for many years, not in crude oil production but in downstream industries, especially in oil refineries (Pan *et al.*, 2017). According to data from British Petroleum (2019), China's oil refining capacity has increased as much as six times from 1980 to 2018, and its share of the world's total refining capacity has grown from less than 0.7–15.6%, ranking second after the United States' 18.8%. However, China's oil refining capacity utilization has been kept at a level of about 65% since the late 1980s, which is 10–20% lower than the world average, and this was especially so during the period from 1994 to 2014 (as shown in Figure 11). Capacity utilizations of the United States and Japan were as high as 90% and 85% over the same period, respectively. With the increasing overcapacity in oil refining, some enterprises turned

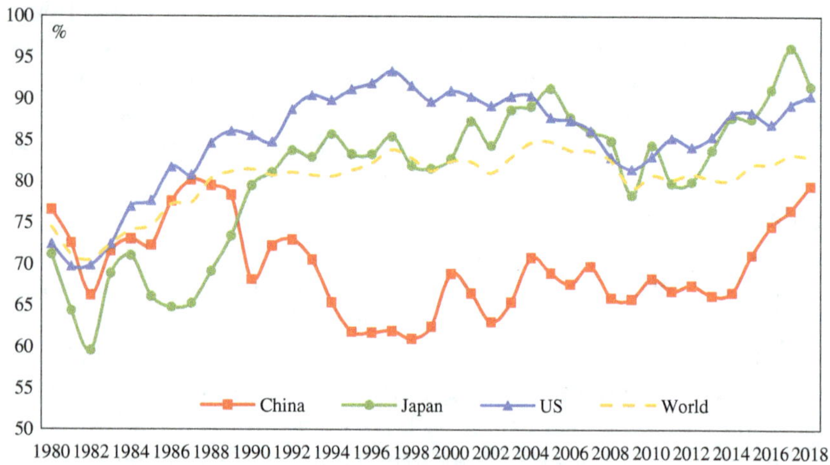

Figure 11: Oil refining capacity utilization in China, US, Japan and the world average.

Source: British Petroleum (2019) and BP World Energy Statistics (2019).

to investing in the chemical industry in 2015; hence, we can note the decrease and even stagnation in oil refining capacity since 2015 along with the sharp increase of refining capacity utilization following that. However, overcapacity was also seen in the chemical industry, despite the fact that China is still in deficit in the foreign trade of chemical products. For instance, the average capacity utilization in the carbon fiber industry has dropped below 40%, and only half the capacity has been utilized in the polyformaldehyde and superabsorbent resin sectors. In fact, excessive investment has been witnessed in plenty of chemical industries, e.g., synthetic plastics, synthetic rubber, synthetic fiber, paraxylene, propylene, polyurethane, general resin, caustic soda, calcium carbide, methanol, nitrogen fertilizer, urea, chloralkali, inorganic salt, etc. (An, 2016; CI Consulting, 2017; Forward Industrial Research Institute, 2018), whereas the demand for some other high-end chemical products such as fine chemicals and synthetic materials still rely on imports (An, 2016).

Overcapacity was not only seen in the production and processing of fossil fuels but also in the renewables industry (Bayaliyev *et al.*, 2011; Liu and Kokko, 2011; Kenderdine, 2017). In the upstream industries of the wind and solar photovoltaic power industry chain, overcapacity in the manufacturing of equipment and components such as polysilicon and wind turbines has existed for many years. For instance, the production of photovoltaic components in China has increased from 4.3 MW in 2001 to 178 GW in 2018, which accounts for more than 75% of the total world's production (Zhang *et al.*, 2016a; Wang, 2016). This massive capacity means China has to export most of its wind and photovoltaic components overseas. However, the overcapacity in wind and photovoltaic components is a global problem, and unsurprisingly, China has encountered investigations of anti-dumping and countervailing from the European Union, the United States, and even India (Xinhuanet, 2013; Sina, 2014; Ministry of Commerce of China, 2016). In the downstream sector, on the one hand, the installed capacity of renewable energy, mainly wind and solar photovoltaic power, increased rapidly. On the other hand, the capacity of the power grid for absorbing the electricity generated from wind and solar energy is really limited, and the price is much higher than electricity from fossil energy. Thus, the overcapacity of renewable power projects is a widespread phenomenon in China (Wang *et al.*, 2014; Zhang *et al.*, 2016b). Similarly, overcapacity has also been witnessed in the industry of new energy vehicles in China, mainly in the field of lithium supply (Shao and Jin, 2020). The global shipments of lithium batteries have increased from 1.08 GWh in 2011 to 62.35 GWh in 2017, and China has become a leader in the global lithium market, occupying more than 60% of the global market share (Olivetti *et al.*, 2017). In 2018, the overall capacity of battery power exceeded 200 GWh. However, only 40% of capacity has been utilized. Meanwhile, high-end battery power is in short supply, which indicates that serious structural overcapacity exists in China's battery power industry (Du *et al.*, 2017).

3. Evolution of China's Policy for Ensuring Energy Supply

The history of China's energy policy since the reform and opening up has experienced three different stages. The first stage was from 1980 to 1998, which followed the diversification strategy centered on electricity. After that, policy has shifted to an energy security strategy focused on energy conservation and efficiency from 1998 to 2015. With the rise of China's position in the international energy market and the rational economic growth in China, the stage of low-carbon and clean energy-oriented transition strategy began after 2015.

3.1. *Diversification strategy focused on electricity (1981–2005)*

After the reform and opening up, the Chinese leadership has realized the importance of the energy industry in supporting economic development. Therefore, China's national energy strategy has been adjusted to serve socialist modernization, and the policy for energy industry distribution has also been changed from a balanced strategy to a focused strategy (Liu, 1995). During the past decades, energy industries have been spread out across the whole country, especially in the undeveloped areas in central and western regions that have weak industrial infrastructure. Due to the focused strategy, the government started to reallocate the energy industries, mainly coal production, by establishing large-scale energy bases in the provinces located in the middle reaches of Yellow River, such as Shanxi, Shannxi, and Inner Mongolia (Shang *et al.*, 2017; Xiang *et al.*, 2017).

At the early stage of the reform and opening up, the proportion of primary energy that was converted into electricity as a share of China's total primary supply was stagnant at about 20%, while that in the member states of International Energy Agency were all above 30% (British Petroleum, 2019). In 1985, the Suggestions of the Central Committee of the Communist Party of China on Formulating the 7th FYP for National Economic and Social Development put forward the energy diversification strategy centered on electricity, which specified that the development of the energy industry should focus on electricity, significantly develop coal-fired power, vigorously exploit hydropower, and gradually develop nuclear power (Zhang *et al.*, 2017a).

During the following several FYPs, a large number of coal power plants were constructed in the major coal-producing areas, coastal provinces, and electricity load centers. As the pillar industry in China's energy sector, the coal industry in China has experienced a boom in growth, mainly due to the liberalization of the energy market. Before the reform and opening up, China implemented a multi-level management system in the coal industry, with the coal products being distributed by national, provincial, municipal, and town governments according to the administrative bodies of the coal mines. In the early 1980s, the trend of declining industrial concentration arose in China, especially in the energy sector. Due to the short supply of energy products, an upsurge in coal mining has crept across the country, with minor coal mines flourishing in small towns all over China. In addition, after the mid-1980s, entry barriers to the coal industry have been greatly reduced, including the qualification examination and approval, minimum investment thresholds, requirements for mining technology and recovery, etc. Moreover, local governments have issued many licenses in order to increase tax revenue and promote employment. Consequently, the number of small coal mines has grown at an alarming rate.

In order to improve energy structure, the policy of reducing oil burning and replacing oil with coal has been implemented all over the country, with further attempts to strengthen the exploration and development of natural gas. Besides, the development of nuclear and renewable energy has also been proposed to diversify the energy mix, and a number of large hydropower stations have been established in the middle and upper reaches of the Yellow River and

Yangtze River as well as their branches, as well as a batch of middle and small hydropower stations in the northeast and east part of China (Xie, 2006). The establishment of nuclear power plants has also made led to great breakthroughs with the operation of Qingshan and Dayawan nuclear power stations in 1991 and 1994, respectively. With the implementation of an electricity-focused energy strategy, the share of electricity (including primary and secondary) in China's total energy consumption grew from 21% in 1985 to more than 37% in 2000, which has greatly reduced the pressure of power supply and supported the adjustment and improvement of industry structure in China.

3.2. *Energy security strategy focused on energy conservation and efficiency (2005–2015)*

In the 1990s, China's energy supply was faced with new problems. On the one hand, serious overcapacity existed in coal production, and the average capacity utilization was stuck at around 70%, even dropping to 65% in the late 1990s, as shown in Figure 10. On the other hand, China became a net oil importer in 1993, and net oil imports increased, surprisingly, year-on-year. By the end of the 2000s, China had imported 60 million tons of crude oil, about 26.7% of its total oil consumption. Besides, long-term extensive economic development caused serious environmental problems, leading to the unsustainability of the national economy (Zhang and Wen, 2008; Chen, 2015). Therefore, energy security became a new issue troubling China's energy supply. In order to protect China's energy security, the Department of Geology and Minerals proposed China's global energy strategy aimed at ensuring long-term, secure and stable energy supply in China. This strategy consisted of three sub-systems (Zhu, 2003). The sub-system of domestic energy supply took coal as the main energy source and diversified the energy mix by including coal, oil, natural gas, hydropower, nuclear power, and other renewable energy sources. The sub-system of foreign energy supply was a comprehensive multi-channel supply system combining international energy trade and direct investment. The strategic energy reserve system took the state as the leading role and included physical energy reserve and proven reserves. During this period, the Chinese government had four main policies to solve the challenges brought about by the energy supply security problems. First and foremost, China's reliance on domestic energy supply to meet energy demand and being energy independent as much as possible. Second, more efforts for increasing domestic energy production as well as energy conservation. Third, renewables energy playing a more important role in increasing domestic energy supply. Lastly, strengthening international collaboration with the main energy-producing and -consuming countries.

Due to the liberalization of the energy market in the1980s, a batch of minor coal mines appeared, exploiting coal resources destructively by grabbing high-quality fat coals and abandoning lean ones without any measures to protect the environment (Shen and Andrews-Speed, 2001; Shi, 2013; Chen, 2015). Thus, these minor coal mines won in the competition with state-owned coal mines due to the low costs brought about by extensive production, resulting in severe waste of resources, overcapacity, as well as a large number of casualties in coal mine accidents. In order to shake up the coal industry and protect the benefits of large state-owned coal mines, the central government has begun to close down some small coal mines and control the total coal outputs since the early 1990s, but this turned out to be a failure due to the inappropriate and rigid management system of state-owned coal mines (Andrews-Speed *et al.*, 2003). This situation finally changed at the end of 1998, when the State Council of China announced the most severe regulation on small coal mines in history, wherein it decided to shut down 258,000 illegal and unsuitable coal mines, cutting down 250 million tons of coal production. This policy has been strengthened in the following years, and immediate results were achieved (Andrews-Speed *et al.*, 2005). The state-owned coal mines have used their capacity more efficiently since then and gradually turned profitable. More importantly, the situation of disordered competition in the coal industry has been stopped, and coal production has increased steadily (Shen *et al.*, 2011).

Oil has become an increasingly important energy source for China owing to its remarkable economic growth. However, secure oil supply has become an important issue since the early 1990s when China became a net oil importer. The dependence on external oil supply has growing since then, as shown in Figure 3. Under the new energy strategy, while developing domestic oil and gas resources, more Chinese petroleum enterprises entered the international oil market to acquire the necessary oil products. (Xie, 2006). In order to deal with energy supply security issues, a series of measures have been taken, for instance promoting the research and utilization of alternative oil resources; reducing unnecessary oil consumption; advocating oil-saving living and consumption; implementing energy diversification strategies, including diversified import sources, oil products, accesses, transportation routes, etc.; creating a peaceful international environment for acquiring foreign oil resources by comprehensively using political, economic, diplomatic, and military efforts; encouraging Chinese enterprises to invest in other countries to get a greater share of overseas oil resources; expanding the openness of the domestic market; and strengthening cooperation with oil-producing countries and multinational corporations.

Renewable energy has been considered the most promising energy sources for the future, and China has made great progress in this regard. In 2006, the Renewable Energy Law was put into force, and started the engine of China's renewable energy development, especially wind and photovoltaic power (Schuman and Lin, 2012). The achievements of China's renewable energy development were obtained mainly due to the strong policies of the Chinese government. First, China has set ambitious goals for renewable energy development. In 2007, the Mid- and Long-Term Development Plan for Renewable Energy (NEA, 2007) was published, proposing that China would increase the share of renewables in total energy consumption to 10% and 15% in 2010 and 2020, respectively, even specifying the capacity goal for each renewable energy source. However, due to the lack of monitoring and compliance requirements, none of these goals were achieved by 2010 (Lo, 2014). To address these problems, an improvement plan, the 12th FYP for Renewable Energy Development, was released in 2012, which set a more conservative goal of 9.5% of renewables in total energy consumption by 2015 and also defined the particular targets for different energy sources. The Chinese government even attended the Paris Summit on Global Climate Change (NEA, 2012). With the booming development of China's renewable energy industry, the Chinese government promised to increase the share of non-fossil fuels in total primary energy supply to 20% at the 2015 Paris Summit on Global Climate Change (Zhou *et al.*, 2019). Besides these steps, another universal policy, feed-in tariff, was even introduced as early as 2003. At the very beginning, the tariff amount was determined on a case-by-case basis through bidding or negotiation, and then baseline prices were set for wind power in 2009 and for solar power in 2011 (NDRC, 2011; Hu *et al.*, 2012). The feed-in tariffs have been adjusted several times according to the practice of renewable energy development in China. In order to encourage the deployment of renewable energy projects, the Chinese government provided generous subsidies to wind and photovoltaic power enterprises in 2009. Considering the declining costs, the subsides followed a slope subsidization mechanism (Ministry of Finance and Ministry of Housing and Urban-Rural Development of China, 2009). In addition, there are also other regulatory policies, fiscal incentives, and public financing policies that have been widely used in China to stimulate the development of renewable energy, e.g., quota obligation in electric utility, transport and heating, tendering, investment or production tax credits, reductions in taxes, and public investment, loans, or grants.

3.3. *Transition strategy focused on low-carbon and clean energy (2015–present)*

Stepping into the 2010s, China's booming economy gradually slowed down, and economic growth fell to the lowest level of 6.9% in the 25-year period, even declining to 6.1% in 2019 (NBSC, 2020). In fact, China's Present Xi proposed the term "new normal" to describe the future trend of China's economy even in 2014 (Zhang, 2015). In this new normal economy, the growth would maintain a medium-high speed, the economic structure would keep improving, and the economic driving force would turn from factors and investment to technology and innovation. Correspondingly, the energy strategy gradually transited away from the fossil energy (mainly coal)-centered system to a more diversified and clean energy system (Zhang *et al.*, 2017a). In addition, China has faced unprecedented levels of air pollution due to massive consumption of coal, and it was imperative for China to undergo a sustainable and clean energy transition (You and Xu, 2010; Wang and Hao, 2012; Hao *et al.*, 2015; Zou *et al.*, 2016).

China's coal production and consumption have begun to decrease from 2014, and despite the returned increase in 2017 and 2018, the levels are still lower than that in 2014. The gradual decline of economic growth led to the shrinking demand for traditional industrial materials, in particular coal, cement, and steel, resulting in severe overcapacity (Zhang *et al.*, 2017a). In fact, the coal capacity has been reduced by more than 500 million tons in the 12th FYP, and the State Council has decided to eliminate another 500 million tons of coal capacity and consolidate to a final 500 million tons of capacity before 2020 (Zhang *et al.*, 2017a). According to the data from the China Coal Industry Association, China has already cut down or consolidated about 810 million tons of coal capacity between 2016 and 2018.

Another obvious change that happened to China's energy system was caused by oil and natural gas. As the second-largest contributor to China's energy mix, oil maintained a relatively stable proportion of about 20% of the total energy mix. China's oil production has increased very slowly since 2005, while the consumption was growing at an amazing speed, resulting in the dependence on external oil supply increasing significantly, even reaching the historically high level of more than 70% in 2019. As a low-carbon and efficient fossil energy source, natural gas did not play an important role in China's energy system traditionally. However, this situation has changed since the 2010s and the Chinese government has started to practice "The Scientific Outlook on Development," which is consistent with sustainable development in connotation. Since then, a faster-growing increase in natural gas's proportion in China's energy consumption has been witnessed—it has risen from 4.4% in 2010 to 7.8% in 2018. Due to the limited economic recoverable reserves of natural gas, gas production failed to catch up with the rolling growth of gas consumption, and China gradually turned from an almost gas self-sufficient state before 2010 to a net gas importer with an external dependence of more than 45% in 2019. In order to ensure energy security, and reduce the negative effect of unexpected interruption of external oil and gas supply, a diversification strategy has been opted. According to data from World Trade Organization, more than 70 countries around the world have exported crude oil to China since 1995, and about half of them have been considered China's regular oil-importing sources, providing more than 99% of China's oil imports. This diversification of importing sources has also been reflected in the external gas supply of China, seeing as how China has imported gas from more than 30 countries. Before 2010, China mostly relied on liquified natural gas (LNG) imports from Australia.

With the operation of the Central Asia–China gas pipelines in 2010 and the Myanmar–China oil and gas pipelines in 2013, pipeline natural gas (PNG) has taken up 40–50% of China's total gas import, and this proportion can be expected to reach even higher when the Russia–China gas pipelines and the fourth route of the Central Asia–China gas pipelines, are put into operations in 2019 and 2021, respectively.

The most obvious transition has happened in the renewable industry sector. After experiencing a significant leading growth, renewable power abandonment and temporary overcapacity have become the main obstacles to the further development of China's renewable energy industry (Wang and Li, 2016). Thus, the investment in renewables gradually slowed down, and even shrank after 2015 (Wang *et al.*, 2020). In order to solve the problem of wind power curtailment, the NDRC (2015) issued the Provisional Announcement on Launching a Pilot Project for the Immediate Consumption of Renewable Energy, which tried to carry out the pilot project of nearby renewable energy consumption in Inner Mongolia and Gansu. In 2016, the Management Measures on Fully Guaranteed Acquisition of Renewable Energy Power (NDRC, 2016) was released, which specified that power grid enterprises should purchase on-grid electricity from renewable power projects within the planned geographical area based on the benchmark electricity price and guaranteed utilization hours determined by the state. In addition to immediate consumption and guaranteed acquisition, the NEA also issued the Guiding Opinions on Establishing a Target Guiding System for the Development and Utilization of Renewable Energy that year, which clearly defined that in all power generation enterprises (not including specialized non-fossil energy enterprises), at least 9% of the total power generation should be provided by non-hydro renewable power by 2020, and this can be accomplished through a certificate transaction system. In 2017, the NDRC, MOF, and NEA (2017) jointly published the Notice on the Implementation of the Legal and Voluntary Subscription and Trading System for Renewable and Green Power Certificates and try to establish a certificate subscription system for renewable power and promote the effective utilization of green and clean energy. The NEA also published monitoring and warning reports on wind power investment to ensure reasonable wind power investment from 2017.

4. Pathways for China's Sustainable Energy Supply

Coal will still play a dominant role in China's energy mix and, in the foreseeable future, oil and natural gas supply will suffer from a high external dependence, while renewable energy sources now possess the best ever chance to distinguish themselves by improving China's energy security. The future path of China's energy transition should be diversification, low carbonization, intellectualization and marketization, integration, and international cooperation.

(1) **Diversification:** A diversification strategy is the most effective path for China to enhance its energy security. Due to its low cost and abundant reserves, coal has dominated China's energy mix over the past several decades, with a share of not less than 65%. In order to enhance China's energy security, renewable energy can carry some of the share that coal now occupies in China's energy system. Although renewable energy has made great progress in China, and the problem of renewable power abandonment has mostly improved, subsidies for renewable energy projects have faced increasing shortages. Despite the fact that China has increased the renewable energy tariff surcharges several times, this shortage is expected to reach 203 billion USD by 2035 (Beijixing, 2019). With the advancement of technology and industrial development, renewable energy costs have fallen significantly. The 13th FYP for Renewable Energy Development proposed that by 2020, wind power prices should fall to the level of the local coal-fired power, and photovoltaic power prices should fall to the level of the selling price of grid enterprises. Therefore, it is necessary to adjust the benchmark prices and subsidy policies in a timely and appropriate manner. In order to promote the consumption of renewable power, a greater scope of quota system implementation, which can be accomplished through actual consumption of renewable power, subscription for green certificate of renewable power, and even quota purchase in the trading market, are matters of great urgency. Although the NEA has tried to collect public ideas about this quota system several times, there is still a long waiting period before this policy can be officially issued. Moreover, small renewable energy power projects can be constructed flexibly in remote rural areas and

independent communities through the distribution of energy supplies, which can not only meet various energy demands locally but also improve rural energy self-sufficiency, and even produce profits by accessing the national power grid.

(2) **Low-carbonization:** A low-carbonization path is preferable than simple decarbonization, as coal will remain a major energy source during this transition. Owning to the low energy density and strong seasonality of renewable energy, the transition from coal to renewable energy is bound to be difficult and lengthy. Thus, a reliable and affordable transitional energy source is needed, and coal could play this role in China's energy system. The experiences of Germany and Japan, who have been recognized as leaders in energy transition, also indicate the transitional role of coal in energy transition, as it occupies a share of 20-30% of the total primary energy supply. Even so, a gradual supply-side reform is an urgent need. To be specific, the government needs to set a binding overall target and schedule for coal consumption in the medium and long term, and break it down to all regions, departments, and industries. Besides, a series of financial and fiscal instruments, e.g., price, tax, and carbon trading system, should be implemented to internalize the external costs (carbon emission and air pollution) from fossil fuel energy consumption, in particular coal, and all kinds of hidden subsidies should be eliminated to increase the costs of coal consumption, and gradually reduce the proportion of coal in China's energy mix. Under the trend of coal electrification, the transitional policy should also focus on coal-fired power plants, e.g., strictly restricting the installation of new coal-fired power capacity, eliminating the low-efficiency thermal power plants, and upgrading the existing coal power units. At the same time, the research and promotion of technologies for safe, green, and efficient coal production, conversion, and utilization need to be accomplished to reduce the negative effects of coal consumption.

(3) **Intellectualization and marketization:** Intellectualization and marketization reform of the power system can improve the resilience of the energy system. At present, the electricity market in China is mainly planned and dispatched, and the rigid power plan of thermal power units has limited the space for renewable power. Thus, a more flexible and marginal cost-based dispatching

should be adopted, where different power sources access the grid according to their marginal costs in ascending order. Obviously, renewable power has the lowest marginal costs and priority to access the power grid. Another barrier is the segmented regional, even provincial, power markets in China, which are self-contained, self-balancing, and relatively closed. The eastern and southern regions are the main power demanders, with plenty of power plants producing intense air pollution while still facing great pressure in the supply of power. By contrast, the western region has abundant energy sources, both fossil fuels and renewables, and low power load and capacity utilization. Thus, it is difficult to effectively dispatch and trade renewable power inter-provincially under the existing provincial market structure and planned dispatching system. Hence, marketization reform should be conducted to promote a nationwide power market to break the provincial, regional, and corporate monopolies and establish a national coordination mechanism for power system planning, power structure adjustment, and power grid establishment. Besides, the intellectualization of the power system can enhance its flexibility. On the power generation side, the current system has very few flexible power sources and the technical scheme and operation mode need upgradation. On the demand side, management and response mechanisms such as time-of-use prices have not yet been established. Because of the intermittent fluctuation of renewable power generation, a more flexible power system should be established to increase the resilience for dissipation and the ability for peak shaving. Therefore, it is necessary to improve the flexibility of thermal power units by establishing a compensation mechanism and conducting technological upgrades.

(4) **Integration:** Comprehensive utilization through integration and technological innovation can help improve energy efficiency. China has already been the largest energy consumer of the world for a decade, and its energy demand will keep increasing with the accelerating process of industrialization and urbanization in the near future. In order to ensure energy security, this growth needs to be well managed by improving energy efficiency, which can be achieved through comprehensive utilization and integration. Presently, different energy sectors in China, including the

power system, heating system, coal sector, oil sector, and gas sector, are basically planned, designed, and operated independently, and so lack inter-sector coordination and mutual transformation. In order to improve energy efficiency, an effective method is integration, such as coordination with combined cooling heating and power system (CCHP) and coal-electricity integration. Traditionally, the CCHP system has already been used in thermal power plants that transmit the waste heat to the heating network to provide heating and cooling services for residents. With the promotion of renewable energy, this type of hybrid energy system is also applicable to renewable power systems. Then based on the performance of different energy sources, the CCHP system with fossil fuels can be effectively associated and intelligently controlled with renewable power units, and the CCHP system can even just play the role of peak shaving when the wind and solar power are sufficient. When the heat from CCHP cannot meet the heating demand, it could be supplemented by electric heating or with a heat pump driven by renewable power. Coal-electricity integration is another energy policy that has been proposed for more than a decade; nevertheless, several attempts turned out to be difficult to implement on a large scale, mainly due to industry barriers, shortsightedness, and focus on short-term interests. Even so, coal-electricity integration is conducive to reducing the transaction costs for both parties, resisting the risk of market fluctuations, and developing a circular mining economy. In order to improve the comprehensive utilization of energy, both financial and non-financial policies are needed. Financial incentives, including fiscal subsidies, financial discounts, and tax reductions, can be provided to enterprises and individuals to promote energy efficiency improvement. Non-financial policies, mainly legislative instruments, which take environment protection, climate change mitigation, energy conservation, and efficiency improvement into consideration, and involve coordination between the central and local governments, needs to be established to form a complete and efficient policy and standard system.

(5) **International cooperation:** International cooperation should be enhanced to improve energy supply security by integration with the global energy industry chain. In fact, the Belt and Road Initiative has already provided a good platform for China

to participate in the global energy industry. In the coal sector, overcapacity does not just exist in coal production, but also in the geological exploration, design, and construction of coal mines, and even equipment, which can be used to invest in foreign coal resources in South East Asia, South Asia, and even Australia. As the biggest oil and gas importer around the world, China has faced great risks of unexpected disruption of oil and gas. Thus, the foreign investment of China's energy enterprises and cooperation with international energy giants can help provide a reliable energy supply and enhance the international competitiveness of Chinese enterprises. In fact, this foreign investment has already made great achievements, and the massive oil and gas imports from Central Asia and Russia are the best evidence for this. In fact, the most needed international cooperation for China lies in the field of renewable energy. Despite the fact that China has the largest renewable energy capacity in the world, the core components of renewable power equipment rely mainly on imports, and the renewable energy policies are not as effective as in some European countries. We shall learn the foreign experiences in promoting renewable energy development; strengthening international cooperation in energy technology, equipment, and engineering services; and promoting the digestion, absorption, and innovation of key technologies. At the same time, China needs to actively participate in global energy governance, such as in major international energy affairs and during meetings discussing the formation of rules, and the construction of global energy networks with various international and regional energy institutions.

Acknowledgments

This research was funded by the Philosophy and Social Science Planning Program in Henan Province, China (2020CJJ094), the Key R&D and Promotion Program (Soft Science Research) in Henan Province, China (202400410068), the Key Scientific Research Project of Colleges and Universities in Henan Province, China (19A790020), research project of Social Sciences Association in Henan Province, China (SKL-2020-2418), and the Nanhu Scholars Program for Young Scholars of XYNU, China.

References

An, P. 2016. Overcapacity, why import in large quantities? – Structural contradictions in the petroleum and petrochemical industry are outstanding and need to be transformed. (产能过剩, 为何大量进口?—石油石化行业结构性矛盾突出亟待转型). *Chemical Management*, 2016 (4), 36. (In Chinese).

Andrews-Speed, P., Yang, M., Shen, L. and Cao, S. 2003. The regulation of China's township and village coal mines: A study of complexity and ineffectiveness. *Journal of Cleaner Production*, 11(2), 185–196.

Andrews-Speed, P., Ma, G., Shao, B., and Liao, C. 2005. Economic responses to the closure of small-scale coal mines in Chongqing, China. *Resource Policy*, 30(1), 39–54.

Bayaliyev, A., Kalloz, J. and Robinson, M. 2011. *Chinas Solar Policy: Subsidies, Manufacturing Overcapacity & Opportunities*. USA: The George Washington University.

Beijixing. 2019. *25 years? How long will China's renewable energy subsidy funding gap continue.* (*25年?中国可再生能源补贴资金缺口将持续多久*). Available at: http://news.bjx.com.cn/html/20190710/991736.shtml (accessed 25 March 2020). (In Chinese).

British Petroleum. 2019. *BP Statistical Review of World Energy*. London: BP (Published 2019). Available at: https://www.bp.com/en/global/corporate/energy-economics/statistical-review-of-world-energy/downloads.html (accessed 10 January 2020).

Chen, J., Liu, G., Kang, Y., Wu, B., Sun, R., Zhou, C. and Wu, D. 2014. Coal utilization in China: environmental impacts and human health. *Environmental Geochemistry and Health*, 36(4), 735–753.

Chen, S. 2015. Environmental pollution emissions, regional productivity growth and ecological economic development in China. *China Economic Review*, 35(35), 171–182.

CI Consulting. 2017. *The development of the petrochemical industry is gradually maturing, and overcapacity has been increasing.* (*石油化工行业发展逐步成熟产能过剩局面已日益加剧*). Available at: http://www.ocn.com.cn/chanye/201706/sceoo21090634.shtml (accessed 22 March 2020). (In Chinese).

Du, J., Ouyang, M. and Chen, J. 2017. Prospects for Chinese electric vehicle technologies in 2016–2020: Ambition and rationality. *Energy*, 120, 584–596.

Feng, D., Wang, S. and Cui, C. 2015. Empirical research for coal industry capacity utilization rate estimation and influencing factors in China. (中国煤炭产业产能利用率估算与影响因素实证研究). *Statistics and Information Forum*, 30(12), 48–55. (In Chinese).

Forward Industrial Research Institute. 2018. *Analysis of the development status of the petrochemical industry: The problem of overcapacity is increasingly prominent.* (*石油化工产业发展现状分析: 产能过剩问题日益凸显*).

Available at: https://bg.qianzhan.com/report/detail/458/180702-a4a649df.html (accessed 22 March 2020). (In Chinese).

Franklin, H. A. 1991. The three C's of a national energy strategy. *Public Utilities Fortnightly*, 127, 12.

Hao, Y., Zhang, Z. Y., Liao, H. and Wei, Y. M. 2015. China's farewell to coal: A forecast of coal consumption through 2020. *Energy Policy*, 86, 444–455.

Hu, Z., Wang, J., Byrne, J. and Kurdgelashvili, L. 2012. Review of wind power tariff policies in China. *Energy Policy*, 53, 41–50.

International Energy Agency. 2019. *World Energy Balances*. Paris: OECD (Published 2019). Available at: https://www.iea.org/reports/world-energy-balances-2019#overview (accessed 30 March 2020).

Ishida, H. 2007. *Energy strategies in China and India and major countries' views*. The Institute of Energy Economics, Japan. Available at: https://eneken.ieej.or.jp/data/en/data/pdf/388.pdf (accessed 30 March 2020).

Ju, Y. and Wang, X. 2019. Understanding the capacity utilization rate and overcapacity of China's coal industry and interprovincial heterogeneity. *IEEE Access*, 7, 111375–111386.

Kenderdine, T. 2017. China's industrial policy, strategic emerging industries and space law. *Asia & the Pacific Policy Studies*, 4(2), 325–342.

Leung, G. C. 2011. China's energy security: Perception and reality. *Energy Policy*, 39(3), 1330–1337.

Liu, J. 2010. Analysis and evaluation of railway coal transportation in different region. (铁路省际煤炭调运的分析与评价). *China Energy*, 32(10), 20–24. (In Chinese).

Liu, Y. and Kokko, A. 2010. Wind power in China: Policy and development challenges. *Energy Policy*, 38(10), 5520–5529.

Liu, Y. and Wang, K. 2015. Energy efficiency of China's industry sector: An adjusted network DEA (data envelopment analysis)-based decomposition analysis. *Energy*, 93, 1328–1337.

Liu, Z. 1995. *Research on China's Productivity Distribution.* (*中国生产力布局研究*). Beijing: China Price Publishing House. (In Chinese).

Lo, K. 2014. A critical review of China's rapidly developing renewable energy and energy efficiency policies. *Renewable and Sustainable Energy Reviews*, 29, 508–516.

Lovins, A. B. 1974. World energy strategies: Facts, issues and options for policies that transcend today's 'Ad-Hocracy'. *Bulletin of the Atomic Scientists*, 30(5), 14–32.

Luo, W. 2019. Research on measurement of coal overcapacity in China based on DEA model. (基于 DEA 模型的中国煤炭产能过剩测度研究). *Coal Economic Research*, 39(12), 48–52. (In Chinese).

Ministry of Commerce of China. 2016. *India Launches Anti-dumping Investigation on Wind Turbine Castings*. (*印度对风力发电机组铸件发起反倾销调查*). Available at: http://www.mofcom.gov.cn/article/ztxx/gwyxx/201602/20160201255299.shtml (accessed 22 March 2020). (In Chinese).

Ministry of Finance and Ministry of Housing and Urban-Rural Development of China 2009. *Opinion on Accelerating the Deployment of Building Integrated Photovoltaic.* (*关于加快推进太阳能光电建筑应用的实施意见*). Available at: http://www.gov.cn/zwgk/2009-03/26/content_1269282.htm (accessed 25 March 2020). (In Chinese).

Mou, D. and Li, Z. 2012. A spatial analysis of China's coal flow. *Energy Policy*, 48, 358–368.

NBSC. 2019a. *China Statistical Yearbook.* Beijing: China Statistics Press.

NBSC. 2019b. *China Energy Statistical Yearbook.* Beijing: China Statistics Press.

NBSC. 2020. *Statistical Bulletin on National Economic and Social Development 2019.* (*中华人民共和国 2019 年国民经济和社会发展统计公报*). Available at: http://www.stats.gov.cn/tjsj/zxfb/202002/t20200228_1728913.html (accessed 25 March 2020), (in Chinese).

NDRC. 2011. *Notice on the Improvement of Photovoltaic Feed-in Tariff Policy.* (*国家发展改革委关于完善太阳能光伏发电上网电价政策的通知*). Available at: http://www.gov.cn/zwgk/2011-08/01/content_1917358.htm (accessed 25 March 2020). (In Chinese).

NDRC. 2015. *Provisional Announcement on Launching a Pilot Project for the Immediate Consumption of Renewable Energy.* (*关于开展可再生能源就近消纳试点的通知(暂行*). Available at: https://www.ndrc.gov.cn/xxgk/zcfb/tz/201510/t20151019_963479.html (accessed 25 March 2020). (In Chinese).

NDRC. 2016. *Management Measures on Fully Guaranteed Acquisition of Renewable Energy Power.* (*可再生能源发电全额保障性收购管理办法*). Available at: https://www.ndrc.gov.cn/xxgk/zcfb/tz/201603/t20160328_963621.html (accessed 25 March 2020). (In Chinese).

NDRC, MOF and NEA. 2017. *Notice on the Implementation of the Legal and Voluntary Subscription and Trading System for Renewable and Green Power Certificates.* (*关于试行可再生能源绿色电力证书合法及自愿认购交易机制的通知*). Available at: http://www.nea.gov.cn/2017-02/06/c_136035626.htm (accessed 25 March 2020). (In Chinese).

NEA. 2007. *Mid- and Long-Term Development Plan for Renewable Energy.* (*可再生能源中长期发展规划*). Available at: http://www.nea.gov.cn/2007-09/04/c_131053171.htm (accessed 25 March 2020) (In Chinese).

NEA. 2012. *Renewable Energy Development Twelfth Five-Year Plan Released.* (*可再生能源发展 "十二五 ?"规划发布*). Available at: http://www.nea.gov.cn/2012-08/08/c_131767651.htm (accessed 25 March 2020). (In Chinese).

Olivetti, E. A., Ceder, G., Gaustad, G. G. and Fu, X. 2017. Lithium-ion battery supply chain considerations: analysis of potential bottlenecks in critical metals. *Joule*, 1(2), 229–243.

Pan, L., Liu, P. and Li, Z. 2017. A system dynamic analysis of China's oil supply chain: Over-capacity and energy security issues. *Applied Energy*, 188, 508–520.

Panwar, N. L., Kaushik, S. C. and Kothari, S. 2011. Role of renewable energy sources in environmental protection: A review. *Renewable and Sustainable Energy Reviews*, 15(3), 1513–1524.

Qiao, X. and Song, L. 2019. Over-capacity in China's coal enterprises — Measurement, evolution characteristics and causes. (中国煤炭企业的产能过剩 — 程度测算, 演变特征与影响因素). *Journal of Beijing Institute of Technology (Social Sciences Edition)*, 5, 19–29. (In Chinese).

REN21. 2019. *Renewables 2019: Global status report.* Paris: REN21 Secretariat. https://www.ren21.net/gsr-2019/ (accessed 30 March 2020).

Schott, S. and Campbell, G. 2013. National energy strategies of major industrialized countries. *International Handbook of Energy Security.*

Schuman S, Lin A. 2012. China's Renewable Energy Law and its impact on renewable power in China: Progress, challenges and recommendations for improving implementation. *Energy Policy*, 51, 89–109.

Sina. 2014. *USS Imposes Anti-dumping Duties on Chinese PV Products.* (*美国对中国光伏产品征收反倾销税*). Available at: http://finance.sina.com.cn/stock/usstock/c/20141218/082621106295.shtml (accessed 22 March 2020). (In Chinese).

Sina Finance. 2014. *Event review: EU imposes anti-dumping duties on photovoltaic products in China.* (*事件回顾：欧盟对华光伏产品征收反倾销税*). Available at: http://finance.sina.com.cn/chanjing/cyxw/20130604/233815695463.shtml (accessed 22 March 2020), (in Chinese).

Shang, Y., Lu, S., Li, X., Hei, P., Lei, X., Gong, J., Liu, J., Zhai, J. and Wang, H. 2017. Balancing development of major coal bases with available water resources in China through 2020. *Applied Energy*, 194, 735–750.

Shao, L. and Jin S. 2020. Resilience assessment of the lithium supply chain in China under impact of new energy vehicles and supply interruption. *Journal of cleaner production*, 252, 119624.

Shen, L. and Andrews-Speed, P. 2001. Economic analysis of reform policies for small coal mines in China. *Resource Policy*, 27(4), 247–254.

Shen, L., Gao, T. and Cheng, X. 2011. China's coal policy since 1979: A brief overview. *Energy Policy*, 40, 274–281.

Shi, X. 2013. China's small coal mine policy in the 2000s: A case study of trusteeship and consolidation. *Resource Policy*, 38(4), 598–604.

Sun, Q., Zhang, J., Zhang, Q. and Zhao, X. 2017. Analysis and prevention of geo-environmental hazards with high-intensive coal mining: A case study in China's western eco-environment frangible area. *Energies*, 10(6), 786.

Tang, X., Jin, Y., Mclellan, B. C., Wang, J. and Li, S. 2018. China's coal consumption declining — Impermanent or permanent? *Resources, Conservation & Recycling*, 129, 307–313.

Wang, D., Wang, Y., Song, X. and Liu, Y. 2018. Coal overcapacity in China: Multiscale analysis and prediction. *Energy Economics*, 70, 244–257.

Wang, D., Wan, K., Song, X. and Liu, Y. 2019. Provincial allocation of coal decapacity targets in China in terms of cost, efficiency, and fairness. *Energy Economics*, 78, 109–128.

Wang, J. and Li, L. 2016. Sustainable energy development scenario forecasting and energy saving policy analysis of China. *Renewable and Sustainable Energy Reviews*, 58, 718–724.

Wang, J., Mohr, S. H., Feng, L., Liu, H. and Tverberg, G. E. 2016. Analysis of resource potential for China's unconventional gas and forecast for its long-term production growth. *Energy Policy*, 88, 389–401.

Wang, K., Su, C., Lobonţ, O. and Moldovan, N. 2020. Chinese renewable energy industries' boom and recession: Evidence from bubble detection procedure. *Energy Policy*, 138, 111200.

Wang, L. 2016. Causes and adjustment of excess capacity of new energy sources: Taking solar energy and wind energy as an example. (新能源产能过剩的原因分析与调整思路 — 以太阳能、风能为例). *Urban and Environmental Studies*, (3), 53–66. (In Chinese).

Wang, S. and Hao, J. 2012. Air quality management in China: issues, challenges, and options. *Journal of Environmental Science-China*, 24(1), 2–13.

Wang, Y. H., Luo, G. L. and Guo, Y. W. 2014. Why is there overcapacity in China's PV industry in its early growth stage? *Renewable Energy*, 72, 188–194.

Wu, Y., Xiao, X. and Song, Z. 2017. Competitiveness analysis of coal industry in China: A diamond model study. *Resource Policy*, 52, 39–53.

Xiang, X., Svensson, J. and Jia, S. 2017. Will the energy industry drain the water used for agricultural irrigation in the Yellow River basin? *International Journal of Water Resources Development*, 33(1), 69–80.

Xie, Z. (2006). *Research on energy policy of People's Republic of China Review and analysis of the evolution of energy policy in China.* (*新中国能源政策研究—对新中国能源政策发展过程的考察分析*). Hefei: University of Science and Technology of China. (In Chinese).

Yang, Q., Hou, X., Han, J. and Zhang, L. 2019. The drivers of coal overcapacity in China: An empirical study based on the quantitative decomposition. *Resources, Conservation & Recycling*, 141, 123–132.

Yong, J. 2017. Current state and prospects of CNPC's oil and gas storage and Transportation. *China Oil & Gas*, 23(4), 28–34.

You, C. A. and Xu, X. C. 2010. Coal combustion and its pollution control in China. *Energy*, 35(11), 4467–4472.

Zhang, H., Zheng, Y., Ozturk, U. A. and Li, S. 2016a. The impact of subsidies on overcapacity: A comparison of wind and solar energy companies in China. *Energy*, 94, 821–827.

Zhang, K. and Wen, Z. 2008. Review and challenges of policies of environmental protection and sustainable development in China. *Journal of Environmental Management*, 88(4), 1249–1261.

Zhang, L., Sovacool, B. K., Ren, J. and Ely, A. 2017a. The Dragon awakens: Innovation, competition, and transition in the energy strategy of the People's Republic of China, 1949–2017. *Energy Policy*, 108, 634–644.

Zhang, L., Yu, J., Sovacool, B. K. and Ren, J. 2017b. Measuring energy security performance within China: Toward an inter-provincial prospective. *Energy*, 125, 825–836.

Zhang, R. 2015. *New Normal.* (*新常态*). China.org.cn. Available at: http://photo.china.com.cn/2015lh/2015-02/10/content_34783843.htm (accessed 25 March 2020). (In Chinese).

Zhang, T., Sun, P. and Xu, W. 2016b. Analysis and policy recommendations for new energy overcapacity problem in China– Wind and solar energy industry as example. *6th International Conference on Electronic, Mechanical, Information and Management* (EMIM 2016).

Zhang, Y., Nie, R., Shi, R. and Zhang, M. 2018. Measuring the capacity utilization of the coal sector and its decoupling with economic growth in China's supply-side reform. *Resources, Conservation & Recycling*, 129, 314–325.

Zhang, Z. 2018. *Empirical Study of Coal Transportation on Multimodal Transport network in China.* (*多式联运下我国煤炭调运问题的实证研究*). Beijing: Beijing Jiaotong University. (In Chinese).

Zhou, N., Price, L., Yande, D., Creyts, J., Khanna, N., Fridley, D., ... and Tian, Z. 2019. A roadmap for China to peak carbon dioxide emissions and achieve a 20% share of non-fossil fuels in primary energy by 2030. *Applied Energy*, 239, 793–819.

Zhu, X. 2003. Dialectical Thinking on China's Energy Strategy. (关于中国能源战略的辩证思考), *China Energy*, 10, 4–12. (In Chinese).

Zou, C., Zhao, Q., Zhang, G. and Xiong, B. 2016. Energy revolution: From a fossil energy era to a new energy era. *Natural Gas Industry B*, 3(1), 1–11.

https://doi.org/10.1142/9781786349224_0002

Chapter 2

Conceptualizing and Redefining Energy Security: A Comprehensive Review

Aliaksandr Novikau
Department of International Relations and Public Administration,
International University of Sarajevo,
Hrasnicka Cesta 15, 71210 Sarajevo,
Bosnia and Herzegovina
anovikau@ius.edu.ba

Abstract

Energy security is a highly contested concept since there is no common agreement about what it means and what elements it should include. On the contrary, the current academic literature is overloaded with a broad spectrum of conceptual and operational definitions of energy security. Nonetheless, in many respects, all these new concepts are essentially the intellectual development of the initial position on energy security as reliable supplies of energy at reasonable prices. Indeed, the essence of energy security is the question of where we are able to get the energy from and what societal costs—economic, political, and environmental—we are ready to pay for it. Since all societal costs are essentially value-laden, any debate about energy security involves assessment of not only technical indicators such as share of imported energy sources or diversity of energy mix but also national values and objectives. A good conceptualization of energy security should thus be built around it.

Keywords: Energy security; Security of supply; Security of demand; Externalities; Values; Energy policy.

1. Introduction

Energy has always been a part of human life. Moreover, it was always a crucial element. Humankind has been using energy from prehistoric times, when early human groups started to control fire. Today's people depend on energy to a tremendous degree. Energy is required in numerous sectors of activity such as production, transportation, and, for some purposes like heating—for human survival. People can hardly imagine their lives without modern forms of energy such as electricity or gasoline. This is not a figure of speech—in the absence of energy, the civilization we know would inevitably collapse within a few months, if not weeks. Undoubtedly, a shortage of energy is a serious threat to human life, and therefore, a threat to security.

At the same time, energy, as any other of society's resources, is scarce, meaning that that society has limited available energy (Mankiw, 2018). Since energy is a scarce resource and its shortage is a serious threat to security, society had to learn how to manage its energy in order to prevent potential risks related to the shortage of energy and mitigate negative consequences if such a shortage happens. We can imagine that the survival of many early human settlements depended on easy and uninterrupted access to flammable materials such as wood. Therefore, a human group that was not be able to get wood to maintain the fire or obtain the wood owing to cost issues would be subject to the threat of energy shortage, and therefore its security would be jeopardized. Thus, it is very likely that early humans somehow considered the availability of flammable materials in their survival strategies. Thus, a concept of energy security can be traced back to those ancient times, though it naturally was not conceptualized as such at that time (Valentine, 2011).

Throughout human history, the importance of energy has increased even more. Simultaneously, the number of threats to uninterrupted energy supply has increased tremendously. The International Energy Agency (IEA) (2014, p. 23) constantly warns about rising energy security concerns around the world: "The global energy system is in danger of falling short of the hopes and expectations placed upon it." Not surprisingly, states and international organizations have included energy security in their strategic plans and agendas. They usually tend to address the energy security challenges in an integrated manner, and often in connection with economic and environmental issues.

Even though energy has always been present in human life and has always been very important for development and even survival of humankind, until recently the concept of energy security was quite a neglected concept in both energy and security scholarships. The attention to energy security conceptualization and operationalization has become undoubtedly visible in scientific literature only in the past few decades.

Even after energy security has been widely acknowledged as an important and working idea, it remains a highly contested concept. An essentially contested concept, by Gallie's (1956, p. 172) definition, is a concept that "not only that different persons or parties adhere to different views of the correct use of some concept but that each party recognizes the fact that its own use of it is contested by those of other parties, and that each party must have at least some appreciation of the different criteria in the light of which the other parties claim to be applying the concept in question".

Similar to the highly contested concept of security in general (see Baldwin (1997) for detailed debates about the concept of security), energy security fits Gallie's definition just as perfectly. Indeed, so far, there is still no common agreement among energy policy scholars about how energy security should be conceptualized. On the contrary, the current literature on energy policy is overloaded with a broad spectrum of definitions that claim a clearer and more precise understanding of this concept than others. In their 2015 study, Ang *et al.* (2015) identified 83 definitions of energy security in the current literature. Taking into account the recent activity in energy security scholarship, it would not be a mistake to say that the number of energy security definitions today has hit three digits. As a result, energy policy literature generates strong debates as to the nature of the concept of energy security and its applicability to different situations. Most importantly, most of the authors writing about energy security recognize other uses of the term and maintain their concept against other uses, though not always aggressively and defensively.

The fact that energy security is somewhat elusive and context-specific can be partially explained by substantial variations among the economic, political, and, naturally, energy systems in the world. Since threats to energy systems are as different as the structures of the energy systems themselves, energy policies inevitably depend on specific public policies that exist within political systems. Moreover, even within a single system, different individuals and groups tend to define energy security quite differently due to the variations in the context, academic disciplines, professions, political ideologies, and motivations. As a result, energy security depends heavily on context and perspectives (Kruyt *et al.*, 2009).

The issue of contested concepts, however, is not unique to energy studies. On the contrary, this is quite typical for any social sciences discipline and, therefore, should not be viewed as a dreadful problem. Despite of differences among energy systems, the fact that energy security means different things to different people at different times, energy systems, and the threats to them have always had common characteristics, and, therefore, a universal concept of energy security can potentially be developed.

Energy experts argue that there is still a strong need for the conceptualization of energy security. Conceptualization refers to taking abstract constructs and defining them by giving theoretical definitions (Neuman, 2014). Concepts, being building blocks of any scientific theory, are extremely important for scientific inquiry. Without good, clearly defined concepts of energy security, scholars would not be able to communicate effectively about energy-related theories. Moreover, without a clear concept, energy security would be an extremely vague term for different and often contradictory policy goals. As a result, policymakers would be not able to formulate effective public policies related to energy, and so there would be no improvement or energy security (Winzer, 2012). Ken Booth (1991, p. 317), while discussing the importance of concepts for security studies in general, said: "If we cannot name it, can we ever hope to achieve it?" Concepts help to communicate ideas, introduce particular perspectives, and explain broad generalizations within a given discipline.

A conceptual definition is a translation of an abstract idea into words or terms that are linked to other ideas or constructs. A good definition has one clear, explicit, and specific meaning (Neuman, 2014). Barry Buzan formulated several common requirements for a concept, irrespective of the discipline it would be used in. According to Buzan, a good concept should hold the following characteristics. First, a concept should be operational in the broadest sense, although its quantification is not necessarily required. Second, a concept should be connected with other concepts. Third, a concept should be connected with theoretically important aspects of the subject matter. Fourth, a concept should allow empirical inquiry.

Finally, it should be capable of being formulated in ordinary language (Baldwin, 1997).

In addition, there is an increasing interest in how energy security should be operationalized or, in other words, measured. This has resulted in numerous indicators and indexes of energy security and, in the same fashion, in debates about the right way to measure energy security (Ang *et al.*, 2015).

Having acknowledged the importance of concepts and operational definitions of security in general and energy security in particular, and most importantly, the possibility to come up with working concepts and measures of energy security, the purpose of this chapter is not to conceptualize and operationalize energy security in an absolutely new way. An old joke says that every time someone comes up with a new standard to replace all ten existing standards, we usually end up with eleven standards rather than with a single one. Aiming not to repeat this mistake, this chapter pursues quite different objectives. It seeks to clarify what energy security means for different actors, individuals, companies, and states. This task is difficult if not impossible without a historical overview of energy security; attempts to conceptualize, measure, and implement it in a form of public policy; and understand the role of values in energy security policymaking.

2. History of Energy Security

Throughout human history, the use of energy has continuously been increasing, both in amount and in the variety of sources. Thus, as Felix Ciută (2010, p. 135) rightfully noted, "energy security is everywhere," meaning that energy can be found in a variety of places—form giant factories to tiny houses—but, most importantly, none of them is free from threats to uninterrupted energy supply in what they can afford. Nonetheless, even though energy has always been a crucial part of human life, the first attempts to conceptualize, measure, and solve energy security in its contemporary sense were made only in the 20th century. Specifically, energy security received special attention from energy policy scholars and professionals at the beginning of the century. This increasing attention to the issue of energy security was primarily caused by the shift of the power source from predominantly local energy sources to imported ones in industrialized countries. Although the shift resulted in increased productivity in many areas such as transportation, it also brought significant problems that were not well known before. For instance, when the British Navy switched from domestic coal to imported oil in the early 20th century, it became vulnerable to attacks on oil fields, transportation lines, and refineries. World War II highlighted the importance of energy security even more. It clearly demonstrated the dangers of depending on imported oil and the need to develop one's own supply. Many battles were aimed specifically to take control over oil fields in distinct parts of the world, thus proving the importance of uninterrupted oil supply for national security. Moreover, even decisions to start a war with a certain country were often dictated by the desire to secure oil supply for military and economic needs.

The importance of energy security did not disappear after World War II. On the contrary, increasing energy consumption in developed countries, especially in such areas as industrial production, transportation, electricity generation, and heating, resulted in the tremendous growth of imported oil from other countries, usually located in other parts of the globe such as the Middle East. Progress in extraction and transportation technologies made the cost of crude oil for western consumers extremely attractive.

Nonetheless, the danger of such strong reliance on oil from foreign sources became obvious in 1973 when many members of the Organization of the Petroleum Exporting Countries (OPEC) imposed an oil embargo on countries supporting Israel during the Yom Kippur War. The quadrupling of oil prices caused a serious energy crisis, and then a long-lasting economic recession in the targeted countries. From that moment, securing oil supplies became a practical policy concern for most of the nations around the globe. Many countries have become concerned about reliable supplies of energy through utilizing different policy mechanisms such as diversification of supply and energy conservation. As a result, the number of studies and public policies concerning energy security has grown exponentially. Also, concerns over energy security during the oil crises of the 1970s caused the creation of several international energy organizations and mechanisms such as the IEA, which was established in 1974 as an autonomous intergovernmental organization in the framework of the Organization for Economic Co-operation and Development (OECD).

During most of the 20th century, energy security was discussed chiefly in the sense of secure supplies of oil for military and economic purposes. Since most of the oil resources were located in potentially unstable regions and countries, energy security was viewed mainly through the lens of geopolitics and focused on securing access to international sources of fossil fuels. Thus, during the 20th century, energy security strongly reflected a dominating state-centric, realist approach to international relations and national security. Initially, the geopolitical approach focused on oil supply disruption from the Middle East to developed countries. Later, energy security started to include other regions such as Europe and Asia, and even other energy types such as natural gas and electricity. Either way, the global realm was viewed as the only legitimate place for energy security discourse. Currently, there is a slight trend to include non-state actors into the analysis of energy security and focus more on global institutions and regimes of global governance, including such issues as global climate change, environmental justice, and many others (Yergin, 1991; Cherp and Jewell, 2011).

At the end of the 20th century, the share of natural gas has increased in the energy balances of many countries. Simultaneously, their energy systems have faced new threats caused because of concerns about the stability of the supply of and prices of the supplied natural gas. Therefore, the current energy security literature, in addition to oil, also focuses on the supply of natural gas, reflecting recent concerns about the stability of the supply of natural gas in Europe and other parts of the world. Some authors propose to include electricity in the analysis of energy security as well because it is the most dominant form of energy supply with a significant share in final energy consumption. Since the characteristics of oil, gas, and electricity supplies differ significantly, and therefore their trade and infrastructure differ too, the meaning of energy security when taking different energy sources into consideration can also vary to a significant degree (Novikau, 2020a).

3. Conceptualizing Energy Security

Before defining energy security, it would not be a bad idea to start with understanding what security is in general. Unfortunately, security remains both a neglected and contested concept itself. Surprisingly, until recently, security has not been an important concept in security studies because most of the scholars were focused on military statecraft and therefore ignoring issues unrelated to military power.

Nonetheless, most of the security scholars agree that security, in its simplest understanding, means something like "the absence of threats." Since the word "threat" is context- and perspective-dependent, the definition of security is not ready for universal use and requires further clarifications such as "Security from what threats?", "How much security?", "Security for who?", and "Security for which values?" (Baldwin, 1997). Nonetheless, the definition of energy security in an absence of threats undoubtedly offers a good point of departure. Based on this definition, security policies, in other words, can be viewed simply as risk management strategies.

One of the major steps in the conceptualization of energy security is the identification of these threats. The problem, however, is that every energy system faces an enormous number of threats of different kinds. Complexity in energy security arises when dealing with the broad spectrum of threats to different aspects of energy use by different energy consumers (Ciută, 2010).

There have been numerous attempts to find integrated solutions to multiple energy security threats (Cherp and Jewell, 2011). The choice of threats and methods of analysis and policy decisions, as has been mentioned earlier, are the major sources of differences in the conceptualization of energy security. Moreover, different scholars and policy professionals prioritize these threats quite differently, which results in further variation (Chester, 2010).

The earliest and still highly influential conceptualizations of energy security were essentially two-dimensional. Yergin (1988, p. 111), in his classical work, focused mainly on *availability* and *affordability* of energy for consumers, stating that "the objective of energy security is to assure adequate, reliable supplies of energy at reasonable prices and in ways that do not jeopardize major national values and objectives." Thus, the definition includes two major components of energy security. The first one is concerned with the physical or geological availability of energy or having sufficient supplies of energy. Yet many energy resources such as oil have become a globally trading commodity, and the simple problem of lack of availability of oil has become quite rare. More often, the question lies in the economic dimension, or affordability, that is, generation of energy services at the lowest cost, maintenance of predictable prices for energy fuels and services, and enabling equitable access to energy services. As Bohi and Toman (1996, p. 1) put it: "energy security refers to the loss of economic welfare that may occur as a result of a change in the price or availability of energy."

There are numerous definitions of energy security that follow the same logic. For instance, Valentine (2010, p. 59) defines energy security as "the aggregate capacity to fulfill energy demand through existing sources of supply."

This conceptualization of energy security focuses chiefly on the economic aspects of energy security. It is viewed as the market outcome and defined in simple market terms-supply and price. Markets are assumed to adjust automatically by finding the equilibrium price at the point at which the demand and supply curves intersect. Thus, energy insecurity was often explained as market failure or mismatch in supply and demand. This may happen, for instance, because of disruption of energy supply due to military conflicts, embargos, sanctions, and other non-economic actions of nations. Consequently, the dominating energy security strategy, in this case, was related to the idea of deregulation of energy supply parts (Chester, 2010; Cherp and Jewell, 2011).

The Asia Pacific Energy Research Center (APERC) defined energy security "as the ability of an economy to guarantee the availability of energy resource supply in a sustainable and timely manner with the energy price being at a level that will not adversely affect the economic performance of the economy" and provided new definitions for the previous definitions as well. In addition to availability and affordability, the authors added two more dimensions to the concept of energy security–accessibility and acceptability (Asia Pacific Energy Research Centre, 2007). Thus, according to the APERC, *availability* is conceptualized as the size of energy reserves, measured through a reserves-to-production ratio. *Accessibility* is defined mainly as an absence of barriers that prevent access of energy consumers to available energy resources. These barriers can be geopolitical, such as political instability in the energy resources region; geographical, such as related to poor transportation infrastructure; technological; financial; or insufficient human resource capacity. Thus, the first two factors are related to the physical elements of energy security. The third dimension of energy security, *acceptability,* is understood from the sense of environmental acceptability, that is the absence of environmental damage from the entire energy supply chain. Finally, *affordability* is explained by the economic affordability of energy resource acquisition and energy infrastructure development.

This so-called "4 A's approach" has become extremely popular among energy policy professionals as a framework for energy security analysis. Moreover, new additional dimensions of energy security have been added by scholars who aim to create a more precise and comprehensive concept of energy security. Most often, additional threats were proposed to be included in the concept of energy security. Recently, the concept of energy security has grown to include not only the stability of fossil fuel supplies but also other related issues such as the environment, politics, and economy.

For example, von Hippel *et al.* (2011) identified six dimensions of energy security: energy supply, economic, technological, environmental, social and cultural, and military/security. Vivoda (2010) added five more dimensions of energy security: demand management, efficiency, human security, international, and policy. In the same vein, Ang *et al.* (2015) identify seven major dimensions of energy security: energy availability, infrastructure, energy prices, societal effects, environment, governance, and energy efficiency.

Sovacool and Mukherjee (2011) identified 20 components of energy security, based on its five dimensions. Security of supply and production, dependency, and diversification are the components of the availability dimension of energy security. Price stability, access and equity, decentralization, and affordability represent the affordability dimension. Technology development is represented by such components of energy security as innovation and research, safety and reliability, resilience, energy efficiency, and investment. Land use, water, climate change, and air pollution represent the sustainability dimension of energy security. Finally, governance, trade, competition, and knowledge for sound regulation represent the regulation and governance dimension.

These are only a few examples of the rapid increase in the number of dimensions. In fact, when discussing energy security, many authors offer their own concepts of energy security that include new and often unique dimensions of energy security.

Sovacool (2010), in addition to the dimensions mentioned earlier, proposed a classification of threats to energy security based on the scales at which they occur. For instance, the macro level includes global threats such as geopolitical issues, war, trade, investment barriers, and transboundary (environmental) externalities. The micro level, i.e., that of individuals and households, includes local energy security threats such as energy poverty. Finally, the meso level includes technology-based energy security threats that cut across the global and local scales.

In addition, some energy security scholars emphasize the importance of considering a temporal dimension of energy security, especially for designing effective energy security policies. Indeed, the preferable energy mix that was in place 50 years back would look ridiculous from today's perspective. For instance, Ang *et al.* (2015) demonstrated a certain shift in the importance of different dimensions of energy security within one decade. Even though the importance of energy availability remained stable over time, the importance of such energy security themes as energy prices, environmental issues, societal effects, governance, and efficiency increased significantly.

Moreover, we should distinguish short-term energy security, such as following blackouts within the electricity supply systems, absence of fuel at gas stations, sudden energy prices spikes for final consumers, etc., as well as long-term energy security, which is usually related to the stability of supply and prices to the national energy system (Kruyt *et al.*, 2009; Valentine, 2010). For instance, Jansen and Seebregts (2010, p. 1654) define long-term energy security as a "proxy of the certainty level at which the population in a defined area has uninterrupted access to fossil fuels and fossil-fuel-based energy carriers in the absence of undue exposure to supply-side market power over a period ahead of 10 years or longer."

In his meta-analysis, Winzer (2012) reviewed several dozens of definitions of energy security definitions and offered his own definition of energy security as the continuity of energy supplies relative to demand. In addition, based on that definition, types of energy security dimensions were proposed. The first dimension, the sources of risk, describes the types of threats to energy security and includes technical, human, and natural threats. The second dimension, the scope of impact, is based on threats to the continuity of energy services and describes how energy security is measured. It includes the continuity of commodities and supplies, continuity of service supplies, economic continuity, human safety, and environmental sustainability. In addition, the author introduced several severity filters to identify whether the level of continuity is secure or not based on the measurements of threat impacts. In particular, Winzer included such filters as speed, size, spread, singularity, and sureness of impacts. Yet he specifically clarified that by no means was this list of filters exhaustive and stated that, therefore, it could be extended further if needed.

4. Operationalization of Energy Security

In addition to the identification of dimensions of energy security, or its conceptualization, there is also a strong need for operational definitions or operationalization of energy security. The purpose of operationalization is to connect an abstract conceptual definition, such as energy security, to a set of measurement techniques or procedures. By connecting an abstract construct to usable indicators and metrics, we create operational definitions or actions (Neuman, 2014). Operationalization of energy security is especially important for the assessment of energy security policies and performance. Hence, the imperative to create severity filters to define a minimum threshold, in which the impacts need to exceed a certain limit, so that it can be used to count as a threat to energy security. Therefore, it is important to identify the base features of energy security that can be quantified. Even though the selection of energy security indicators and construction of composite indexes is a subjective process, there is a general consensus that having comparative indicators of energy security is definitely required for setting agendas and making policies (Sovacool, 2010; Winzer, 2012; Ang *et al.*, 2015).

The energy security literature is filled with numerous attempts to quantify and assess energy security. Approximately half of the energy security studies try to measure energy security performance. The number of indicators of energy security varies from one to several hundred. There are both advantages and disadvantages of using a large number of indexes. A small number of indicators results in poor stability of an index when a change in a single indicator causes a significant change of the entire index. An increase in the number of indicators improves the stability of an index but results in poor sensitivity when a change in an important indicator can be muted by unchanging ones. Thus, the choice of the number of energy security indicators is always a trade-off between the stability and sensitivity of an index. As a result, the majority of studies include no more than 20 indicators of energy security.

There are also numerous attempts to combine indicators into a single composite index of energy security that would allow us to easily assess the dynamics of energy security in a country or perform a cross-country analysis. For the purpose of construction of a composite index, normalization, weighting, and aggregation of individual indicators are usually required (Ang *et al.*, 2015). At the same time, some authors discourage the construction of aggregated indexes that combine different types of energy. It is argued that the vulnerability of different countries, even those which belong to a single region like the EU, varies significantly in relation to different types of energy sources. As a result, aggregated indexes of energy security can be misleading (Le Coq and Paltseva, 2009).

Sovacool and Brown (2010) offered 10 indicators, representing four dimensions of energy security, that constitute an Energy Security Index. The *availability* dimension is represented by such indicators as oil import dependency, natural gas import dependency, and dependence on petroleum transport fuels. The *affordability* dimension is represented by retail electricity prices and retail gasoline/petrol prices. The *energy and economic efficiency* dimensions are represented by energy intensity, per capita electricity use, and on-road fuel intensity of passenger vehicles. Finally, *environmental stewardship* is represented by SO_2 and CO_2 emissions.

These indicators were further extended by Sovacool and Mukherjee (2011) who offered 320 simple and 52 complex indicators of energy security grouped into 20 components of energy security that have been previously mentioned.

Several approaches to the operationalization of energy security attempted to specifically measure the diversity of energy supply and suppliers. For instance, Jansen and Seebregts (2010) developed four composite diversity indices of long-term energy security based on the Shannon-Wiener diversity index. The four indices are as follows:

(1) diversification of energy sources in energy supply; (2) diversification of imports with respect to imported energy sources; (3) long-term political stability in regions of origin; and (4) fuel resource base in regions of origin, including the home region. These indicators are normalized to a 0–100 range, with a lower value indicating an inferior energy security situation. The criticism of the index is based on the fact that it lacks common ground and, therefore, is arbitrary (Kruyt *et al.*, 2009).

Because of the historical factors described in the previous sections, the very first of attempts were focused on energy import dependency or the proportion of energy that comes from abroad. Also because of historical factors, such as the vulnerability of the energy market to OPEC decisions and instability in the Middle East, most of the early operationalization was focused mainly on oil. This measure can be applied to other specific fuels such as natural gas and coal, or to the entire energy mix of a given country (Cherp and Jewell, 2010; Löschel *et al.*, 2010).

For instance, the IEA introduced a multi-fossil-fuels energy security measurement based on two indicators. The first indicator is based on physical availability of energy resources, and so the initial indicators are adjusted to account for political stability in the export countries. The most important limitation is that they only refer to international fossil fuel markets (Kruyt *et al.*, 2009; Jansen and Seebregts, 2010).

Le Coq and Paltseva (2009) introduced the risky external energy supply index that is focused on the diversity of supply as a measure of short-term energy security. The authors considered the situation of a sudden disruption in energy supply that cannot be fixed by market mechanisms and used a Herfindahl–Hirschman approach to evaluate market concentration.

Gupta (2008) developed an oil vulnerability index on the basis of market and supply risk indicators. The market indicators included the oil imports to GDP ratio, oil consumption per unit of GDP, GDP per capita, and share of oil in total energy supply. The three supply risk indicators included the ratio of the oil reserves to consumption; exposure to geopolitical oil risks as measured by import dependence, diversification of supply, and political risk in oil-exporting countries; and market liquidity. The composite oil vulnerability index was calculated as the weighted average of these indicators, where weights were derived using a multivariate technique of principal component analysis.

A supply/demand (S/D) index is an energy security indicator for a defined region in the medium and long run that sets out to integrate major underlying supply-side and demand-side factors. This index is normalized to a 0–100 scale, with a lower value indicating an extremely low-security situation and the highest value indicating extremely high security. The index covers final energy demand, energy conversion and transport, and primary energy sources supply and, therefore, covers the entire energy system (Kruyt *et al.*, 2009; Jansen and Seebregts, 2010).

There have also been attempts to measure energy security in a country through the "willingness to pay" metrics. It is based on the idea of measuring how much a certain country would pay (as a share of GDP) to reduce risks to energy security. It is assumed that this willingness to pay would be higher for severe threats to energy security, related to the high share of imported energy, a high share of fossil fuels in the energy mix, and high energy intensity of the national economy (Kruyt *et al.*, 2009).

5. Energy Security for Who?

In many respects, the definition with an explicit focus on the absence of threats can explain the differences in conceptualizing security and therefore arriving at its single denominator. Indeed, since threats to security are different for different individuals and groups, their specific understanding of security would vary as well. Therefore, without specifying a "referent object", a concept of security would make no sense. In other words, there would be no practical use of the concept of security without specifying security for whom and from what threats (Baldwin, 1997). Following the same logic, Cherp and Jewell (2014) emphasized the importance of identifying a reference object and threats for energy security as well. Indeed, since the dimensions of energy security discussed earlier are essentially value-laden and without a reference object, none of them makes much sense.

The primary subject of energy security in its traditional understanding is an energy consumer. The most widespread notion of energy security is end-user oriented and, therefore, focuses on the interests of energy consumers. Not surprisingly, as we can see from the previous sections, most of the definitions of energy security in current literature are focused on the continuity of commodity supplies or, in other words, on the security of supply. As a result, the notions of security of supply and energy security are often used interchangeably (Kruyt *et al.*, 2009; Winzer, 2012).

The security of supply is important for many direct and indirect consumers of energy. Because of the clear linkage between energy and economic growth, energy security is often viewed in relation to national economy. Thus, the answer to the question "energy security for who" is often "for the national economy". Again, because energy systems vary around the globe, national governments identify these threats quite differently (Dorian *et al.*, 2006).

At the same time, some researches discuss so-called international energy security alongside the national one. They argue that global reliance on fossil fuels as a primary source of energy jeopardizes energy security of all countries. At the same time, some countries are more vulnerable than others, and challenges to their energy system also vary to different degrees. According to von Hippel *et al.* (2010), the main differences between countries in relation to energy security are determined by the following factors: the number of local energy resources, the role of the state in determining energy prices, and the focus, i.e., whether on short-term or long-term energy security goals.

It is worth mentioning that there are many voices in energy security literature arguing that the supply-side-centered approach to energy security reflects the interests of industrialized countries only and ignores the energy systems of energy exporters. For those countries, as some scholars argue, energy security means not only a stable functioning of their energy systems but also the availability of sufficient energy export at reasonable prices. Since the export of hydrocarbons generates a significant share of the government revenues in those countries, it directly affects the security of their citizens. This is why these countries insist on including the security of demand in the notion of energy security. That view is supported by many energy policy scholars who include security of demand in their definitions and metrics of energy security. The concept of security of demand usually includes the availability of customers, price fairness, and energy transit security issues, such as control over pipelines.

This brings us to the important question—can the security of demand be legitimately viewed as a component of energy security? Even though the interests of energy exporters should be acknowledged, the idea to represent their interests through the introduction of a concept of energy supply can be grossly misleading for debates on the concept of energy security.

Indeed, for the end energy consumers, both in energy-importing and energy-exporting countries, the concept of security of demand makes little or no sense. Thus, specifically for them, energy security would mean mainly security of supply and, therefore, would not go far beyond the 4 A's, even though energy exports play a significant role in governmental revenues and, therefore, in national security, which inevitably affects the security of every citizen. This can affect the security of supply for domestic consumers as well—for instance, through governmental subsidies. Yet, exports of any other products or services would have a similar effect. On the contrary, for energy exporters, what matters is the security of demand; the security of supply is not important.

6. Energy Security Policies

Although energy security is not a policy but rather a concept, it clearly reflects some strategic policy intents. One of the unique characteristics of energy as a commodity is the presence of factors that inhibit its efficient allocation through market mechanisms. In other words, global energy is characterized by inherent market failure. It is usually believed that one of the legitimate reasons for a government to intervene in the economy is to correct market failures and, as a result, improve the efficiency of resource allocation (Fisher and Rothkopf, 1989). There are two major causes of market failure—externalities and market power.

Externalities are usually defined as the impact of one person's actions on the well-being of others. If the impact on the other person is beneficial, it is called positive externality, and when adverse–negative externality. Pollution is a classic example of negative externality because manufacturers do not consider the full cost of the pollution they create in their production process, and therefore tend to pollute much without governmental intervention (Mankiw, 2018).

A well-known by-product of fossil fuel use is pollution. As a matter of fact, most air pollution is energy related. Other types of energy are not free from negative externalities either. The emergence of nuclear power, on the one hand, reduced the dependency on carbon-based fossil fuels and cut carbon emission. On the other hand, nuclear accidents, such as the ones at Three Mile Island, Chernobyl, and Fukushima, have brought new threats to energy security. Finally, the 21st century has been characterized by the increasing role of renewables in the energy mix. Because of their unique features, renewable energy sources are often viewed as a practical way to improve energy security. At the same time, under certain circumstances, renewables can potentially generate new risks to energy security (Jonsson *et al.*, 2015; Novikau, 2020b). As a result, governmental intervention is always required to regulate pollution caused by energy.

The second cause of market failure is the so-called market power, that is, the ability of a single person or a group of people to influence market prices. A competitive market consists of many buyers and sellers trading identical products so that each buyer and seller is a price taker and firms can freely enter or exit the market. Market power is a situation where there is no competitive market, and therefore imperfect competition exists. For example, monopolies on both supply and demand sides have significant market power and, therefore, the ability to influence market prices (Mankiw, 2018).

The energy market is characterized by the existence of market power and, therefore, imperfect competition. Although different types of energy resources have their own market features, in general, major consumer markets on the supply side are more vulnerable to the exercise of monopolistic market power by major energy exporters (Jansen and Seebregts, 2010). For example, the cartels of the OPEC have the ability to influence the global supply of crude oil and, therefore, to affect market prices. As a result, the opportunity cost of oil can exceed real market price. Other types of energy such as natural gas or electricity are characterized by imperfect competition to an even greater degree. Since energy suppliers and consumers are often located in different countries, the ability of the national governments to intervene in order to fix the market failure is quite limited because of the anarchic nature of the international system (Bohi and Toman, 1996; Goldthau, 2012).

Since energy is characterized by several externalities, the sum of externalities not internalized in the energy price is measured on an equivalent basis and is referred to as "premium", which can serve as useful guidelines for policymakers (Bohi and Toman, 1996).

It is imperative that the societal responses to threats to energy security require political decisions. As von Hippel *et al.* (2010, p. 86) put it "a key goal of energy policy is to improve energy security—whether broadly or narrowly defined–and thus to reduce existing (or looming) energy insecurity." Curbing the use of fossil fuels, in a socio-economically efficient way over longer timescales, is the main lever towards achieving a more secure energy economy. It is important to note that energy security policies do not exist in vacuum and always depend on other public policy goals in a country, such as economic performance, public health, foreign policy, and many others.

7. Redefining Energy Security

So what is the best conceptual and operational definition of energy security? Does it really need to be redefined? If so, then how? As the chapter demonstrates, the literature on energy security is extremely rich with various conceptual and operational definitions of energy security. Yet, regardless of the number of energy security dimensions, they are never viewed as isolated categories but rather strongly interconnected.

Yet, in many respects, all these new concepts of energy security are essentially the intellectual development of Yergin's initial position on energy security as "reliable supplies of energy at reasonable prices." Indeed, the essence of energy security is the question of where we are able to get the energy from and what price we have to pay for it. It would, however, be a dreadful mistake to understand the word price and, therefore, affordability in a narrow sense, like the US dollars we pay for a barrel of crude oil. In this case, the introduction of other dimensions of energy security is absolutely needed.

We should rather think about affordability in the sense of all combined costs associated with obtaining the energy. Indeed, most, if not all, dimensions of energy security described, albeit too briefly, in this chapter represent the societal costs related to energy—economic, political, environmental, human capital, foreign policy, and many others. In other words, by consuming energy we all pay the cost—with money, with economic crises, with global climate change, with environmental degradation, with political instability at home, with civil wars overseas, with military conflicts, and the list goes on. Part of these costs are paid by energy consumers, and parts of the costs, which are defined as externalities, are paid by other society members, and a part is paid by all humankind, including future generations. They are all the costs we have to pay. Essentially, these are the costs that form the true question of affordability—can we afford these costs? Naturally, the costs associated with different types of energy are different. They also vary significantly across nations. Even within a society, there are a variety of opinions about what price we can pay for energy. Nonetheless, the question remains about the cost we pay. Does it mean that all the conceptual and operational definitions of energy created so far are useless? Absolutely not! As was mentioned earlier, these dimensions of energy security are essentially the different dimensions of costs. Thus, the questions of cost and how it should be measured remain quite important.

It is important to emphasize the second part of Yergin's definition of energy security, which often remains neglected in energy security debates –"in ways that do not jeopardize major national values and objectives." Values play a crucial role in agenda-setting and policy formulation by guiding policymakers about what is important or desirable. As was mentioned in the very first section of this chapter, since the society's resources are scarce, public policy choices are always about the allocation of available resources and, therefore, shaped by trade-offs among different values in a society. Since values constitute the underlying principles for the individual's formation of political preferences, it is not surprising that values have a central place in most theories about policy processes. In many respects, public policy is just an authoritative allocation of values. Even though policymakers can agree that a certain issue exists in a society, they may disagree about whether the issue is appropriate for a government to regulate, and if it is what courses of action should be chosen. Thus, values can be important or even determinative in shaping policymakers' behavior and, therefore, the possibilities and limitations of policymaking.

Energy security policy, as any other public policy, is value laden. Essentially, any policy debate about an environmental issue involves a debate not only on "hard" evidence such as the share of imported energy sources or diversity of energy mix but also on its consequences, particularly social, political, and economic ones. Social values, as Cherp and Jewell (2014) point out, "is a central question for contemporary energy security." Thus, the definition of energy security should be built around it.

References

Ang, B. W., Choong, W. L. and Ng, T. S. 2015. Energy security: Definitions, dimensions and indexes. *Renewable and Sustainable Energy Reviews*, 42, 1077–1093.

Asia Pacific Energy Research Centre. 2007. *A Quest for Energy Security in the 21st Century: Resources and Constraints*. Tokyo: Institute of Energy Economics, Japan.

Baldwin, D. A. 1997. The concept of security. *Review of International Studies*, 23(1), 5–26.

Bohi, D. R. and Toman, M. A. 1996. *The Economics of Energy Security*. Dordrecht: Springer Netherlands.

Booth, K. 1991. Security and emancipation. *Review of International Studies*, 17(4), 313–326.

Cherp, A. and Jewell, J. 2010. Measuring energy security. In Sovacool, B. K. (ed.) *The Routledge Handbook of Energy Security*. Routledge, pp. 330–355.

Cherp, A. and Jewell, J. 2011. The three perspectives on energy security: Intellectual history, disciplinary roots and the potential for integration. *Current Opinion in Environmental Sustainability*, 3(4), 202–212.

Cherp, A. and Jewell, J. 2014. The concept of energy security: Beyond the four As. *Energy Policy*, 75, 415–421.

Chester, L. 2010. Conceptualising energy security and making explicit its polysemic nature. *Energy Policy*, 38(2), 887–895.

Ciută, F. 2010. Conceptual notes on energy security: Total or banal security? *Security Dialogue*, 41(2), 123–144.

Dorian, J. P., Franssen, H. T. and Simbeck, D. R. 2006. Global challenges in energy. *Energy Policy*, 34(15), 1984–1991.

Fisher, A. C. and Rothkopf, M. H. 1989. Market failure and energy policy a rationale for selective conservation. *Energy Policy*, 17(4), 397–406.

Gallie, W. B. 1956. Essentially contested concepts. *Proceedings of the Aristotelian Society*, 56(1), 167–198.

Goldthau, A. 2012. A public policy perspective on global energy security: Public policy perspective on global energy security. *International Studies Perspectives*, 13(1), 65–84.

Gupta, E. 2008. Oil vulnerability index of oil-importing countries. *Energy Policy*, 36(3), 1195–1211.

International Energy Agency (IEA). *World Energy Outlook 2014*. Paris, France: OECD Publishing; International Energy Agency.

Jansen, J. C. and Seebregts, A. J. 2010. Long-term energy services security: What is it and how can it be measured and valued? *Energy Policy*, 38(4), 1654–1664.

Jonsson, D. K. *et al.* 2015. Energy security matters in the EU energy roadmap. *Energy Strategy Reviews*, 6, 48–56.

Kruyt, B. *et al.* 2009. Indicators for energy security. *Energy Policy*, 37(6), 2166–2181.

Le Coq, C. and Paltseva, E. 2009. Measuring the security of external energy supply in the European Union. *Energy Policy*, 37(11), 4474–4481.

Löschel, A., Moslener, U. and Rübbelke, D. T. G. 2010. Indicators of energy security in industrialised countries. *Energy Policy*, 38(4), 1665–1671.

Mankiw, N. G. 2018. *Principles of Economics*. 8th edition. Australia; Boston, MA, USA: Cengage Learning.

Neuman, W. L. 2014. *Social Research Methods: Qualitative and Quantitative Approaches*. 7th edition. Harlow: Pearson.

Novikau, A. 2020a. Energy security: Evolution of a concept. In Romaniuk, S. Thapa, M. and Marton, P. (eds.) *The Palgrave Encyclopedia of Global Security Studies*. Cham: Springer International Publishing, pp. 1–4.

Novikau, A. 2020b. Energy security strategies. In Romaniuk, S. Thapa, M. and Marton, P. (eds.) *The Palgrave Encyclopedia of Global Security Studies*. Cham: Springer International Publishing, pp. 1–4.

Sovacool, B. K. 2010. Introduction: Defining, measuring, and exploring energy security. In Sovacool, B. K. (ed.) *The Routledge Handbook of Energy Security*. London; New York: Routledge, pp. 19–42.

Sovacool, B. K. and Brown, M. A. 2010. Competing dimensions of energy security: An international perspective. *Annual Review of Environment and Resources*, 35(1), 77–108.

Sovacool, B. K. and Mukherjee, I. 2011. Conceptualizing and measuring energy security: A synthesized approach. *Energy*, 36(8), 5343–5355.

Valentine, S. V. 2010. The fuzzy nature of energy security. In Sovacool, B. K. (ed.) *The Routledge Handbook of Energy Security*. London; New York: Routledge, pp. 56–73.

Valentine, S. V. 2011. Emerging symbiosis: Renewable energy and energy security. *Renewable and Sustainable Energy Reviews*, 15(9), 4572–4578.

von Hippel, D. F., Savage, T. and Hayes, P. 2011. Introduction to the Asian energy security project: Project organization and methodologies. *Energy Policy*, 39(11), 6712–6718.

von Hippel, D. F. *et al.* 2010. Evaluating the energy security impacts of energy policies. In Sovacool, B. K. (ed.) *The Routledge Handbook of Energy Security*. Routledge, pp. 74–95.

Vivoda, V. 2010. Evaluating energy security in the Asia-Pacific region: A novel methodological approach. *Energy Policy*, 38(9), 5258–5263.

Winzer, C. 2012. Conceptualizing energy security. *Energy Policy*, 46, 36–48.
Yergin, D. 1988. Energy security in the 1990s. *Foreign Affairs*, 67(1), 110.
Yergin, D. 1991. *The Prize: The Epic Quest for Oil, Money, and Power.* New York: Simon & Schuster.

https://doi.org/10.1142/9781786349224_0003

Chapter 3

Historical Energy Security Performances of China: A Bi-Level Analysis

Yuzhuo Huang[*,‡], Caixia Li[*,§], and Ken'ichi Matsumoto[*,†,¶]

[*]Graduate School of Fisheries and Environmental Sciences, Nagasaki University, Japan

[†]Research Institute for Global Change, Japan Agency for Marine-Earth Science and Technology, Japan

[‡]bb53420006@ms.nagasaki-u.ac.jp

[§]bb53419006@ms.nagasaki-u.ac.jp

[¶]kenichimatsu@nagasaki-u.ac.jp

Abstract

With the rapid global economic development, energy demand has increased sharply in the past few decades. China depends on a large amount of energy to stimulate its economic development as the largest developing country. Energy security is of vital importance for China and its provinces. In this chapter, we evaluated the historical energy security performance at both national (1992–2018) and provincial levels (1995–2016). Particularly, we applied three energy security indicators, including diversity of energy sources, energy import, and country risks ($S1$–$S3$). We elucidated that at the national level, $S1$ (the indicator based on diversity of energy sources) and $S2$ ($S1$ with energy import) both increased in the period 1992–2002, then decreased from 2002 to 2006. However, $S3$ ($S2$ with country risks) basically decreased from 1996 to 2006. After 2006, all the three indicators increased, but with fluctuation in their levels. At the provincial level, we found that the energy security levels largely differed by province. From the further evaluation of the six selected provinces with obvious characteristics of energy security performance (Guangdong, Qinghai, Beijing, Sichuan, Fujian, and Heilongjiang), we found that the energy security performances of five provinces (except Heilongjiang) improved because the demand for fossil fuels declined and that for renewable energy increased over time. Heilongjiang was the only one province with negative growth of energy security during the study period, because it is rich in fossil fuel resources but not in renewables. To improve the energy security, China needs to use more renewable energy to diversify energy sources, improve the diversification of energy imports, and reduce the imports from high-risk countries.

Keywords: Energy security; Indicator; China; National-level analysis; Provincial-level analysis.

1. Introduction

1.1. *Background*

The oil crisis in the 1970s aroused the attention of policymakers and the general public on the topic of energy security. In 1974, the International Energy Agency defined the concept of energy security for the first time, and it was further deepened in the Kyoto Protocol in 1997, namely supply stability, price economy, and cleanliness were added (Ren and Li, 2017). In terms of supply, the annual increase in world oil reserves reached its peak in the 1960s, and has been in a downward spiral for half a century since then (Zhang and Lu, 2015). As for the price, "fluctuation" has become the main topic of price changes in the international crude oil market. Since the beginning of the 21st century, the international crude oil market has experienced an "inflection point" in oil prices, which started during the global financial crisis in 2008. Energy security has been more critical due to the sharp changes in energy prices and the disruption of supply chains. With respect to cleanliness, the energy structure has gradually changed from a high-carbon one to a low-carbon one. From 1995 to 2018, the share of oil in global energy consumption continued to decline, shifting from 39% to 33% (BP, 2019b). However, the shares of natural gas and renewable energy in the global energy demand have been steadily rising. Between 1995 and 2018, the share of natural gas demand rose from 21% to 24%, while that of renewable energy demand rose from 0.4% to 4.1%.

The global economic landscape has profoundly changed in the 2010s, with developing countries having a prominent role in the world economy and their dependency substituted by significant shares in world trade and foreign direct investment flows (Gechev, 2018). Because of the economic growth in developing countries, the pattern of world energy supply and demand has also changed. The pattern of energy supply has been changed with the shale revolution catapulting the United States to pole position as the world's largest producer of oil and gas, and the rapid growth of liquefied natural gas (LNG) transforming how natural gas is transported and traded around the world (BP, 2019a). On the demand side, energy consumption in non-OECD (Organisation for Economic Co-operation and Development) countries has grown rapidly and the global center of energy consumption has shifted faster to Asia with the expanding middle classes in Asia (BP, 2019a). Emerging economies have been the dominant driving force in the current global energy demand growth, with energy demand growth of non-OECD countries overtaking that of the OECD countries in 2008, which have since been the absolute driver of demand growth (Kong and Li, 2015). As the world's second largest economy, China's energy demand and choice will undoubtedly have an increasingly important impact on the rest of the world (Leung, 2011).

Since the beginning of the 21st century, China's gross domestic product (GDP) has maintained a high-speed and stable growth. In 2016 and 2017, its GDP reached 74.05 trillion yuan and 82.48 trillion yuan, with growth rates of 6.7% and 6.9%, respectively (National Bureau of Statistics of China, 2018). However, in the context of rapid economic development, the growth rate of energy demand has shown a three-stage downward trend in the 21st century. During the period 2000–2010, China's annual growth rate of energy demand was 9.4%, but it dropped to 4.3% during 2011–2014 and to 1.5% during 2015–2017. The continuous improvement of energy efficiency is one of the important reasons to slow down the growth of energy demand. In this case, China's energy demand per unit GDP maintained a reducing trend, from 8.8 to 6.8 tons of coal equivalent per thousand yuan, during 2010–2016.

The spatial distribution of energy resources in China is extremely unbalanced, and there is a large spatial distribution gap between areas where energy resources are concentrated and those where energy is consumed. Therefore, energy products need to be traded between regions. Regional differences in energy distribution lead to energy flows that meet the energy needs of different provinces. Therefore, there are some provinces with more energy production than energy consumption and vice versa. The regions with high energy security performances are mainly located in the middle reaches of the Yellow River and northwest, southwest, and northeast China, while the regions with weaker energy security are mainly distributed in coastal areas (Liu *et al.*, 2012). Specifically, Shanxi, Inner Mongolia, Shaanxi, Heilongjiang, Xinjiang, and Guizhou have the highest surplus of energy supply. Meantime, the surplus of energy supply in the above-mentioned provinces has been increasing over time, in all places except Heilongjiang. In contrast, Jiangsu, Guangdong, Hebei, Shandong, Zhejiang, Hubei, and Liaoning have the highest gap between energy supply and demand. Each of these provinces had an energy supply shortfall of more than 100 million tons of standard coal in 2009 (Shen *et al.*, 2010). Moreover, the gap between supply and demand in these provinces is widening annually.

Safe and stable energy supply is an important basis for guaranteeing energy security (Lu *et al.*, 2014). For the energy security of China, ensuring energy supply is even more important. China's energy supply consists of domestic production, imports, and reserves. In terms of domestic production, by the end of 2016, China's proven coal reserves were 1598 billion tons, oil reserves were 3.5 billion tons, and natural gas reserves were 54536.5 billion cubic meters (Ministry of Natural Resources of the People's Republic of China, 2017). Coal resources still occupy the majority of China's energy reserves. However, China does not occupy a dominant position in the reserves of crude oil and natural gas when compared with the rest of the world. As of 2017, China's proven reserves of crude oil and natural gas account for only 1.5% and 3.1% of the world's proved reserves (BP, 2019b). Meantime, crude oil and natural gas are also major sources of China's energy imports. In 2017, China's external dependence on oil and natural gas reached 69% and 52%, respectively. In order to ensure the stability of crude oil and natural gas import, China completed three cross-border oil import pipelines in 2015, i.e., China–Russia, China–Kazakhstan, and China–Myanmar. In the same year, China established the ABC line in Central Asia, the China–Myanmar cross-border natural gas import pipeline, and even began construction of the East China–Russia line and the Central Asia D line. Energy storage is an important aspect of China's energy security to avoid energy risk. In addition, China's energy storage mainly focuses on petroleum reserves. In 2004, China began to build the first phase of the national strategic petroleum reserve bases, and during the 12th Five-Year Plan (FYP) period, it began to build the second phase. After the completion of the first- and second-phase bases in 2020, China will have a total strategic reserve capacity of 44.6 million cubic meters (Yang and Li, 2015).

Energy price is one of the most important factors affecting energy security. Stable energy price has a profound impact on regulating the vitality of the domestic energy market and enhancing the influence on international energy price (Cao and Bluth, 2013). Since the 21st century, China's energy prices have shown an overall trend of rising volatility, among which that of the coal market price is the most obvious (Lin and Mou, 2008; He *et al.*, 2016). The fluctuation of coal price increased starting with the global financial crisis in 2008, but it began to decline significantly since 2014. In 2016, the coal supply reform pushed down the production capacity and output, while the coal price gradually recovered under the guidance of the price policy. Because of the decline in China's domestic coal production in 2017 from the 2016 level, the import volume increased rapidly, which also saw a rise in the international coal market price (He *et al.*, 2016).

In the 21st century, China's demand for energy is no longer limited to production and development, and also includes the concept of sustainable development. Promoting the cleanness of energy structure has been a new chapter of China's energy security development. The actual situation of its energy shows that in the future economic development process, coal will still be the main energy source. However, because of environmental concerns and other factors, the total coal demand will be controlled. In the internal composition of energy demand, the proportion of high-carbon energy has gradually declined, while the proportion of natural gas and non-fossil energy sources have been increasing. Specifically, during 2000–2018, the proportion of coal in energy demand decreased from 68% to 59%, while that of natural gas and non-fossil energy sources increased from 9.5% to 22% (National Bureau of Statistics of China, 2019).

1.2. *Literature review*

Many studies have applied various types of methodologies to evaluate energy security performance. Considering the spatial dimension, we subdivided all the previous studies into two categories: international and national level. Among these studies, most of the energy security studies at the international level focus on energy diversity, energy efficiency, and the impact of climate change on energy security, while those at the national (Chinese) level stress the impact of energy structure and energy policy on energy security.

1.2.1. *International-level studies*

As an indispensable part of economic security, energy security has long been the top priority of research in various countries (Duan and Wang, 2018); thus, there are many international-level studies on energy security. Using subjective and objective weight allocation, Wang and Zhou (2017) evaluated the energy security of global countries and found that the countries with good and excellent energy security performance were concentrated in western Europe and north America, while those with weak and poor energy security were concentrated in Asia and Africa. Matsumoto, Doumpos and Andriosopoulos (2018) applied energy security indicators and hierarchical clustering to analyze the energy security performance of EU countries and further confirmed that primary energy diversification was the main means of improving energy security, and import-related factors (the share and diversity of import sources) were also shown to have a significant impact on energy security. Bahgat and Gawdat (2006) concluded that geopolitical and economic developments in the first decade of the 21st century had heightened Europe's sense of vulnerability with respect to its energy supply. In terms of energy security in Asia, Tongsopit *et al.* (2016) suggested that increased development of renewable energy and energy efficiency technologies would move the Association of Southeast Asian Nations in a positive direction toward achieving energy security and sustainable energy policy goals. Li, Shi, and Yao (2016) analyzed energy security in four Asian economies, i.e., Singapore, South Korea, Japan, and Taiwan, which were resource-poor yet economically advanced countries, and proposed that the development of renewable resources and the liberalization of the power sector are important ways to strengthen energy security. Kitamura and Managi (2017) quantified Japan's energy security in the event of energy resource supply disruption in exporting countries for Japan and proposed that while the oil reserves of the government and enterprises played an important role in energy security, the unexpected shutdown of the nuclear power plant after the Fukushima accident in 2011 reduced the security of Japan's energy supply. Matsumoto (2018) further demonstrated that the Fukushima nuclear leakage event led to the continuous decline of Japan's energy security since 2011 and argued that energy security was mainly affected by the diversity of major energy sources. Moreover, some recent studies also found that climate change mitigation would be able to improve energy security performances by shifting the energy structure from a fossil-fuel-centered to a more renewable-energy-centered one (Matsumoto, 2013; Matsumoto and Andriosopoulos, 2016; Matsumoto and Shiraki, 2018).

1.2.2. *National-level studies*

The presence of rich natural resources does not fundamentally solve China's energy issue because the uneven regional distribution of energy has always been the root cause of the imbalance between energy supply and demand. Moreover, the huge population intensifies the severity of China's energy security. The problems of China's energy security are mainly reflected in the following five aspects: the significant pressure in energy supply, the relative scarcity of energy resources, the shortage of green energy, the relative backwardness of energy technology, and the drastic change in the international energy market (Luo, 2011). From the perspective of China's main energy types, Lin *et al.* (2012) showed that China's coal production would peak in 2030 and the net import of coal would continue to increase due to the rapid growth of GDP. Wang *et al.* (2018) argued that renewable energy was an effective tool to support China in maintaining energy independence and mitigating climate change. Furthermore, a strong and sustainable renewable energy policy will contribute to the sustainable development of China's energy. In terms of resource availability, resource affordability, economic efficiency, and environmental impact, Lu *et al.* (2019) suggested that China's energy security has improved over the last five decades. However, Geng and Ji (2014) found that during 1994–2008, because of increasing international energy market monopoly and high volatility of international crude oil prices, China's energy supply security declined. In addition, the economic development model also has a potential impact on the development of energy security. Yao and Chang (2015) deemed that China's macroeconomic reform had restricted the formation of China's energy policies and determined its energy security level. Energy security in the new era is gradually influenced by climate change. Duan and Wang (2018) proposed that climate policy could help reduce the systematic risk of China's energy system based on time-scale-independent indicators such as energy intensity, energy expenditure, and per capita energy consumption. In addition, Matsumoto (2015) applied a computable general equilibrium model to verify the performance of China's energy security in the business-as-usual and climate mitigation scenarios and further confirmed that energy security improved with the progress of climate change mitigation. In studies targeted at specific provinces, Yao (2008) analyzed the relationship between energy security and energy efficiency in Zhejiang from 1990 to 2005 and put forward the notion that the optimization of energy structure and industrial structure was the main reason for the enhancement of energy security in Zhejiang. Wang, Zhao and Xing (2014) predicted the coal input of Liaoning during 2012–2019 by using an autoregressive integrated moving average model and proposed that the main reasons for the slow enhancement of energy security in Liaoning were the single-energy demand structure and expansion of primary energy demand gap. Liu, Shen and Zhang (2011) made a comparative analysis of the energy security of Guangdong and Shaanxi from 1995 to 2008 and further emphasized that the external dependence of coal and the ratio of coal supply and demand were the key factors affecting the stability of regional energy security. Qiang and Chen (2016) built an energy security index based on a principal component analysis to evaluate Fujian's energy security and argued that both the energy supply security and energy utilization security significantly affected the overall energy security.

1.3. *Purpose of the study*

The literature review on energy security at the international and national (Chinese) levels showed that most of the studies analyzed energy security from the perspective of energy demand and energy diversity. On one hand, the analyses of energy demand mostly targeted the domestic aspect of energy demand, ignoring the impact of energy exporters on the stability of energy import. On the other hand, most of the studies focused on a single point in time, lacking comprehensive and long-term historical analysis of energy security. Moreover, literature on China's energy security mainly stressed energy security at the national level but lacked the energy security perspective that targeted all the provincial administrative units.

Thus, the energy security performance needs to be considered with consideration of impacts from multiple dimensions (Geng and Ji, 2014). Long-term historical analysis is important to understand what contributes to improving energy security. Thus, with relevant data pertaining to energy demand during the period 1992–2018, we used three energy security indicators based on the Shannon–Wiener diversity index to quantify China's overall energy security performance. Because there were no data on energy import at the provincial level, we only applied one of the three energy security indicators, which focuses on energy diversity, to quantify the energy security performance at the provincial level during 1995–2016.[1] While providing the energy security performance of all provincial administrative units in China, our findings can also demonstrate the impact of international energy markets on China's overall energy security. Therefore, this study contributes to the development of a comprehensive and historically grounded understanding of energy security in China, which will help to strengthen the theory and feasibility of China's energy security policy. Furthermore, considering that developing countries will be the main area for future economic development, China's development of energy security, as a representative of emerging economies, will provide insights to international applicability for the future development of energy security in developing countries.

The remaining parts of this chapter are organized as follows. Section 2 describes the methodology and data, Section 3 presents the results and discussion, and Section 4 presents the conclusions and policy implications based on our findings.

[1]Due to the different availability of energy security-related data at the national and provincial levels, our time series at the national and provincial levels are different.

2. Methodology and Data

Many methods were used to estimate energy security performance in the previous studies, as mentioned earlier. Here, we conducted simple indicator analyses to realize China's historical energy security performance at both national and provincial levels.

2.1. *Energy security indicators*

We used three energy security indicators $S1$, $S2$, and $S3$ to evaluate the historical transition of energy security performance according to energy supply in China (Matsumoto *et al.*, 2018). These indicators enabled us to analyze historical energy security development by mainly taking into consideration energy availability as well as country risks.

The first indicator $S1$ (Equation (1)) evaluates the diversity of primary energy sources based on the Shannon–Wiener index, which is applied to both national- and provincial-level analyses. In this study, energy sources were divided into ten types (i.e., coal, oil, natural gas, wind, nuclear, hydro, solar, geothermal, biomass, and others (i.e., other renewable energy)) for the national-level analysis and into seven types (i.e., coal, oil, natural gas, hydro, nuclear, wind, and solar) for the provincial-level analysis. The diversity of energy sources is a very important factor for maintaining a high level of energy security. This is because if some energy sources decrease because of some reason, there is the possibility of it being compensated for by other energy sources. Therefore, it is necessary to improve energy diversity for ensuring that energy security is partly preserved.

$$S1 = -\sum_{i=1}^{N} p_i \ln(p_i), \tag{1}$$

where i denotes the type of primary energy source, p_i denotes the share of primary energy i, and N denotes the number of primary energy types.

Diversity is not the only factor to affect energy security; thus, we considered energy import dependence and import origins in the second indicator $S2$ (Equations (2)–(5)). Note that only fossil fuels are imported but other energy sources are domestic. Therefore, the imports considered in $S2$ (and also $S3$) only include coal, oil, and natural gas.

$$S2 = -\sum_{i=1}^{N} c2_i p_i \ln(p_i), \tag{2}$$

$$\text{where } c2_i = 1 - dm_i \left(1 - \frac{IM2_i^m}{IM2_i^{\max}}\right), \tag{3}$$

$$IM2_i^m = -\sum_{j=1}^{M} m_{ij} \ln(m_{ij}), \tag{4}$$

$$IM2_i^{\max} = -M\frac{1}{M} \ln\left(\frac{1}{M}\right), \tag{5}$$

where j denotes the origin of the primary energy imports, dm_i denotes the share of imports of primary energy i, m_{ij} denotes the share of imports of primary energy i from country j, and M denotes the number of origins of primary energy imports (this differs by energy source).

As for the third indicator $S3$ (Equations (6)–(10)), risks of energy exporters are added to $S2$ to develop it. This is because energy sources imported from lower-risk countries are more important for ensuring the country's energy security.

$$S3 = -\sum_{i=1}^{N} c3_i p_i \ln(p_i), \tag{6}$$

$$\text{where } c3_i = 1 - dm_i \left(1 - \frac{IM3_i^m}{IM3_i^{\max}}\right), \tag{7}$$

$$IM3_i^m = -\sum_{j=1}^{M} A_j m_{ij} \ln(m_{ij}), \tag{8}$$

$$IM3_i^{\max} = -M\frac{1}{M} \ln\left(\frac{1}{M}\right), \tag{9}$$

$$A_j = \frac{r_j}{\max_j r_j}, \tag{10}$$

where r_j denotes the risk indicator for country j.

The three indicators were calculated for each year from 1992 to 2018 at the national level. However, because the data for country risks were only available from 1996 to 2018, $S3$ was calculated from 1996 to 2018. At the provincial level, the energy security performance was calculated with $S1$ only from 1995 to 2016, because of the data availability.

2.2. *Data*

The data on China's demand and import of primary energy (used to calculate the share of primary energy p_i and dependence on imports dm_i) were extracted from two data sources: the Statistical Review of World Energy (BP, 2019b) and the UN Comtrade Database (United Nations, 2018). According to the Statistical Review of World Energy (BP, 2019b), we aggregated the demand data into ten types of primary energy. Data on the import of fossil fuels (coal, oil, and natural gas) were taken from the UN Comtrade Database (United Nations, 2018). In addition, this study applied the average of six governance indicators (control of corruption, government effectiveness, political stability and absence of violence/terrorism, regulatory quality, rule of law, and voice and accountability) from the World Governance Indicators (World Bank, 2019) for the risk indicator r_j. Because the governance indicators ranged from -2.5 to 2.5, they were converted into a scale of 0–1, with values closer to 0 indicating higher risk. Not all risk data were available after 1996. However, to increase the period of the analysis, data available for the closest years or average of the two closest years were used to make up the missing data from 1996 to 2018.

As for the provincial-level data, the primary energy demand (from 1995 to 2016) was taken from the National Bureau of Statistics of China (National Bureau of Statistics of China, 2019).

Figure 1 shows the energy demand structure of the country from 1992 to 2018 (BP, 2019b). China shifted from being a net oil exporter to a net oil importer in 1993 (Jianxin, 2006). Since then, it has become the second largest net oil importer after the United States (Leung, 2011). China depends on more and more oil and natural gas (Figure 1). It is apparent that China's primary energy demand is increasing over time. Despite the slower economic growth than what was seen in the past years, China's primary energy demand rose by

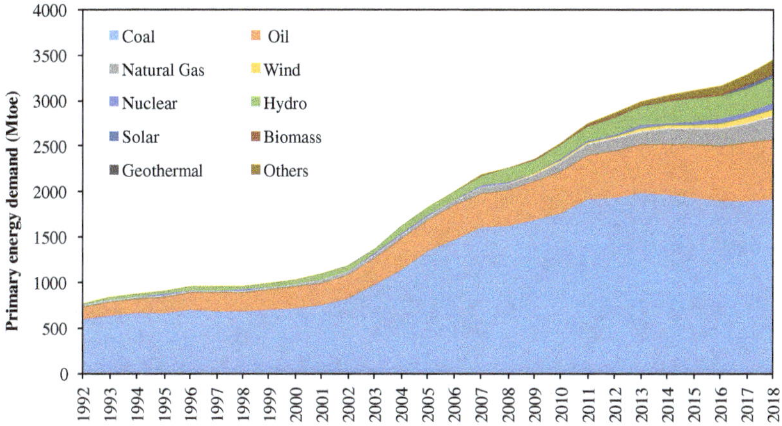

Figure 1: Structure and transition of primary energy demand in China. "Others" means other renewable energy.
Source: BP (2019b).

4.3% in 2018, the highest since 2012 (BP, 2019b). In addition, the demand for coal occupies a huge percentage of overall energy demand because China is the largest producer and consumer of coal in the world (BP, 2019b). Although China has reduced the demand for coal in order to protect the environment, the share of coal was 56% of the energy mix in 2018 (BP, 2019b). Because the coal demand declined, the demands for other primary energy sources have increased over time.

The provincial data showed differences in the primary energy structure based on the province (see for example Figure 6 in Section 3.2 for the primary energy structure of the six selected provinces). As can be seen, Beijing depends mostly on fossil fuels, while the other five provinces depend not only on fossil fuels but also on other primary energy sources. The types and demands of primary energy have also increased in every province over time (Figure 6).

Figure 2 shows China's import dependence rate for fossil fuels (United Nations, 2018) and the self-sufficiency rate of fossil fuel use (BP, 2019b). Figure 2(a) shows that the dependence rates of imported fossil fuels have increased at different rates over time. The dependence on imported oil has stably increased, with some exceptions. As China is the largest coal producer, the country has enough coal production to maintain its coal self-sufficiency (Figure 2(b)).

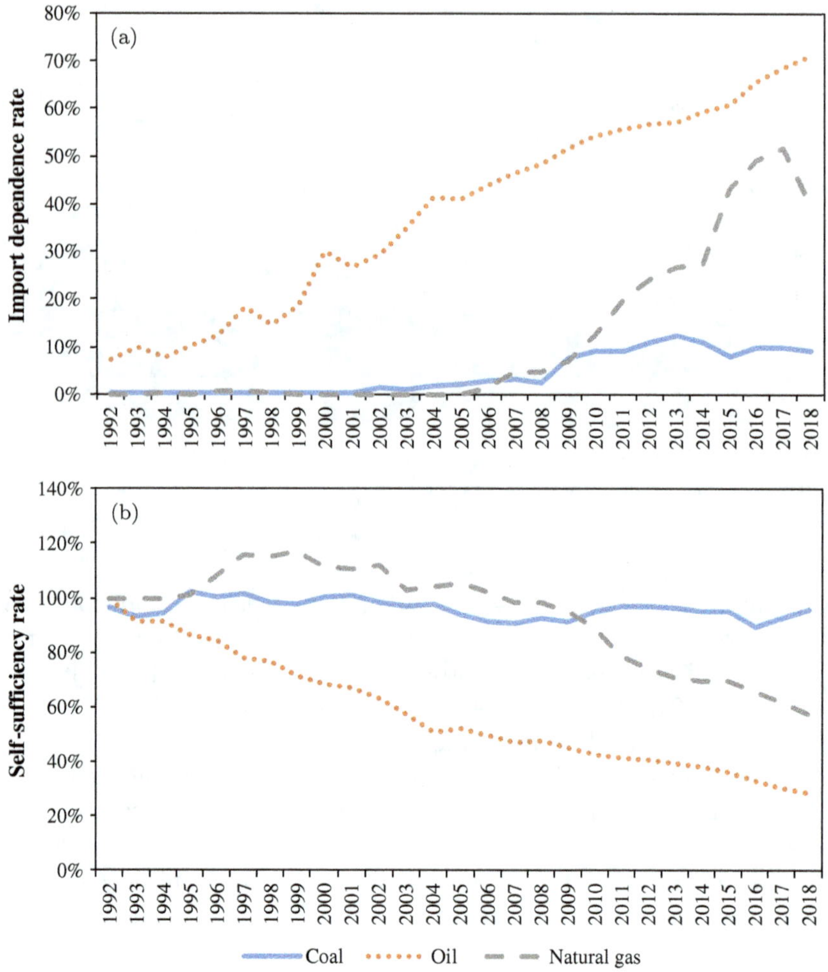

Figure 2: Dependence on import (a) and self-sufficiency rate (b) of fossil fuels. *Source*:United Nations (2018) for panel (a) and BP (2019b) for panel (b).

In addition, import dependence of coal is lower than that of oil and natural gas (Figure 2(a)). Self-sufficiency in natural gas demand was seen before 2007. Indeed, gas production actually exceeded its consumption during 1996–2006 (Lin and Wang, 2012). China had imported little natural gas before 2005. However, natural gas import dependence rose quickly after 2005 (Figure 2(a)), mainly because Chinese authorities were concerned about the environment

(Chai *et al.*, 2018). Dependence on imported natural gas suddenly declined in 2018, because of the China-United States trade war (Downs, 2019).

3. Results and Discussion

In this section, the results at the national level and those at the provincial level are presented in Sections 3.1 and 3.2, respectively.

3.1. *Energy security performance at the national level*

Using data on primary energy demands and imports, as well as the country risk indicators, we calculated the three energy security indicators ($S1$, $S2$, and $S3$) from 1992 to 2018 ($S3$ from 1996 to 2018). As shown in Figure 3, the first indicator, $S1$, increased from 1992 to 2002, and then it slightly decreased in the period 2002–2006. After that, it tended to increase, except for the period from 2008 to 2011, showing some fluctuations. The energy security performance wave from 2008 to 2011 was due to the global financial crisis outbreak, which affected the world economy. The global financial crisis reduced the global energy demand (Umbach, 2010). Eventually, this reduced energy demand, which made the energy diversity unstable in terms of China's energy demand structure.

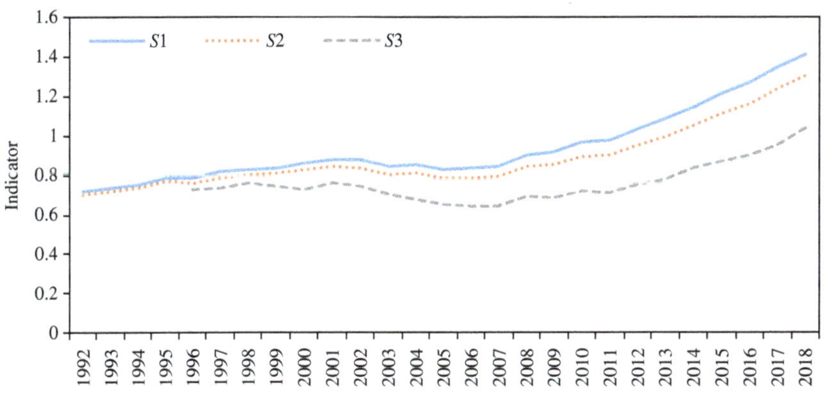

Figure 3: Primary energy security trends with respect to the three indicators in China during 1992–2018.

The second indicator, $S2$, revealed that the energy security, from primary energy diversity together with fossil fuels imports, increased stably during the period 1992–2002. $S2$ also encountered a small fluctuation between 2008 and 2011, and then increased smoothly after 2011. As mentioned earlier, the observed peak in 2008 was due to the impact of the global financial crisis on China's import of primary energy. Indeed, the growth rate of primary energy from fossil fuel imports was 2.5% in 2008, 15.5 percentage points less than that in 2007 (BP, 2019b). Although $S1$ and $S2$ both evaluated energy security from ten types of primary energy source, $S2$ also included the import of fossil fuels. The gap between $S1$ and $S2$ has grown larger over time. As China imports more energy, $S1$ will be greater than $S2$. As mentioned in Section 2.2, when the domestic energy production could not meet the demand, China started importing more primary energy, which started in 1993. Consequently, import of fossil fuels caused a widening of the gap between $S1$ and $S2$.

The third indicator, $S3$, was neither similar to $S1$ nor $S2$. $S3$ showed a decreasing trend during the period 1996–2006 with a fluctuation from 1998 to 2002. Because the Asian financial crisis occurred during 1997–1999, several oil-exporting countries faced a decline of about 50% in their national incomes within one year (Umbach, 2010). With the oil price declining, energy demand also decreased (Umbach, 2010). Because China was a net oil-importing country, the Asian financial crisis caused a general decrease in energy imports and also energy import in China (United Nations, 2018). Decreasing energy imports resulted in $S3$ reaching a peak in 1998. After 2006, $S3$ stably increased, except for a fluctuation observed in the period 2008–2011. In addition, the differences between $S2$ and $S3$ have grown larger over time. According to United Nations (2018) and World Bank (2019), China's import partners were increasing over time and, at the same time, the countries' risk level also increased. Therefore, since China imported more fossil fuels from higher-risk countries, the differences between the two indicators grew over time.

For further discussion, we chose 1996, 2001, 2006, and 2018 to analyze the changes in these three indicators. Figure 4 shows the energy demand structure of the four years (BP, 2019b). As can be seen from Figure 3, the three indicators reached their peaks in 2001 and dropped until 2006. We considered the primary energy structures of 2001 and 2006 as turning points in terms of the energy security

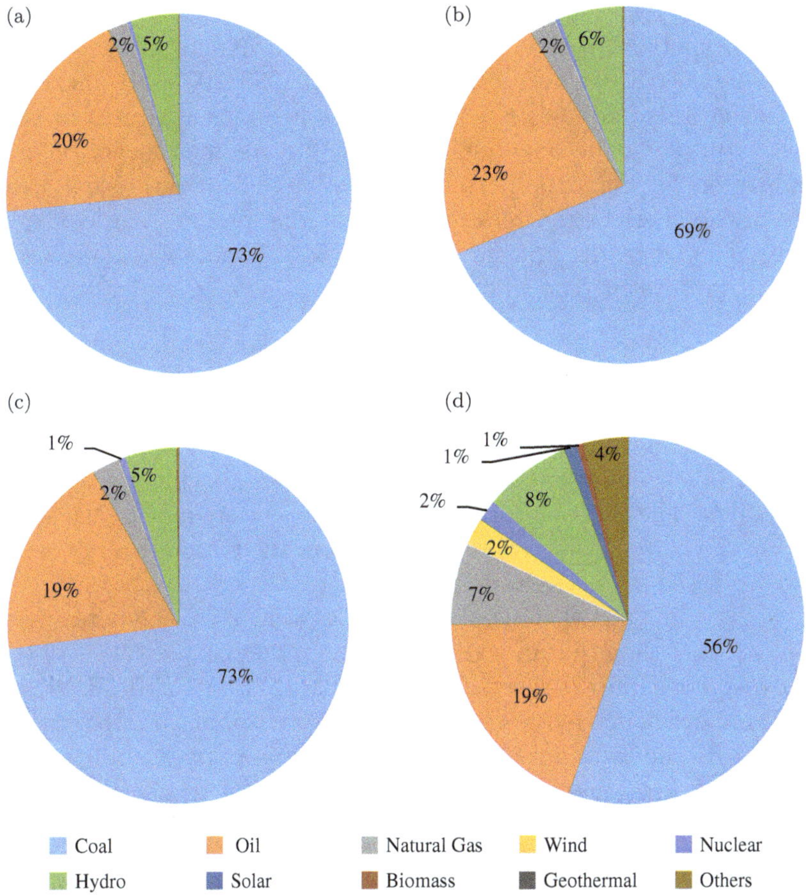

Figure 4: Primary energy demand structure in 1996 (a), 2001 (b), 2006 (c), and 2018 (d).

Source: BP (2019b).

performance. The energy structure of 2018 shows the current situation of China's energy demand (Figure 4(d)). Analyzing the energy demand structures during these years will enable us to provide future directions of the energy demand structure.

(1) 1996–2001:

Comparing Figure 4(a) with Figure 4(b), we can see that China's coal demand was 69% in 2001, which was 4 percentage points lower than that in 1996. The shares of other energy sources were almost the same in 1996 and 2001 (except for oil increasing 3 percentage points from 1996 to 2001). Because of these changes in the shares, the energy security increased in the period 1996–2001 ($S1$ and $S2$).

During this period (1996–2001), the self-sufficiency rates of coal and natural gas became high (Figure 2). As mentioned before, China's energy imports increased over time. Also, the risk indicators of the energy exporters increased in this period (World Bank, 2019). Therefore, the upward trend in risk of import was the reason for the downward trend of $S3$.

(2) 2001–2006:

When comparing Figure 4(b) with Figure 4(c), we can see that the share of coal demand was 73% in 2006, which was 4 percentage points higher than that in 2001. The shares of oil demand declined 1 percentage point while that of hydropower demand declined 4 percentage points. The shares of other energy sources were almost the same during these two years. These changes were the reasons energy security decreased in this period ($S1$ and $S2$).

China's oil import dependence was 44% in 2006, 17 percentage points higher than that in 2001. In addition, the risk indicators of the oil-exporting countries increased as well (World Bank, 2019). Increase in oil import dependence was the main threat to oil import security (Zhang, Ji and Fan, 2013). In contrast, the import dependences of coal and natural gas were much lower than that of oil (Figure 2); thus, the main cause of the downward trend of $S3$ was the risk of the oil exporters.

(3) 2006–2018:

The primary energy diversity in 2018 was much higher than that in 2006 (Figure 4(c)(d)). The share of coal demand declined from 73% in 2006 to 56% in 2018. The share of natural gas demand increased from 2% to 7% and that of hydropower demand increased from 5% to 8% in the same period. In addition, China has expanded wind, nuclear, solar, biomass, and other renewable energy sources (Figure 4(d)). Thus, $S1$ steeply increased during the period 2006–2018.

The import dependence of fossil fuels (especially oil and natural gas) increased rapidly during this period. However, $S2$ also increased during this period. This may be because the effect of energy diversity was strong enough to increase the $S2$ indicator. Furthermore, during this period, the risk levels of important oil exporters, such as Iran and

Iraq, stayed high (World Bank, 2019) and the share of oil imported from Iran and Iraq increased (16.1% in 2018). Such increases in the share of imports from high-risk countries widened the gap between $S3$ and the other indicators, although the $S3$ indicator also showed an increase.

From these results on national-level analyses, it can be elucidated that not only diversification of primary energy diversity but also a decrease in energy imports from high-risk countries is essential to improve energy security.

3.2. *Energy security performance at the provincial level*

Using primary energy demand data of each province, we obtained the energy security performance based on the energy security indicator $S1$ (Equation (1)) for 30 provinces (Figure 5). Note that because different types of primary energy sources were used to calculate $S1$, the results for the national and provincial levels are not comparable. The energy security performance of most provinces gradually increased with time. However, energy security performance of Heilongjiang gradually weakened after reaching its peak in 2001. Because of limited space to discuss the results of all the provinces, we selected provinces with particularly significant growth in energy security performances, i.e., Guangdong, Qinghai, Beijing, Sichuan, and Fujian (marked by black rectangles in Figure 5), for further discussion. In addition, as Heilongjiang is the only province with a negative growth in energy security performance since 1995, this was also selected for discussion (marked by a red rectangle in Figure 5). Figure 6 shows the primary energy demand structure of the above-mentioned six provinces.

Figure 5 shows that Guangdong experienced the highest energy security performance among the 30 provinces in 2016. Because $S1$ expresses the diversity of primary energy sources, we can speculate that the primary energy diversity of Guangdong increased from 1995 to 2016. According to primary energy demand structure shown in Figure 6(a), the growth rate of coal demand in Guangdong began to slow down in 2007 and the demand for natural gas started to increase significantly in the same year. In 2011, the coal demand decreased for the first time. Meanwhile, the growth of nuclear energy

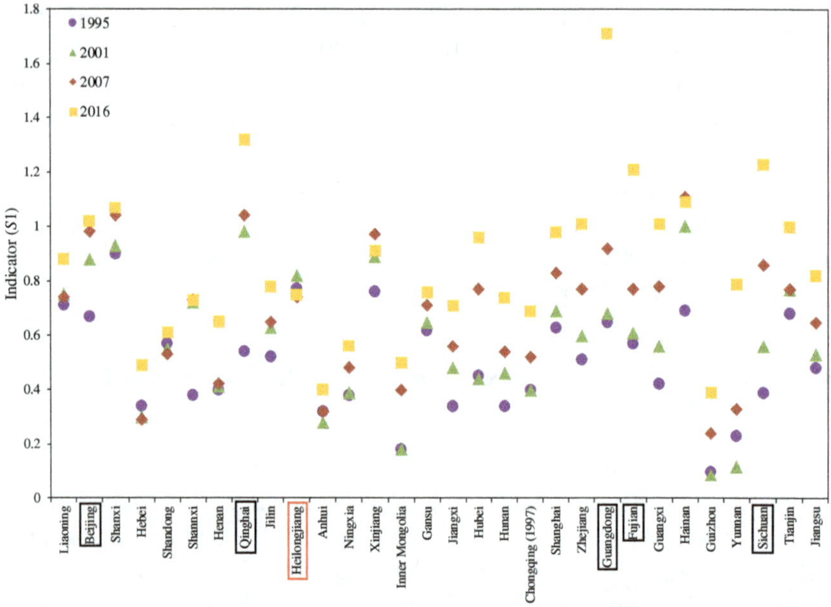

Figure 5: Energy security performance based on $S1$ in 1995, 2001, 2007, and 2016 at the provincial level.

demand accelerated, and the demand for hydropower started to show a steady growth. Overall, the energy structure of Guangdong shifted from a high-carbon one to a low-carbon one, with the most obvious change in energy structure being the significant increase in nuclear power (Figure 6(a)). With the continuous acceleration of economic development, the decoupling of energy demand and economic growth has gradually intensified. As China became part of the World Trade Organization during the 10th FYP (2001–2005) period, Guangdong's economy saw rapid development, with an average annual gross regional product growth of 146.4 billion yuan in 2001–2016 (Bureau of Statistics of Guangdong Province, 2019). However, Guangdong was short on fossil-fuel reserves and production, with almost 100% coal dependency on other provinces. In 2006, the power gap in Guangdong was as high as 4.24 GW (Guo and Li, 2009). In order to ensure energy security to maintain sustainable and stable economic development, Guangdong gradually adjusted the power generation structure that was reliant on coal-fueled power. Under this

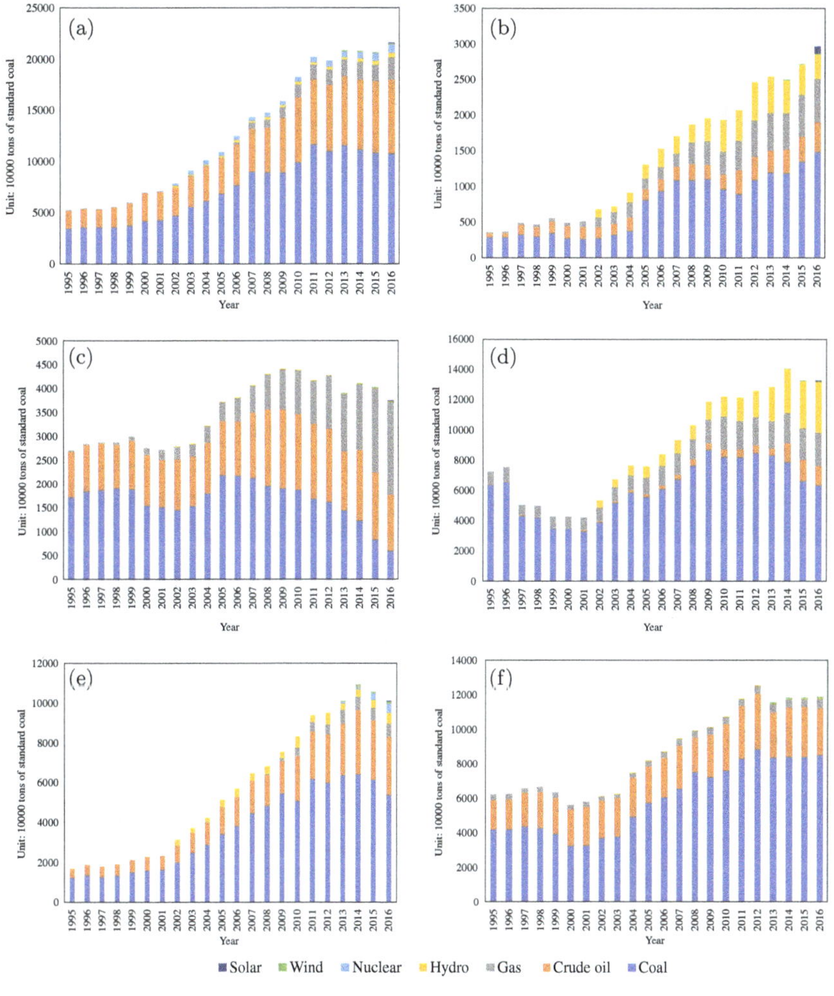

Figure 6: Primary energy demand structure of Guangdong (a), Qinghai (b), Beijing (c), Sichuan (d), Fujian (e), and Heilongjiang (f).
Source: National Bureau of Statistics of China (2019).

condition, nuclear power has become an effective way to solve the problem of power generation in Guangdong, where energy resources are scarce but energy demand is very high (Li, 2018). According to the 11th FYP for the development of nuclear power in Guangdong, from 2005 to 2020, the installed capacity of new nuclear power will reach 20 GW. Actually, during the first eight months of 2018,

Guangdong's nuclear power generation was 55.16 TWh, accounting for 30.6% of the national total nuclear power.

The province with the lowest total population during 1995–2016 (National Bureau of Statistics of China, 2018) and the one with a relatively backward economic development, leading to the lowest energy demand, was Qinghai. However, compared with the energy structure of other provinces (Figure 6), Qinghai's energy structure was obviously diversified. In addition, because of the diversified development of primary energy sources, Qinghai's energy security performance rapidly grew during 1995–2016, and it ranked second in energy security performance among the 30 provinces in 2016 (Figure 5). After 2008, the demand for clean energy in Qinghai has gradually increased, especially the proportion of hydropower, which reached a peak of 22.8% in 2010. The reason behind the increase in clean energy is that, in 1999, Qinghai issued relevant policies to implement the national law on the prevention and control of air pollution and actively developed and promoted clean energy such as hydropower, natural gas, and solar power, which gradually replaced coal. In addition, Qinghai is extremely rich in hydropower, the proportion of which has continuously increased in the entire clean energy mix in the power supply structure. As shown in Figure 6(b), solar energy started to show significant growth in 2016. Because of its abundant solar energy[2], the Qinghai provincial government also emphasized the importance of solar energy in the development of clean energy in the 12th FYP (2011–2015). Therefore, the installed photovoltaic power generation of the province reached 4 GW by 2015, accounting for about 15% of the total installed power generation of the whole province.

Sichuan ranked third among 30 provinces in terms of energy security performance in 2016, and its energy demand structure was similar to that of Qinghai, with hydropower accounting for a large proportion of its total energy demand. Although the proportion of clean energy increased in both provinces, the low-carbon development of energy demand structure in Sichuan was more obvious.

[2]Qinghai is rich in solar energy, especially in Qaidam Basin, with an annual sunshine duration of 3200–3600 hours, and the annual total radiation is 7000–8000 MJ/m^2.

Specifically, compared with Qinghai, after 2008, the coal demand of Sichuan showed a significant downward trend. Sichuan has the second largest hydropower resources in China after Yunnan, and it also has the largest reserves of natural gas with the best conditions for further development (Lou and Li, 2016). However, Sichuan does not have an advantage in traditional energy (i.e., coal and oil). The production of coal is far less than demand, and the topography of the basin results in little oil reserves, so about 90% of its crude oil supply is imported from other provinces. During the 12th FYP, the Sichuan government set goals of developing clean energy, optimizing the energy demand structure, and reducing the proportion of high-carbon fuels. The low-carbon development of energy structure promoted the diversification of energy structure in Sichuan by reducing Sichuan's dependence on coal resources and greatly enhancing the energy security performance. In addition, the optimization of the energy demand of industries was also one of the important factors for the enhancement of Sichuan's energy security performance. The energy demand in the secondary industries continuously decreased, while the energy demand in the tertiary industry sector steadily increased, which to a large extent reduced the demand for fossil energy in industrial activities and promoted the circulation of clean energy in the market (Shen *et al.*, 2019).

Compared with Guangdong and Qinghai, Beijing's energy security performance in 2016 was not so prominent, and even lagged behind the energy security performance of some other provinces (e.g., Hebei and Yunnan). However, Beijing had a strong energy security performance in the early stage. The reason for this phenomenon is closely related to Beijing's energy supply. In the early period, Beijing's strong energy security performance benefited from its energy structure. In 2005, the executive meeting of the state council adopted the Beijing urban master plan (2004–2020) that aimed to reduce the use of high-carbon energy and increase the proportion of clean energy. As of 2016, Beijing's natural gas demand accounted for 31% of the total energy demand, an increase of 17 percentage points compared with 2010 (Bureau of Statistics of Beijing, 2017), and natural gas has now become one of the main energy sources. Although Beijing's energy security performance was relatively high at the beginning, the enhancement of Beijing's energy security performance after 2007 was not obvious. The weakening of its energy security performance in the later stages was closely related to energy production. From 1995 to 2016, the total energy demand in Beijing was always greater than the total energy production. Since 2000, the annual energy production in Beijing has been stable while the growth rate of energy demand has been increasing to reach levels higher than that of energy production (Bureau of Statistics of Beijing, 2006, 2017). In 2016, the total energy demand increased by 1.67 times compared with the 2000 level (Bureau of Statistics of Beijing, 2017), resulting in a widening gap between demand and production. This imbalance between demand and production has increased Beijing's dependence on external sources of energy. In addition, Beijing's energy dispatch was concentrated on natural gas and coal, leading to the development and introduction of renewable energy being slower than in other provinces after 2007. Eventually, the lagging development of renewable energy weakened the increase in Beijing's energy security performance.

Compared with the initial stage, Fujian's energy security performance in 2016 has greatly improved, ranking it fourth among the 30 provinces. However, the time distribution of energy security enhancement in Fujian showed a certain degree of imbalance, with a trend similar to the change in energy security enhancement in Guangdong. Before 2007, the enhancement of energy security was weak, but after 2007, the enhancement was significant. Before 2007, the proportion of oil and coal in the energy structure of Fujian remained more than 80% (Figure 6(e)). Although Fujian is one of the representatives of China's coastal developed provinces, it lacks fossil fuel production and relies heavily on the imports of fossil fuels from other provinces. From 2000 to 2014, Fujian's energy self-sufficiency rate gradually decreased from 56% to 24% (Bureau of Statistics of Fujian Province, 2017). From 2015, the energy self-sufficiency rate began to increase slightly. Since its energy demand depends on the input from other provinces, the energy security of Fujian is largely controlled by the stability of the external energy supply, resulting in the weak energy security performance from 1995 to 2007. After 2007, strengthening the development and utilization of clean energy in Fujian to reduce the dependence on external energy supply was the main driving force to enhance Fujian's energy security. In the special plan for energy development during the 12th FYP period, Fujian put forward the diversification of its power supply structure and the development of new energy to improve the ability to guarantee energy supply. During 12th FYP period, the power and energy structure in Fujian was continuously optimized and clean energy sources, such as hydropower, wind power, and nuclear power, developed rapidly, accounting for 61% of the total energy production in 2014 (Qiang and Chen, 2016). Moreover, as the proportion of coal power generation in the total power mix decreased and the dependence of coal demand on external supply gradually weakened. From 2006 to 2016, hydropower showed stable development in Fujian, accounting for 40% of the total energy production annually (Ji and Xi, 2018). In addition, owing to its location on the southeastern coast, Fujian is also rich in wind power due to the narrow pipe effect of the Taiwan strait. In 2015, the installed wind power capacity reached 1.76 GW, an increase of 141% over 2010 (Huang, 2019). Fujian began to use nuclear power in 2013 and, as of 2015, its total installed nuclear power capacity accounted for 11% of the total installed capacity (Ji and Xi, 2018). As stated, during the 12th FYP period, the development of renewable and clean energy has enhanced the diversity of energy in Fujian, reduced the external dependence of energy, and greatly enhanced the energy security.

The top five provinces in energy security performance in 2016 mentioned herein have some of the following points in common: the demand for fossil fuel energy has gradually decreased, the share of clean energy demand has grown steadily, and the scale of renewable energy demand has expanded. Heilongjiang, the only province with negative growth in energy security performance during the study period, does not have these characteristics. The proportion of coal demand in Heilongjiang has increased since 2000 while that of clean energy remained small. In terms of the energy resources, Heilongjiang is rich in mineral resources, especially coal and crude oil, which led to the fact that in the secondary industry of Heilongjiang, resource-based heavy industry enterprises represented by coal and crude oil, has always occupied a leading position (Sun *et al.*, 2016). Moreover, the share of secondary industry, which is dominated by resource-based industries, in its gross regional product was above 51% before 2011 (Bureau of Statistics of Heilongjiang Province, 2017). Regarding clean energy, Heilongjiang is rich in natural gas resources, with proven reserves of about 139.1 billion cubic meters. Meanwhile, Heilongjiang is also one of the nine largest wind power bases in China with the most abundant wind energy resources. However, because of the superiority of coal resources, a coal-thermal power has more cost advantages, thus negatively affecting diversification of energy structure (Cai and Cui, 2017). Although coal demand slightly decreased during the 12th FYP period, it still occupies a high share in total energy mix. The proportion of natural gas in 2016 was only 4.1%, which was lower than the national average (Bureau of Statistics of Heilongjiang Province, 2017). Although Heilongjiang is rich in fossil fuels, its recoverable reserves have been seriously depleted since 2003 due to the early exploitation of resources and the long-term intensive exploitation (Zhang and Qin, 2013; Wang and Song, 2017). Furthermore, Heilongjiang's energy diversity is weak. Specifically, the energy structure has been dominated by high-carbon energy, and the introduction of clean energy is slow (Figure 6(f)). The above factors ultimately led to the negative growth of energy security in Heilongjiang after 2007.

4. Conclusions

Although China is abundant in energy resources, it is also a large energy consumer with rapid economic development and the aim of environmental pollution reduction. In this chapter, we evaluated the historical energy security performance of China at both national and provincial levels by using the three energy security indicators. At the national level, the energy security performance evaluated by the three energy security indicators mostly showed an improvement since 2006, except for a slight fluctuation between 2008 and 2011 because of the global financial crisis. At the provincial level, we evaluated the energy security performance with the $S1$ indicator. The results showed that the demand for fossil fuels has gradually decreased with the share of clean energy demand growing steadily and the scale of renewable energy demand expanding. At both the national and provincial levels (except Heilongjiang), energy diversity showed increase after 2006.

China's primary energy demand structure is not optimum in terms of energy security defined herein as it has a large share of coal and a small share of other primary sources of energy, particularly renewable energy. Similarly, the energy demand structures of the six selected provinces also indicated that the provinces rely too much on coal.

To further improve energy security in China, two policy implications are provided.

1. Increasing the share of renewable energy is necessary to balance primary energy structure, not only for the country but also for every province in China. Actually, the degree of primary energy diversity is significantly different among provinces. In this case, energy balance is also of vital importance in every province. For example, the Chinese government can adopt measures to guide people to use more renewable energy instead of traditional coal, such as by reducing the prices of renewable energy to stimulate renewable energy demand.
2. Considering the origin of energy import and reducing imports from high-risk countries are also important strategies to improve energy security. China is a large energy producer (especially the largest coal producer) and also a large energy consumer. For stimulating economic development, China should collaborate positively with other countries rich in energy resources to secure enough energy imports. In addition, considering the risks of fossil-fuel-exporting countries is an effective way for reducing imports from high-risk countries.

Acknowledgments

This study was partially supported by Integrated Research Program for Advancing Climate Models Grant Number JPMXD0717935457 from the Ministry of Education, Culture, Sports, Science and Technology, Japan, and JSPS KAKENHI Grant Numbers JP18K11754 and JP18K11800.

References

Bahgat, G. 2006. Europe's energy security: Challenges and opportunities. *International Affairs*, 82(5), 961–975.

BP. 2019a. *BP Energy Outlook 2019 edition, BP Energy Outlook.* Available at: https://www.bp.com/en/global/corporate/search-results.html?q=BP

Energy Outlook 2019 edition&hPP=10&idx=bp.com&p=0&fR%5BbaseUrl%5D%5B0%5D=%2F (accessed 26 February 2020).

BP. 2019b. *BP Statistical Review of World Energy, The Editor BP Statistical Review of World Energy*. Available at: https://www.bp.com/content/dam/bp/business-sites/en/global/corporate/pdfs/energy-economics/statistical-review/bp-stats-review-2019-full-report.pdf (accessed 26 February 2020).

Bureau of Statistics of Beijing. 2006. *Beijing statistical yearbook (2006)*. Available at: http://nj.tjj.beijing.gov.cn/nj/main/2006_ch/index.htm (accessed 26 February 2020).

Bureau of Statistics of Beijing. 2017. *Beijing statistical yearbook (2017)*. Available at: http://nj.tjj.beijing.gov.cn/nj/main/2017-tjnj/zk/indexch.htm (accessed 16 February 2020).

Bureau of Statistics of Fujian Province. 2017. *Fujian statistical yearbook (2017)*. Available at: http://tjj.fujian.gov.cn/xxgk/ndsj/ (accessed 16 February 2020).

Bureau of Statistics of Guangdong Province. 2019. *Guangdong statistical yearbook (2019)*. Available at: http://stats.gd.gov.cn/gdtjnj/content/post_2639622.html (accessed 16 February 2020).

Bureau of Statistics of Heilongjiang Province. 2017. *Heilongjiang statistical yearbook (2017)*. Available at: http://www.hlj.stats.gov.cn/tjsj/tjnj/ (accessed 26 February 2020).

Cai, Y. and Cui, Y. 2017. Investigation and analysis on the current situation and existing problems of energy industry in Heilongjiang Province. *Business Economy*, 6, 22–23.

Cao, W. and Bluth, C. 2013. Challenges and countermeasures of China's energy security. *Energy Policy*, 53, 381–388.

Chai, J. *et al.* 2018. The Future natural gas consumption in China: Based on the LMDI-STIRPAT-PLSR framework and scenario analysis. *Energy Policy*, 119, 215–225.

Downs, E. 2019. *High Anxiety?: The Trade War and China's Oil and Gas Supply Security.*

Duan, H. and Wang, S. 2018. Potential impacts of China's climate policies on energy security. *Environmental Impact Assessment Review*, 71(80), 94–101.

Gechev, V. 2018. The economic rise of developing countries. *SSRN Electronic Journal.*

Geng, J. B. and Ji, Q. 2014. Multi-perspective analysis of China's energy supply security. *Energy*, 64, 541–550.

Guo, X. and Li, J. 2009. The advantages and perspectives of unclear power plant in Guangdong. *Energy Technology*, 30(3), 169–172.

He, L. *et al.* 2016. Comparison of the regulatory effects of domestic and foreign energy prices on energy consumption of China. *Journal of Natural Resources*, 31(1), 1–16.

Huang, X. 2019. Current situation and outlet of power and energy industry in Fujian Province. *Development Research*, 6, 73–79.

Ji, X. and Xi, Y. 2018. Study on building a clean, low-carbon, safe and efficient modern energy system in Fujian Province. *Energy and Environment*, 5, 14–20.

Jianxin, Z. 2006. *Oil Security Reshapes China's Foreign Policy.*

Kitamura, T. and Managi, S. 2017. Energy security and potential supply disruption: A case study in Japan. *Energy Policy*, 110, 90–104.

Kong, X. and Li, L. 2015. The new global energy landscape and China's policy. *Northeast Asia Forum*, 5, 47–57.

Leung, G. C. K. 2011. China's energy security: Perception and reality. *Energy Policy*, 39(3), 1330–1337.

Li, B. 2018. Energy security evaluation of China's economically developed provinces-taking Guangdong and Fujian Provinces as an example. *Coal Economic Research*, 38(7), 31–35.

Li, Y., Shi, X. and Yao, L. 2016. Evaluating energy security of resource-poor economies: A modified principle component analysis approach. *Energy Economics*, 58, 211–221.

Lin, B., Liu, J. and Yang, Y. 2012. Impact of carbon intensity and energy security constraints on china's coal import. *Energy Policy*, 48, 137–147.

Lin, B. and Mou, D. 2008. The impact of energy price increases on macro-economy: An analysis based on cge method. *Economic Research Journal*, 11, 88–101.

Lin, B. and Wang, T. 2012. Forecasting natural gas supply in China: Production peak and import trends. *Energy Policy*, 49, 225–233.

Liu, L. *et al.* 2012. Evaluation and spatial-temporal evolution of energy security in China. *Acta Geographica Sinica*, 67(12), 1634–1644.

Liu, L., Shen, L. and Zhang, Y. 2011. Regional differences in energy security of China: A case study of Guangdong and Shaanxi Provinces. *Resources Science*, 33(12), 2386–2393.

Lou, Y. and Li, Q. 2016. On energy utilization and structure of Sichuan Province. *Tianjin Science & Technology*, 43(02), 16–18+21.

Lu, H. *et al.* 2019. Emergy-based analysis of the energy security of China. *Energy*, 181, 123–135.

Lu, W. *et al.* 2014. Assessment of energy security in China based on ecological network analysis: A perspective from the security of crude oil supply. *Energy Policy*, 74, 406–413.

Luo, Y. 2011. Research on the current situations and countermeasures for the energy security in China. *Energy Procedia*, 5, 261–265.

Matsumoto, K. 2013. Change in energy structure and energy security under climate mitigation scenarios, in Leal, W. and Voudouris, V. (eds.) Global Energy Policy and Security, 45–57. London: Springer.

Matsumoto, K. 2015. Energy structure and energy security under climate mitigation scenarios in China. *PLoS ONE*, 10(12), 1–17.

Matsumoto, K. 2018. Energy security performance in Japan: Historical and scenario analysis, in Hsu, S. (ed.) Routledge Handbook of Sustainable Development in Asia, 596–610. Oxon and New York, NY: Routledge.

Matsumoto, K. and Andriosopoulos, K. 2016. Energy security in East Asia under climate mitigation scenarios in the 21st Century. *Omega*, 59, 60–71.

Matsumoto, K., Doumpos, M. and Andriosopoulos, K. 2018. Historical Energy security performance in EU countries. *Renewable and Sustainable Energy Reviews*, 82, 1737–1748.

Matsumoto, K. and Shiraki, H. 2018. Energy security performance in Japan under different socioeconomic and energy conditions. *Renewable and Sustainable Energy Reviews*, 90, 391–401.

Ministry of Natural Resources of the People's Republic of China. 2017. *China Mineral Resources Report 2017*. Available at: http://g.mnr.gov.cn/201710/t20171017_1629178.html (accessed 12 February 2020).

National Bureau of Statistics of China. 2018. *China statistical yearbook (2018)*. Available at: http://www.stats.gov.cn/tjsj/ndsj/ (accessed 10 February 2020).

National Bureau of Statistics of China. 2019. *China statistical yearbook (2000–2019)*. Available at: http://www.stats.gov.cn/tjsj/ndsj/ (accessed 12 February 2020).

Qiang, W. and Chen, A. 2016. The evolution and characteristics of Fujian's energy security. *Journal of Fujian Normal University*, 32(5), 96–105.

Ren, Z. and Li, C. 2017. Goal-oriented assessment of China's energy security. *International Petroleum Economics*, 11, 28–35.

Shen, L., Liu, L. and Zhang, Y. 2010. Theoretical analysis framework and empirical research on the complexity of regional energy security. *Research and Approach*, 32, 30–36.

Shen, Y. *et al.* 2019. Analysis on the dynamic characteristics of energy consumption structure in Sichuan Province. *Energy Conservation*, 4, 147–150.

Sun, F., Guo, P. and Luo, J. 2016. On Current situation and countermeasures of China's new low-carbon development of urbanization-based on the investigation in Heilongjiang province. *Journal of Liaoning Technical University (Social Science Edition)*, 18(2), 144–148.

Tongsopit, S. *et al.* 2016. Energy security in ASEAN: A quantitative approach for sustainable energy policy. *Energy Policy*, 90, 60–72.

Umbach, F. 2010. Global energy security and the implications for the EU. *Energy Policy*, 38(3), 1229–1240.

United Nations. 2018. *UN Comtrade, United Nations Statistical Office*. Available at: https://comtrade.un.org/data/ (accessed 15 February 2020).

Wang, B. *et al.* 2018. Role of renewable energy in China's energy security and climate change mitigation: An index decomposition analysis. *Renewable and Sustainable Energy Reviews*, 90, 187–194.

Wang, H. and Song, J. 2017. Study on the economic development of resource-based cities in Heilongjiang Province. *China Journal of Commerce*, 13, 121–122.

Wang, Q. and Zhou, K. 2017. A framework for evaluating global national energy security. *Applied Energy*, 188, 19–31.

Wang, Y., Zhao, Y. and Xing, H. 2014. Coal resource flow of Liaoning Province based on energy security. *Geography and Geo-Information Science*, 30(6), 82–87.

World Bank. 2019. *The World Governance Indicators*. Available at: https://datacatalog.worldbank.org/dataset/worldwide-governance-indicators (accessed 26 February 2020).

Yang, Z. and Li, W. 2015. Development situation and needs of China's petroleum reserve system. *International Petroleum Economics*, 23(9), 69–77.

Yao, L. and Chang, Y. 2015. Shaping China's energy security: The impact of domestic reforms. *Energy Policy*, 77, 131–139.

Yao, X. 2008. Energy efficiency and energy security-analysis based on Zhejiang Province. *Zhejiang Social Science*, 4, 33–39.

Zhang, H. Y., Ji, Q. and Fan, Y. 2013. An evaluation framework for oil import security based on the supply chain with a case study focused on China. *Energy Economics*, 38, 87–95.

Zhang, S. and Qin, J. 2013. Analysis of energy sustainable development in Heilongjiang Province. *Economic Forum*, 513(4), 46–47.

Zhang, Y. and Lu, B. 2015. Prediction of global energy trend and analysis on energy technology innovation characteristics. *Natural Gas Industry*, 35(10), 1–10.

https://doi.org/10.1142/9781786349224_0004

Chapter 4

Measuring Energy Security for China: A Multi-Dimensional Approach

Thai-Ha Le[*,§], Nguyen Phuc Canh[†,¶], and Wei Hao[‡,||]

[*]Fulbright School of Public Policy and Management, Fulbright University Vietnam, Vietnam
[†]University of Economics Ho Chi Minh City, Vietnam
[‡]Massey University, Wellington Campus, New Zealand
[§]ha.le@fulbright.edu.vn
[¶]canhnguyen@ueh.edu.vn
[||]w.hao@massey.ac.nz

Abstract

There have been very few studies that evaluate multiple dimensions of energy security in China. This study thus aims to extend the line of research on energy security for the case of China from 1980 to 2014. For this purpose, the 4-A quantitative evaluation framework from Yao and Chang (2014) was employed as the main stream of analysis. We then conducted an overall energy security index based on a total of sixteen indicators. The results indicate that: (i) the availability and applicability dimensions show a stable increasing trend over the entire investigation period; (ii) the acceptability dimension increased strongly over the period 1980s to 1995 before gradually increasing afterwards; (iii) the affordability dimension improved steadily from 1980 to 1992 and from 1999 to 2008, while showing a decline in other periods. Notably, China's overall energy security improved during the period 1990–1995, but decreased sharply over the years 1994–2000. Furthermore, it fluctuated from 2000 to 2009 before exhibiting a rising trend in recent years. The findings of this study imply that actions need to be taken on various dimensions for China to improve its overall energy security.

Keywords: Energy security index; China; 4-A evaluation framework; Principal component analysis; Normalization.

1. Introduction

Of the 17 sustainable development goals (SDGs) adopted by all United Nations (UN) Member States in 2015, energy is at the heart of many of them (UN, 2019). Indeed, energy security has been a critical issue that is the focus of significant attention from scholars and regulators (Le and Canh, 2019). Le and Canh (2019) find that energy security has positive impacts on economic growth, while energy insecurity presents a negative effect, as seen for instance during the period 2002–2013. As the world's fastest-growing regional economy, energy security is a crucial challenge facing Asia (Le *et al.*, 2019). By constructing an energy insecurity index based on 12 selected indicators for many countries in the region over the period 1990–2014, Le *et al.* (2019) indicate rising energy insecurity in most of the Asian countries (i.e., Bangladesh, China, India, Indonesia, Malaysia, Nepal, Pakistan, Saudi Arabia, Sri Lanka, Thailand, and Vietnam).

This chapter aims to measure the energy security index (ESI) for China. In 2010, with a GDP of US$5,879.9 billion, China officially surpassed Japan to become the second largest economy in the world after USA. To maintain this strong economic growth rate, China always needs a stable source of energy to ensure the operation of a sustainable growing economy. Furthermore, taking into consideration the energy issue is critical to achieve multiple development goals, that is, to ensure stable economic growth, prevent crises, and formulate security policies, and to restore and protect the environment as a mandatory condition of sustainable development. Therefore, in the process of national security strategy planning, the country always takes into account the energy security strategy. China has set specific goals for energy security strategy, which has served as an important premise for the country to take measures to ensure national energy security.

China is an emerging case for empirical studies of energy security due to its large-scale economy and large energy consumption base (Fang *et al.*, 2018; Hu *et al.*, 2014). Hu *et al.* (2014) noted that the economic growth of China was still heavily reliant on energy-intensive industries, which thus put strong pressure on energy security during the period 2000–2011. Interestingly, Yao and Chang (2014) proposed a 4-A quantitative evaluation framework (availability, technological applicability, acceptability, and affordability) to analyze China's energy security situation over the period 1981–2010. They found that energy security in China was at its best during the period 1981–1985 before deteriorating until 2010. Fang *et al.* (2018) extended the energy security analysis to five dimensions by adding developability to the aforementioned four categories[1] and carried out an empirical analysis for China over the period 2005–2015. They indicated that China's sustainable energy security was at risk over the period 2008–2012.

Traditionally, analysis of energy security have focused on the challenges of meeting energy demand because the competition for seemingly limited resources can result in conflict and undermine cooperation (Le *et al.*, 2019). Energy security analysis should be viewed as being multifaceted and should thus be extended beyond traditional themes such as ensuring the supply of fossil fuels and the efficacy of energy markets (Sovacool, 2011). However, there have been very few studies that evaluate the multiple dimensions of energy security for China. Furthermore, the evaluation of each dimension of energy security and the construction of a composite ESI are relatively scarce in the existing literature.

Therefore, this study extends the line of research on energy security for the case of China from 1980 to 2014. We employ four main dimensions (i.e., 4-A quantitative evaluation framework) from Yao and Chang (2014) as the main method of analysis. We then construct a composite ESI based on all the four components of the 4-A framework for empirical analysis and policy implication. Finally, an analysis of and discussion on the trend and fluctuation in each dimension of energy security as well as the overall ESI are carefully undertaken.

Empirically, the study constructs the availability (AV) dimension of energy security from five indicators, the applicability (AP) of technology from three indicators, the acceptability (AC) from three indicators, and the affordability (AF) from five indicators. The overall ESI is then constructed from these 16 indicators. The results show that: (i) the availability and applicability dimensions show a stable increasing trend over the whole period; (ii) the acceptability increased strongly over the period starting in the 1980s and continued till 1995 before increasing at a more gradual pace afterward; (iii) the affordability increased steadily in the periods 1980–1992 and

[1]More details on the definition of each dimension are provided in Le and Canh (2019).

1999–2008, while other periods witnessed a decreases in this indicator. Notably, the overall ESI shows that, overall, China's energy security improved during the period 1990–1995, while it decreased sharply in the period 1994–2000. In addition, it fluctuated over the years 2000–2009 before showing an increasing trend in recent years. The findings of this study support those by Tongsopit *et al.* (2016) who showed that to improve overall energy security, actions need to be taken in various dimensions.

The rest of this chapter is structured as follows. Section 2 reviews the related literature. Section 3 presents the data sources and methodology. Section 4 discusses the results and implications. Section 5 concludes with possible suggestions to improve China's energy security.

2. Literature Review

2.1. *Concept of energy security*

Although energy security has been studied extensively in the literature, there are very few studies that provide a clear, comprehensive, and commonly acceptable definition of energy security. The concept of energy security was initiated by the International Energy Agency (IEA) when confronting the threat of unstable oil supply after the first oil crisis in 1973. Since then, there has been growing interest in studying energy security among researchers, businesses, and policymakers. Initial studies conceptualized energy security as securing oil supplies (see, for example, Yergin (1988) and Fried and Trezise (2010) among others), while later studies expanded the concept of energy security to the entire infrastructure of energy supply to support the global economy (Stringer, 2008). The initial concept of supply security, with a focus mostly on the physical existence of energy resources, was also later extended to incorporate the price element owing to economic interest (Jenny, 2007; Kruyt *et al.*, 2009). As a result, the expanded definition "the reliable and adequate supplies of energy at reasonable prices" has become a more widely cited definition in the energy security literature (Chang and Lee, 2008; Yao and Chang, 2014; Wang and Zhou, 2017).

With the economy developing continuously, technology advancing and environmental awareness increasing, more contemporary studies are introducing multiple dimensions to interpret and assess the traditional concept of energy security. In 2007, Asia Pacific Energy Research Center (APERC) first proposed the inclusion of the 4-A dimensions in the concept of energy security. These four dimensions refer to the following: (1) Availability dimension (referring to the geological existence of energy resources); (2) Accessibility dimension (considering the geopolitical issues related to energy security); (3) Affordability dimension (relating to the economic factors of energy security); (4) Acceptability dimension (covering the environmental and societal aspects of energy security). These four dimensions are also adopted in the academic literature to evaluate the situation of energy security. For example, Kruyt *et al.* (2009) projected the future energy security in Western Europe for the next few decades using these four dimensions as the conceptual framework. Ren and Sovacool (2014) evaluated the four dimensions of energy security and the multiple metrics used under each dimension. The conclusion from this study was that the availability and affordability dimensions of energy security are the most important and influential elements for a country's energy security, and this holds for China and for other countries.

While there are numerous studies attempting to evaluate energy security qualitatively or quantitatively, "no set of energy indicators can be final and definitive," and "indicators must evolve over time to fit country-specific conditions, priorities and capabilities" (Narula and Reddy, 2016; IEA, 2005). Energy security is a highly context-dependent concept. Its definition can vary with special circumstances, level of economic development, perception of risks, robustness of the energy system, and prevailing geopolitical issues within the specific country or region of study (Kruyt *et al.*, 2009; Ang *et al.*, 2015). Existing studies have explored different sets of dimensions and metrics to conceptualize or quantify energy security.

For example, Sovacool and Brown (2010) examined energy security in the United States (US) and 21 Organization for Economic Cooperation and Development (OECD) countries by conceptualizing energy security based on accessibility, affordability, efficiency, and environmental stewardship. In the analysis of developing countries, Narula and Reddy (2016) quantified sustainable energy security based on dimensions of availability, affordability, efficiency, and acceptability. Von Hippel *et al.* (2011) look beyond the original four dimensions and include six dimensions (namely, energy supply, economic, technological, environmental, socio-cultural, and military security dimensions) and various other attributes to measure the sustainability of energy security in Northeast Asia. Built on the conceptual work of Von Hippel *et al.* (2011), Vivoda (2010) extended the concept of energy security to seven dimensions (with human security, public relations, and energy security policy as the additional three dimensions) and proposed 44 attributes to measure the performance of energy security in Asia. Further extending Vivoda (2010)'s work, Sovacool (2011) identified 20 dimensions and 200 attributes for policymakers to consider when assessing the energy security issues in Asia.

2.2. *Energy security in China*

China has become a net importer for all fossil-fuel energy sources since 1990. Specifically, China became a net crude oil importer in 1996, a net natural gas importer in 2007, and a net coal importer in 2009. This rapid growth in energy demand has brought both challenges and opportunities to China's energy security. As China's energy demand continues to increase and its impact on global energy market becomes increasingly profound, more and more researchers have turned their attention to studying and evaluating the energy security situation in China.

Wei *et al.* (2019) analyzed the energy security situation in China and identified the main challenges currently confronting China's energy security. First, challenges of rapid energy consumption can cause a series of problems in energy production and safe use. Second, there are new factors threatening energy security, such as price, transport, technology, investment, geopolitics, natural disasters, etc. In addition, there is a challenge in diversifying the energy mix and transforming from traditional, single energy use to the use of multiple energy sources. Moreover, global climate change and environmental protection need to be considered when producing and consuming energy. Finally, China needs to control total energy consumption, but setting the control objective at a reasonable level can be extremely difficult.

Wu *et al.* (2012) constructed an index of energy security based on indicators for energy supply security and indicators for energy usage security, and their composite index shows an uptrend, downtrend, and a final uptrend of energy security over the periods 1996–2002, 2003–2005, and 2006–2009, respectively. According to Wu *et al.* (2012), the implementation of the "energy-saving and emission reduction" policy was found to have a positive impact on the improvement of energy security over the investigation period, indicating that climate protection and energy security — two critical goals — can be achieved in a win–win manner in China.

Yao and Chang (2014) also examined the energy security performance in China, but documented different trends based on the new evaluation framework. In particular, they pointed out that existing concepts of energy security defined in the prior literature were either lacking comprehensive dimensions or had duplicate dimensions. Therefore, they proposed and constructed a new quantitative 4-A framework to assess the energy security in China over the period 1981–2010. Their 4-A analytical framework included the dimensions of availability of energy resources (AV), applicability of technology (AP), acceptability by society (AC), and affordability of energy resources (AF), with each A dimension proxied using five indicators. According to Yao and Chang (2014), this framework used the least number of indicators but was comprehensive enough to reflect the real nature of energy security in the context of China.[2] They examined the performance of China's energy security over seven five-year time spans, each of which corresponded to one of China's Five-Year Plan.[3] Their results indicated that China's energy security had not improved due to economic reform in the last 30 years. The best performance in energy security was identified during the period 1981–1985, followed by a deterioration until 1995. Improvement was witnessed over the periods 1995–2000 and 2001–2005, but the situation worsened again over the years 2005–2010.

Further investigating the underperformance of China's energy security, Yao and Chang (2015) related energy policies to energy security from the macroeconomic reform perspective and found that

[2]This 4-A framework was also used to quantitatively evaluate the energy security in ASEAN countries in a more recent study (see Tongsopit *et al.*, 2016).

[3]China's Five-Year Plans are a series of five-year national development agendas focused on social and economic development.

macroeconomic reform was the key variable affecting China's energy security. China's energy policies were a passive reaction to the macroeconomic reforms, which restricted the development of energy security in China.

Extending the analysis to the year 2014, Song *et al.* (2019) introduced a new aggregated evaluation index (China energy security index, CESI) based on the energy supply dimension, the economic–technical dimension, and the environmental dimension. Consistent with Yao and Chang (2014)'s findings, their results also showed that China's energy security demonstrated an 'N' trend, with the worst energy security performance identified in 2010 and the best identified in 2000. In the same vein, Fang *et al.* (2018) proposed five dimensions (availability, accessibility, affordability, acceptability, and developability) to assess China's energy security from 2005 to 2015. They showed that the availability and developability dimensions, which are the most important to China's energy security, exhibited a downward trend and an inverted U-shaped trend, respectively, during the sample period.

Based on provincial-level data, Zhang *et al.* (2017) studied the energy security in 30 Chinese provinces by utilizing 20 metrics based on five dimensions (availability and diversity, affordability and equality, technology and efficiency, environmental sustainability, and governance and innovation). Their results showed that no province performed well in all five dimensions and that all provinces faced threats and challenges related to energy availability and diversity.

In a more recent study, different trends of China's energy security were illustrated. Lu *et al.* (2019) introduced *energy* into the assessment of energy security and developed an *energy*-based index. Their overall results demonstrated that China's energy security improved over the last five decades in terms of resource availability, resource affordability, economic efficiency, and environmental impact perspectives.

Song *et al.* (2019) conducted a strengths, weaknesses, opportunities, and threats (SWOT) analysis to identify the strength and weakness associated with China's energy security situation. The strength was the installed capacity generated by renewable energy, whereas the weakness arose from indigenous energy availability and energy dependence. This analysis opened a new avenue for China to further improve energy efficiency and optimize the energy structure, such as by exploiting and using clean and renewable energy to support the sustainable development of energy and power industries.

Further extending the quantitative analysis to 24 Asian countries, Le *et al.* (2019) depicted increasing energy insecurity for China along with 10 other countries in Asia over the period 1990–2014, a period that was considered as a critical challenge to Asia's economic growth.[4]

3. Data and Methodologies

3.1. *Data and variables*

This study attempts to develop a comprehensive and quantifiable ESI for China, based on a 4-A framework considering four aspects: AV, AP, AC, and AF. Principal component analysis is then performed to evaluate which of the selected indicators has the biggest individual impact on this composite index for China.

Constructing a composite ESI has two main challenges in terms of analysis, namely, the indicators to be included and the methodology to be used. If the construction is only based on very few indicators, one might question the stability of the index. This is because a sudden change in an indicator may lead to a significant fluctuation in the composite index (Desmond, 2014). However, if too many indicators are included, minor fluctuations in some indicators might be drowned out by the majority of unchanged indicators (Le *et al.*, 2019). As such, the more common practice in literature tends to suggest the use of a representative set of 10–25 indicators so that a balance between the stability and sensitivity of the index can be achieved. At the same time, the constructed index is made so as to ensure that it conveys the comprehensiveness of the energy security situation (Desmond, 2014). Furthermore, a basket of 10–25 indicators translates into an average weight from 4% to 10% for each indicator (assuming that all the indicators carry equal weights), which seems reasonable

[4]There is a strand of literature focusing on examining the impact of energy security on economic viability and sustainability. Energy security is found to positively contribute to economic growth in Japan (Gasparatos and Gadda, 2009), Pakistan (Mahmood and Ayaz, 2018), 26 EU countries (Balitskiy *et al.*, 2014), and in a global sample of 74 countries (Le and Canh, 2019).

Table 1: Description of variables and data sources.

Indicator	Description	Source	Period	Note
Availability (AV) Indicators				
AV-1	Coal reserve-to-production (R/P) ratio	BP Statistical Review of World Energy	1981–2018 (production data)	
AV-2	Oil import dependence: Imports of crude oil: 1,000bbl/d	BP Statistical Review of World Energy June 2019.	1993–2018	Imports of oil are collected from BP Statistical Review of World Energy June 2019
AV-3	Natural gas reserve-to-consumption ratio	BP Statistical Review of World Energy June 2019	1980–2018	Natural gas consumption data are available from 1965-2018
AV-4	Availability factor of conventional thermal electricity	EIA	1980–2016	
AV-5	Availability factor of non-thermal electricity	EIA	1980–2016	Non-thermal electricity generation in billion kilowatt-hour (including renewables and electricity)
Applicability (AP) Indicators				
AP-1	Energy intensity: Total primary energy consumption per dollar of GDP (1,000 Btu per year 2010 US dollars (purchasing power parities))	EIA	1980–2016	
AP-2	Efficiency of energy processing and conversion	National Bureau of Statistics of China (NBS)	1983–2015	The efficiency (%) data is sourced from National Bureau of Statistics of China (NBS). National Data is used
AP-3	Crude oil distillation capacity (thousand barrels per day)	EIA	1986–2015	Distillate fuel oil 1000 barrels/day

Acceptability (AC) Indicators				
AC-1	Share of China's CO_2 emissions in global CO_2 emissions	BP Statistical Review of World Energy June 2019	1980–2018	China's CO_2 emission in the world's total CO_2 emissions
AC-2	Share of renewable energy in total electricity generation	EIA	1980–2016	Renewable power generation as a part of total electricity generation
AC-3	Share of nuclear energy in total electricity generation	EIA	1980–2016	Nuclear power generation as a part of total electricity generation
Affordability (AF) Indicators				
AF-1	Growth rate of ex-factory price index (previous year = 100) for coal	National Bureau of Statistics of China (NBS)	1980–2014	LBNL China Energy Databook
AF-2	Growth rate of ex-factory price index (previous year = 100) for petroleum	National Bureau of Statistics of China (NBS)	1980–2014	LBNL China Energy Databook
AF-3	Growth rate of ex-factory price index (previous year = 100) for electricity	National Bureau of Statistics of China (NBS)	1980–2014	LBNL China Energy Databook
AF-4	Volatility of coal prices	National Bureau of Statistics of China (NBS)	1997–2018	LBNL China Energy Databook Volatility is calculated based on the formula given by Yao and Chang (2014) Volatility is calculated based on a 5-year rolling window
AF-5	Energy consumption per capita: Non-productive use (SCE kg)	National Bureau of Statistics of China (NBS)	1983–2016	Annual per capita energy consumption of households

Table 2: Summary of statistical descriptions of selected variables: 1986–2014.

Variable	Obs	Mean	Std.	Min	Max
AV-1	29	72.89	31.64	28.81	128.08
AV-2	29	1920.76	2012.76	9.15	6192.83
AV-3	29	0.05	0.02	0.03	0.07
AV-4	29	1579.55	1198.53	333.79	3984.92
AV-5	29	416.73	363.98	93.56	1407.23
AP-1	29	11.73	3.61	8.05	19.85
AP-2	29	69.65	2.38	65.20	73.50
AP-3	29	1654.91	1081.96	457.00	3578.68
AC-1	29	0.18	0.06	0.10	0.28
AC-2	29	0.19	0.02	0.16	0.24
AC-3	29	0.01	0.01	0.00	0.02
AF-1	29	108.20	11.37	88.70	139.70
AF-2	29	112.86	18.00	83.10	171.30
AF-3	29	106.70	9.60	100.20	139.50
AF-4	29	0.15	0.10	0.00	0.31
AF-5	29	185.08	73.68	119.00	346.10

(Desmond, 2014). Subject to the availability and quality of the data, we finally decided on the exact number of indicators.

Based on the above-mentioned framework, we proceeded with the study by selecting the indicators to be included into the ESI for China. As mentioned earlier, our ESI is built upon the 4-A framework, consisting of the four essential dimensions of AV, AP, AC, and AF. Based on data availability, 16 indicators were selected and are presented in Table 1. The summary of statistical descriptions of the selected variables is presented in Table 2.

3.2. *Methodology*

Since the selected indicators rely on different units and different scales, they need to be normalized before being aggregated into a composite index. In this study, the normalization of the indicators was conducted through the well-known z-transformation. In the standardization procedure, scaling was performed based on deviation from the mean.

Normalization using standardized z-score was performed as follows:

$$\text{Zee} = \frac{X_i - \bar{X}}{\sigma}, \tag{1}$$

where $\bar{X}$ is the group average and σ is the standard deviation.

Next, principal component analysis (PCA) was conducted to process the data. PCA enables us to evaluate how fluctuations in certain variables impact the final outcome. PCA is widely used to analyze strong predictors in a data set since it reveals the data structure and explains the variations (Le *et al.*, 2019; Radovanovic *et al.*, 2018). In the existing literature, PCA has seldom been used to quantify the level of energy security (Radovanovic *et al.*, 2018). However, its use in the analysis of the phenomena influenced by a group of variables has justified the use of PCA in this study to measure the impacts of different components of energy security on its level.

Following Jolliffe (2002), the construction of one PCA is performed as follows: Assume a random vector X whose values are taken in $\Re^m$, that has a mean μ_X and covariance matrix of $\sum_X$. Eigenvalues of $\sum_X$ in descending order are $\lambda_1 > \lambda_2 > \cdots > \lambda_m > 0$, so that the i-th eigenvalue of $\sum_X$ is the ith largest of them. Similarly, a vector α_i that corresponds to the i-th eigenvalue of $\sum_X$ is the ith eigenvector of $\sum_X$. Next, we derive the form of principal components by maximizing $\text{var}[\alpha_1^T X] = \alpha_1^T \sum_X \alpha_1$, subject to $\alpha_1^T \alpha_1 = 1$. This optimization problem is then solved by applying the Lagrange multiplier method, as follows:

$$L(\alpha_1, \phi_1) = \alpha_1^T \sum_X \alpha_1 + \phi_1(\alpha_1^T \alpha_1 - 1),$$

$$\frac{\partial L}{\partial \alpha_1} = 2 \sum_X \alpha_1 + 2\phi_1 \alpha_1 = 0 \Rightarrow \sum_X \alpha_1 = -\phi_1 \alpha_1$$

$$\Rightarrow \text{var}[\alpha_1^T X] = -\phi_1 \alpha_1^T \alpha_1 = -\phi_1. \tag{2}$$

Since $-\phi_1$ is the eigenvalue of $\sum_X$, with α_1 being the corresponding normalized eigenvector, $\text{var}[\alpha_1^T X]$ is maximized by choosing α_1 to be the first eigenvector of $\sum_X$. In this case, $z_1 = \alpha_1^T X$ is the first principal component of X, while α_1 is the vector of coefficients for z_1, and $\text{var}(z_1) = \lambda_1$.

To find the second principal component, $z_2 = \alpha_2^T X$, the optimization problem of maximizing $\text{var}[\alpha_2^T X] = \alpha_2^T \sum_X \alpha_2$ subject to

z_2 being uncorrelated with z_1 is solved. Because $\text{cov}(\alpha_1^T X, \alpha_2^T X) = 0 \Rightarrow \alpha_1^T \sum_X \alpha_2 = 0 \Rightarrow \alpha_1^T \alpha_2 = 0$, solving this problem is equivalent to solving the maximization of $\alpha_2^T \sum_X \alpha_2$, subject to $\alpha_1^T \alpha_2 = 0$, and $\alpha_2^T \alpha_2 = 1$.

The Lagrange multiplier method is also applied.

$$\begin{aligned}
L(\alpha_2, \phi_1, \phi_2) &= \alpha_2^T \sum_X \alpha_2 + \phi_1 \alpha_1^T \alpha_2 + \phi_2(\alpha_2^T \alpha_2 - 1), \\
\frac{\partial L}{\partial \alpha_2} &= 2 \sum_X \alpha_2 + \phi_1 \alpha_1 + 2\phi_2 \alpha_2 = 0, \\
&\Rightarrow \alpha_1^T \left(2 \sum_X \alpha_2 + \phi_1 \alpha_1 + 2\phi_2 \alpha_2 \right) = 0 \Rightarrow \phi_1 = 0, \\
&\Rightarrow \sum_X \alpha_2 = -\phi_2 \alpha_2 \Rightarrow \alpha_2^T \sum_X \alpha_2 = -\phi_2.
\end{aligned} \tag{3}$$

Because $-\phi_2$ is the eigenvalue of $\sum_X$, and α_2 is the corresponding normalized eigenvector, $\text{var}[\alpha_2^T X]$ is maximized by selecting α_2 to be the second eigenvector of $\sum_X$. In this case, $z_2 = \alpha_2^T X$ is the second principal component of X, while α_2 is the vector of coefficients for z_2, and $\text{var}(z_2) = \lambda_2$. Following a similar procedure, the ith principal component $z_i = \alpha_i^T X$ could be constructed by choosing α_i to be the ith eigenvector of $\sum_X$, and this has a variance of λ_i. The main outcome of PCA are the principal components, which are a set of values of linearly uncorrelated variables that have orthogonal vectors of coefficients.

In short, the ESI is constructed as follows:

$$ESI_{it} = a_1 E_1 + a_2 E_2 + \cdots + a_{16} E_{16}, \tag{4}$$

where E denotes the 16 input indicators for constructing the composite index and $a_1, a_2, \ldots$ are the coefficients (the eigenvectors) derived from the PCA analysis for the first principal component after the variables are standardized.

In determining the outcome of PCA, weights are assigned to each variable included in the formation of the composite index. The first principal component is regarded as the best representative of the value of the composite index, which is newly built based on the given variables. The resulting weights indicate the degree of correlation between an input factor and the composite index. Based on the weights, we can identify the variables that explain a significant part of the composite index. As a result of the standardization approach, all principal components have zero mean. The standard deviation for each component is the square root of the eigenvalue.

Before performing the PCA, two tests, namely, Bartlett's test of sphericity and Kaiser–Meyer–Olkin (KMO) test of sampling adequacy, were conducted to examine the suitability of these data for factor analysis (Hair *et al.*, 1998; Tabachnick *et al.*, 2007). Bartlett's test of sphericity was conducted to check if the correlation matrix used in the PCA is an identity matrix. The test statistics must be significant ($p < 0.05$) in order to justify the use of factor analysis (Hair *et al.*, 1998; Tabachnick *et al.*, 2007). In addition, the KMO test was employed to assess the sampling adequacy of factor analytic data matrices. This statistic indicates the proportion of common variance among variables that might be caused by underlying factors. The value of the KMO index ranges from 0 to 1, with a value greater than 0.5 generally indicating suitability for factor analysis (Hair *et al.*, 1998; Tabachnick *et al.*, 2007). The results of KMO Measure of Sampling Adequacy and Bartlett's Test of Sphericity are presented in Table 3. As can be seen, the KMO values are found to be greater than 0.5 for all the cases. For the Bartlett's test of sphericity, the computed p-values were 0.000. Thus, the results of both tests support the use of PCA in this study.

There are two steps in the empirical PCA. The first stage involves identifying the factors with the lowest correlation pairwise and calculating the total variance of the variable contributed by these factors. The purpose here is to extract the factors that contribute to

Table 3: Results of Bartlett's test of sphericity and KMO measure of sampling adequacy.

	Bartlett's Test of Sphericity			**KMO Measure Sampling of Adequacy**
	Chi-square	**Degrees of Freedom**	**p-Value**	
Energy Security Index: Dimensions				
AV	365.724	10	0.000	0.763
AP	66.446	3	0.000	0.734
AC	54.229	3	0.000	0.496
AF	51.957	10	0.000	0.640
Energy Security Index: Composite				
ESI	968.562	120	0.000	0.790

the largest portion of the variation in the original variables. The first factor explains the highest total variation. Next, the second factor that accounts for the largest portion of the remaining unexplained variance is extracted. The first factor and the second factor have no correlation. This procedure is continued until the number of identified components equals the number of variables originally included in the construction of the composite index. Afterward, we can extract the components that explain a portion of variance above a certain threshold level, which is often set at one (Mundfrom *et al.*, 2005).

4. Empirical Results

Table 4 reports the estimated factors and their eigenvalues. Based on these results, we consider the first three factors for the PCA on China's ESI, since they together contribute almost 90% of the total variance of the ESI. The magnitudes of the coefficients, presented in Table 5, indicate the impacts of each selected indicator to that component. The magnitudes of the coefficients vary by the variances of the corresponding variables.

Table 4: Total variance explained for China's ESI.

Component	Eigenvalues	% of Variance	Cumulative Variance %
1	10.440	65.252	65.252
2	2.538	15.863	81.114
3	1.388	8.678	89.792
4	0.543	3.396	93.188
5	0.338	2.115	95.303
6	0.250	1.565	96.868
7	0.197	1.230	98.099
8	0.151	0.944	99.042
9	0.105	0.653	99.696
10	0.024	0.148	99.843
11	0.010	0.062	99.905
12	0.008	0.050	99.955
13	0.003	0.020	99.975
14	0.002	0.013	99.988
15	0.001	0.008	99.996
16	0.001	0.004	100.000

Table 5: Impact assessment of selected indicators on the principal components of China's composite energy insecurity index.

Normalized Variables Using Standardized z-Score			
	Principal Component		
Variable	**1**	**2**	**3**
AV1	−0.978	−0.173	−0.009
AV2	0.969	−0.093	0.204
AV3	−0.921	−0.114	0.056
AV4	0.970	−0.078	0.205
AV5	0.924	−0.209	0.303
AP1	−0.799	−0.342	0.204
AP2	0.906	−0.087	−0.084
AP3	0.989	−0.013	0.100
AC1	0.982	0.049	0.139
AC2	−0.100	−0.768	0.548
AC3	0.864	0.294	−0.155
AF1	−0.326	0.752	0.290
AF2	−0.295	0.702	0.481
AF3	−0.477	0.521	0.548
AF4	0.694	0.529	−0.317
AF5	0.919	−0.154	0.302

Because of standardization, all principal components will have zero mean. There is also zero correlation between the principal components themselves.

To interpret the principal components, we identify those variables that are most significantly correlated with each component. In this study, a correlation above 0.6 — in either direction from zero — is deemed significant. The principal component results will then be interpreted with respect to the value that we have considered statistically significant.

The first principal component is found to be strongly correlated with 12 of the normalized variables. The first principal component increases with increasing AV2, AV4, AV5, AP2, AP3, AC1, AC3, AF4, and AF5 and decreasing AV1, AV3, and AP1 scores. This suggests that these twelve criteria vary together. For instance, if energy consumption per capita (AF5) increases then oil import dependence (AV2) tends to increase, and thus share of China's CO_2 emissions in the global CO_2 emission scale (AC1) tends to increase as well.

Furthermore, the first principal component seems to correlate most strongly with crude oil distillation capacity (AP3). We can also note that the correlations of crude oil distillation capacity (AP3) (+), share of China's CO_2 emissions in the global CO_2 emission (AC1) (+), coal reserve-to-production (R/P) ratio (AV1) (–), availability factor of conventional thermal electricity (AV4) (+), and oil import dependence (AV2) (+) with this principal component are not significantly different.

The second principal component increases with AF1 and AF2 (growth rates of ex-factory price index for coal and petroleum, respectively) but decreases with AC2 (share of renewable energy out of total electricity generation). This implies that the growth rates of ex-factory price index for coal and petroleum — two non-renewable energy sources — tend to move in the opposite direction with the use of renewable energy in electricity generation, which is expected in theory. The third principal component weakly increases with increasing AC2 and AF3.

The plots of the four dimensions of China's ESI as measured by principal component analysis are presented in Figure 1. As previously discussed, the principal components are based on normalized variables using z-score standardization. We present four plots of principal component scores for four aspects of the 4-A framework, namely, AV, AP, AC, and AF.

We found a trend of increasing availability and applicability for China (see Figure 1). The performance in the availability dimension could be attributable to the advantages of China's national oil companies, which received support from the state-owned banks for high-risk projects. Thanks to this strategy, China's energy shortages have been relieved to some extent (Yao and Chang, 2014). Besides, China should realize the diversification of energy import. Diversifying energy sources (i.e., avoiding over-dependence on a single source of energy such as coal or oil) and broadening the list of countries that supply energy resources (i.e., importing oil from different countries) are useful means of reducing risk in the availability dimension. Zhang *et al.* (2013) proposed that promotion of diversity in import energy sources ensures stability of energy supply. China should thus adjust its strategies actively and shift the energy dependence from politically unstable regions to politically stable regions. Also, Wei *et al.* (2019) suggested that policymakers in China be made

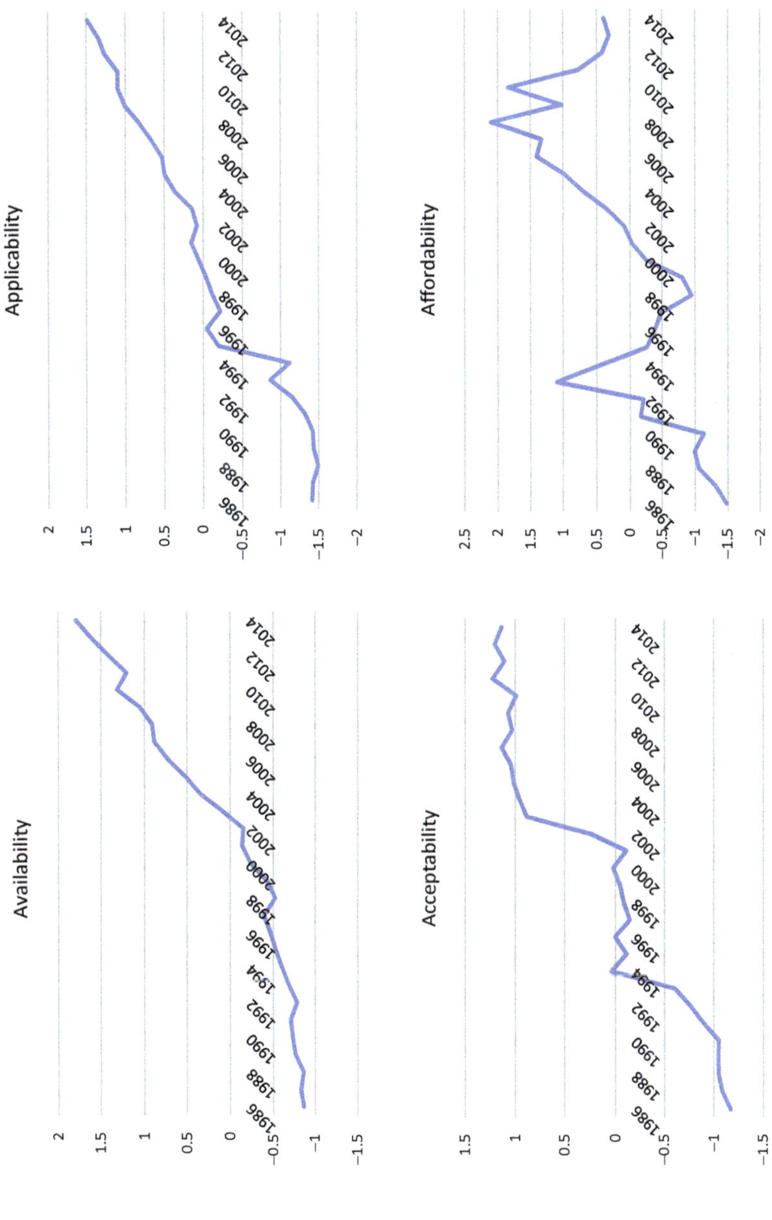

Figure 1: Trend in China's ESI performance: Dimensions (1986–2014).

aware of the risks associated with importing resources when drafting and implementing energy import strategies.

Nevertheless, increased reliance on oil and gas imports is certainly not a reliable approach to sustained energy supply. It is important that China strengthens its exploitation and development of renewable energy resources, particularly given the rapid depletion of domestic fossil fuel resources. In the same vein, the improvement in China's applicability indicator reflects the country's success in deploying technologies to improve energy efficiency and to harness crude oil — a critical energy resource. To reduce risks and limit the increase in energy imports, China has implemented a series of energy-saving measures. For instance, domestic oil savings have been implemented in a strict manner. In addition, the country has set priority tax and credit measures to stimulate the production of energy-efficient products and technologies.

The trend for acceptability has been rising several years (1986–1994 and 2002–2003) while remaining relatively stable for certain years. Note that since we consider environmental aspects in our acceptability index, our findings could be explained by the fact that this country has been the largest global emitter of CO_2 for years (*Satista*). Coal is a major source of electricity in China due to its cheap cost (Yao and Chang, 2014). Despite measures to address the increased efficiency of energy use, in absolute terms, China's coal consumption has continued to increase in line with a rise in the country's energy demand. This increase represents a critical challenge to carbon emissions and climate goals. As such, to alleviate environmental pollution, policymakers in China should integrate CO_2 emission reduction measures into their national energy development programs (Tongsopit *et al.*, 2016). In this regard, developing renewable energy, nuclear energy, and other alternative energy sources is also one focus of China's energy security strategy. Regarding renewable energy, China is now speeding up the construction of wind power generation equipment and hydropower plants to increase electricity production. Regarding nuclear energy — the only energy that can replace large-scale petrochemical energy while reducing emissions of gases and material into the environment — China is one of the world's largest producers with 46 nuclear reactors in operation as of March 2020. In addition, China is also intensifying research into new technologies from fossil fuels and waste.

Besides availability, affordability is regarded as one of the two most essential dimensions in improving China's energy security (Ren and Sovacool, 2014). Our study found that the trend of affordability of energy resources in China is quite volatile. Specifically, it was on the rise during the periods 1986–1993, 1999–2008 (reached its peak in 2008), and 2009–2010. On the other hand, it had fallen during 1994–1998, 2008–2009, and from 2010 onwards. In this study, the "volatility of coal prices" was used as a proxy to measure the stability of energy prices in China. The results indicate that this is a critical factor that moves in tandem with the composite index. Due to the full liberalization of the coal sector in China, coal pricing is subject to the forces of supply and demand (Yao and Chang, 2014). Meanwhile, a second key AF indicator is "energy consumption per capita: non-productive use (SCE kg)", which reflects consumers' sensitivity to price changes. Our results are similar to Yao and Chang (2014)'s finding that, overall, there was an improvement in the affordability dimension after 1995 and until 2010.

Taken together, policies and actions should be in place to stabilize the energy price in China. For example, China should eliminate monopolies and promote energy price reform and decentralization to improve market liquidity and ensure price stability (Ren and Sovacool, 2014), optimize the oil futures market and oil marketing information system (Zhang *et al.*, 2013), and formulate strategic and proactive plans to improve the energy price system (Wei *et al.*, 2019).

As regards China's overall ESI, we find a strong fluctuation throughout the investigation period (see Figure 2). Specifically, the results indicate that China's energy security was relatively stable between 1986 and 1992 before surging briefly during the period 1992–1993. Afterward, it deteriorated for about five years until it hit higher levels again between 1998 and 2000. Since then, the energy security situation appears to have fluctuated quite a bit, but generally showed an increasing trend. The fluctuation in China's energy security status could be attributed to the differences in the country's policy priority over the investigation period.

Our results are similar to those obtained by Yao and Chang (2014) who also depicted a fluctuating but downward trend in energy security for the country during period 1995–2010. Our findings are also consistent with those of Yamaguchi *et al.* (2013), who showed that energy security has been deteriorating in most developing countries

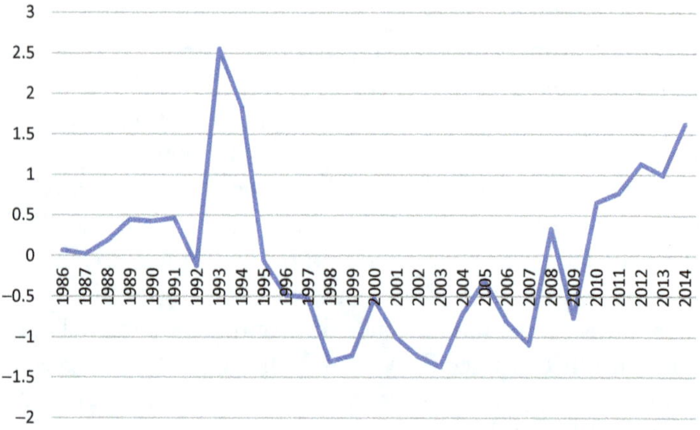

Figure 2: Trend in China's ESI performance: Composite (1986–2014).

in Asia during the same period as ours. The explanation for this could be follows: in most developing countries in Asia, (1) energy self-sufficiency rates have gradually dropped, (2) these countries are overly reliant on a single energy source, (3) there is much room for improvement in energy efficiency, and (4) they carry a high environmental load (Yamaguchi *et al.*, 2013). All these factors are relevant to China also.

5. Conclusion

This study attempted to measure a composite ESI for China during the 1986–2014 period. Based on the 4-A analytical framework, we performed principal component analysis on 16 selected indicators to construct a composite index for energy security. The variables were standardized using z-score normalization before being used as inputs in the principal component analysis to build different measures of energy security.

Empirical results revealed the trend of increasing availability of energy resources and applicability of technology in China. On the other hand, the results showed that the trend of acceptability by society is a fluctuating trend, but shows signs of improvement recently. Meanwhile, the trend of fluctuating but recently decreasing affordability of energy resources was also observed in China. Overall,

China's ESI showed a strong fluctuation throughout the investigation period. Specifically, it was relatively stable between 1986 and 1992, before surging briefly during the period 1992–1993. Afterward, it deteriorated for about five years until it again rose between 1998 and 2000. Since then, the energy security situation seems to be volatile but is generally on the rise.

With the rapid growth of China's economy, energy is expected to continue to play a critical role in the coming years. As such, China should optimize its storage and transportation system and strengthen cooperation with energy-exporting countries (Wei *et al.*, 2019). Diversity in transport modes can also help maintain the safety and stability of energy transportation, while enhanced cooperation with energy producers can safeguard energy security (Zhang *et al.*, 2013; Ren and Sovacool, 2014).

There is a close relationship between energy security and national economic development (Le *et al.*, 2019). Meanwhile, an underdeveloped economy faces challenges in providing good social security. Energy security is thus inextricably linked to the environment, education, and health. In this regard, ensuring energy security is important not only for the industrial activities of an economy but also for the development of social infrastructure, including healthcare and education. Therefore, policymakers should ensure national energy security and social harmony.

The empirical results of this study necessitate the development of a "comprehensive operating definition of energy security", combined with "a workable framework for analysis of energy security policy" as opined in a recent study on Asia-Pacific's energy security situation by Vivoda (2010). The development of renewable energy sources is essential, not only in extending the use of traditional energy resources but also in protecting the environment in China. For example, Ren and Sovacool (2014) suggest that China should increase the fraction of renewable energy in total primary energy supply, with such sources as hydropower, solar power, biomass, and wind power, to improve its availability dimension in energy security. To improve energy security performance at the provincial level, Zhang *et al.* (2017) suggested that China should develop renewable energy sources and diversify its energy mix, improve energy efficiency, enhance awareness on environment quality, and adjust the energy strategy to balance the development among different provinces. In a similar vein,

Wang *et al.* (2018) pinpointed the importance of renewable energy in securing energy independence and mitigating climate change in China and suggested that promoting renewable energy should be the top priority in China in order to enhance energy supply security.

Last but not least, since energy security is a transnational endeavor, in addition to individual national solutions, strong regional or international cooperation to address this problem is also essential.

References

Ang, B. W., Choong, W. L. and Ng, T. S. 2015. Energy security: Definitions, dimensions and indexes. *Renewable and Sustainable Energy Reviews*, 42, 1077–1093.

Balitskiy, S., Bilan, Y. and Strielkowski, W. 2014. Energy security and economic growth in the European Union. *Journal of Security and Sustainability Issues*, 4.

Chang, Y. and Lee, J. L. 2008. Electricity market deregulation and energy security: A study of the UK and Singapore electricity markets. *International Journal of Global Energy Issues*, 29, 109–132.

Desmond, C. W. L. 2014. *Energy Security Indexes: A Survey with Application to Singapore.*

Fang, D., Shi, S. and Yu, Q. 2018. Evaluation of sustainable energy security and an empirical analysis of China. *Sustainability*, 10, 1685.

Fried, E. R. and Trezise, P. H. 2010. *Oil Security: Retrospect and Prospect*, Brookings Institution Press.

Gasparatos, A. and Gadda, T. 2009. Environmental support, energy security and economic growth in Japan. *Energy Policy*, 37, 4038–4048.

Hair, J. F., Black, W. C., Babin, B. J., Anderson, R. E. and Tatham, R. L. 1998. *Multivariate Data Analysis*, Prentice Hall Upper Saddle River, NJ.

Hu, H., Zhang, X.-H. and Lin, L.-L. 2014. The interactions between China's economic growth, energy production and consumption and the related air emissions during 2000–2011. *Ecological Indicators*, 46, 38–51.

IEA, E. 2005. EEA. Energy indicators for sustainable development: Guidelines and methodologies. *Vienna, International Atomic Energy Agency*, 1–28.

Jenny, F. 2007. Energy Security: A market oriented approach, presentation at the OECD Forum on innovation, growth and equity. Paris, May 14–15, 2007.

Jolliffe, I. T. 2002. Graphical representation of data using principal components. *Principal Component Analysis*, 78–110.

Kruyt, B., Van Vuuren, D. P., De Vries, H. J. and Groenenberg, H. 2009. Indicators for energy security. *Energy Policy*, 37, 2166–2181.

Le, T.-H., Chang, Y., Taghizadeh-Hesary, F. and Yoshino, N. 2019. Energy insecurity in Asia: A multi-dimensional analysis. *Economic Modelling*, 83, 84–95.

Le, T.-H. and Canh, N. P. 2019. Is energy security a driver for economic growth? Evidence from a global sample. *Energy policy*, 129, 436–451.

Lu, H., Xu, F., Liu, H., Wang, J., Campbell, D. E. and Ren, H. 2019. Emergy-based analysis of the energy security of China. *Energy*, 181, 12–135.

Mahmood, T. and Ayaz, M. T. 2018. Energy security and economic growth in Pakistan. *Pakistan Journal of Applied Economics*, 28, 47–64.

Mundfrom, D. J., Shaw, D. G. and Ke, T. L. 2005. Minimum sample size recommendations for conducting factor analyses. *International Journal of Testing*, 5, 159–168.

Narula, K. and Reddy, B. S. 2016. A SES (sustainable energy security) index for developing countries. *Energy*, 94, 326–343.

Radovanović, M., Filipović, S. and Golušin, V. 2018. Geo-economic approach to energy security measurement–principal component analysis. *Renewable and Sustainable Energy Reviews*, 82, 1691–1700.

Ren, J. and Sovacool, B. K. 2014. Quantifying, measuring, and strategizing energy security: Determining the most meaningful dimensions and metrics. *Energy*, 76, 838–849.

Song, Y., Zhang, M. and Sun, R. 2019. Using a new aggregated indicator to evaluate China's energy security. *Energy Policy*, 132, 167–174.

Sovacool, B. K. 2011. Evaluating energy security in the Asia Pacific: Towards a more comprehensive approach. *Energy Policy*, 39, 7472–7479.

Sovacool, B. K. and Brown, M. A. 2010. Competing dimensions of energy security: An international perspective. *Annual Review of Environment and Resources*, 35, 77–108.

Stringer, K. D. 2008. Energy security: Applying a portfolio approach. *Baltic Security and Defence Review*, 10, 121–142.

Tabachnick, B. G., Fidell, L. S. and Ullman, J. B. 2007. *Using Multivariate Statistics*, Pearson Boston, MA.

Tongsopit, S., Kittner, N., Chang, Y., Aksornkij, A. and Wangjiraniran, W. 2016. Energy security in ASEAN: A quantitative approach for sustainable energy policy. *Energy Policy*, 90, 60–72.

UN. 2019. Sustainable development goal 12: Responsible consumption and production [Online]. United Nations. Available: https://sustainabledevelopment.un.org/sdg12 [Accessed 12 February 2020].

Vivoda, V. 2010. Evaluating energy security in the Asia-Pacific region: A novel methodological approach. *Energy Policy*, 38, 5258–5263.

Von Hippel, D., Suzuki, T., Williams, J. H., Savage, T. and Hayes, P. 2011. Energy security and sustainability in Northeast Asia. *Energy Policy*, 39, 6719–6730.

Wang, Q. and Zhou, K. 2017. A framework for evaluating global national energy security. *Applied Energy*, 188, 19–31.

Wang, Z., Danish, Zhang, B. and Wang, B. 2018. Renewable energy consumption, economic growth and human development index in Pakistan: Evidence form simultaneous equation model. *Journal of Cleaner Production*, 184, 1081–1090.

Wei, Y.-M., Liang, Q.-M., Wu, G. and Liao, H. 2019. Challenges and Outlook of China's Energy Security. *Energy Economics*, 415–432.

Wu, G., Liu, L.-C., Han, Z.-Y. and Wei, Y.-M. 2012. Climate protection and China's energy security: Win–win or tradeoff. *Applied Energy*, 97, 157–163.

Yamaguchi, K. *et al.* 2013. *Study on the Development of an Energy Security Index and an Assessment of Energy Security for East Asian Countries.*

Yao, L. and Chang, Y. 2014. Energy security in China: A quantitative analysis and policy implications. *Energy Policy*, 67, 595–604.

Yao, L. and Chang, Y. 2015. Shaping China's energy security: The impact of domestic reforms. *Energy Policy*, 77, 131–139.

Yergin, D. 1988. Energy Security in the 1990s. *Foreign Aff.*, 67, 110.

Zhang, H.-Y., Ji, Q. and Fan, Y. 2013. An evaluation framework for oil import security based on the supply chain with a case study focused on China. *Energy Economics*, 38, 87–95.

Zhang, L., Yu, J., Sovacool, B. K. and Ren, J. 2017. Measuring energy security performance within China: Toward an inter-provincial prospective. *Energy*, 125, 825–836.

https://doi.org/10.1142/9781786349224_0005

Chapter 5

Evaluating Energy Security in China: A Subnational Analysis

Huijuan Xiao*, Zhengnan Zhang†, Anting Wang‡, and Jingzheng Ren§

Department of Industrial and Systems Engineering, The Hong Kong Polytechnic University, Hong Kong SAR, China

*hui-juan.xiao@connect.polyu.hk

†17082567d@connect.polyu.hk

‡17082086D@connect.polyu.hk

§jzhren@polyu.edu.hk

Abstract

China, a high energy-consuming and large country, is characterized by unbalanced socio-economic development among provinces, inevitably leading to a great disparity in energy security. It is of utmost importance to evaluate the subnational energy security situation in China to formulate effective measures to enhance energy security. This study first analyzed China's energy situation from 2000 to 2017 in terms of energy consumption by fuel types, energy consumption flows, and energy production, providing a basis for the better understanding of China's energy demand and supply status. The energy security of China's 30 provinces from 2011 to 2017 was then evaluated using 21 indicators based on the drivers-pressure-state-impact-response (DPSIR) model. We found that: (1) the average of provincial energy security was relatively low and experienced a slight decrease from 2011 to 2017. The energy security degree reduced to 0.57 in 2017, and the imbalance of the energy security scores of the five dimensions could possibly be the reason for the low level of the overall evaluation of energy security, especially the low level of "response". (2) For specific provinces, the top five highest levels of energy security of the provinces in 2017 were Tianjin (0.73), Beijing (0.66), Shanghai (0.64), Heilongjiang (0.64), and Jilin (0.63).

Guizhou, Ningxia, Xinjiang, Qinghai, and Hebei had the lowest level of energy security in 2017, at 0.51, 0.50, 0.49, 0.49, and 0.47, respectively. (3) Energy-abundant provinces were not the ones that necessarily performed best in terms of energy security. Since energy security performance measurement is a multidimensional evaluation, some energy-abundant provinces, such as Guizhou, Ningxia, and Xinjiang performed poorly in terms of energy security. Some policies have been put forward to enhance these provinces' energy security effectively.

Keywords: Energy security; China; DPSIR; Energy indicator system.

1. Introduction

According to British Petroleum (BP, 2019), China's primary energy consumption experienced a rapidly increasing trend, rising from 1010.9 Mt in 2000 to 3132.2 Mt in 2017. China became the world's largest energy consumer starting in 2008 and its share of primary energy consumption increased from 10.08% in 2000 to 23.18% in 2017 (BP, 2019). Moreover, China became a net oil importer since 1993 and a net natural gas importer since 2007 and then a net coal importer after 2009, thus increasing the uncertainty and threat of China's energy supply chain. Therefore, it is of utmost importance to evaluate the energy security situation of China to formulate effective measures to enhance China's energy security. Based on Hoogeveen and Perlot (2007), energy supply is a general term to indicate the access to and availability of energy at all times. Supply can be disrupted for several reasons, for example, owing to physical, economic, social, and environmental risks.

China, a large and high energy-consuming country, has unbalanced socio-economic development, which inevitably leads to a variation of energy security among provinces. For example, some provinces are rich in fossil fuel reserves, such as Shanxi and Inner Mongolia, while some provinces are service-based provinces that are supported by imports from these energy-abundant provinces (Bao and Fang, 2013; Chen *et al.*, 2010; Kasman and Duman, 2015; Zhang *et al.*, 2012). Because of these disparities, subnational energy security evaluation is crucial for implementing targeted strategies and national energy security is quite different from sub-national ones. Most studies have evaluated China's energy security at the national level (Bambawale and Sovacool, 2011; Geng and Ji, 2014; Liu, 2014; Ren and Sovacool, 2014; Wu *et al.*, 2012; Yao and Chang, 2014). For example, Ren and Sovacool (2014) examined China's energy security in terms of availability, affordability, acceptability, and accessibility using a Fuzzy Decision-making Trial and Evaluation Laboratory method. Geng and Ji (2014) measured China's energy supply and its dynamic change from 1994 to 2011 and found out that China's energy supply security first experienced a decreasing trend before 2008 followed by an increase during 2008–2011. Yao and Chang (2014) evaluated China's energy security through the 4-As assessment framework from 1981 to 2010 and suggested that China's energy security performed the best from 1981 to 1985 and decreased from 2006 to 2010. Yang and Chen (2015) constructed an evaluation framework from five aspects to measure China's energy security situation from 2002 to 2010.

Given the existing literature, the temporal analysis of energy security of Chinese provinces is far from enough, not to mention that the analysis carried out so far were all purely temporal analysis of provincial energy security. To fill this gap, this study first analyzed China's energy situation from 2000 to 2017 in terms of energy consumption by fuel types, energy consumption flows, and energy production, which can provide a basis for better understanding of China's energy demand and supply status. The energy security of China's 30 provinces from 2011 to 2017 was then evaluated using twenty-one indicators based on the drivers-pressure-state-impact-response (DPSIR) model. Lastly, the level and dynamic change of 30 the provinces' energy security are presented and some policies are put forward to enhance these provinces' energy security effectively.

The structure of this chapter is as follows. Section 2 presents methodology and data and introduce the DPSIR model. Section 3 explains the evaluation results of 30 provinces' energy security, and Section 4 presents the main conclusion and puts forward some policy implications.

2. Methodology and Data

2.1. *DPSIR model*

In this study, the DPSIR model was adopted to estimate the scores of Chinese energy security from 2011 to 2017. According to the DPSIR framework, there is a chain of links beginning from "driving forces" (social factors and environmental factors) through "pressures" (increasing demand for resources) to "states" (physical, chemical, and biological states) and "impacts" on ecological systems, living environment, and human health, finally resulting in "responses" (target setting, policy implications, and actions).

Figure 1 depicts the complete DPSIR framework in terms of energy security. "Driving force" is the starting point of the whole chain. Examples of driving forces for a country's energy security can be rising population and social development, which further increase the need for fossil fuel and electricity consumption. Driving forces exert "pressures" on both society and environment because of the changing production or consumption activities. Therefore, the pressures can have a significant impact on the "states" of the environment, such as increasing total waste discharged and increased common industrial solid waste and sulfur dioxide emissions, and the society, such as higher energy consumption elasticity and electricity consumption elasticity. These changes in the physical, chemical, or biological states of the environment and society determine the quality of ecosystems and the welfare of human beings. In other words, changes in the state may have environmental or economic "impacts" on the functioning of ecosystems, their life-supporting abilities, and ultimately on human health and the economic and social performance of society.

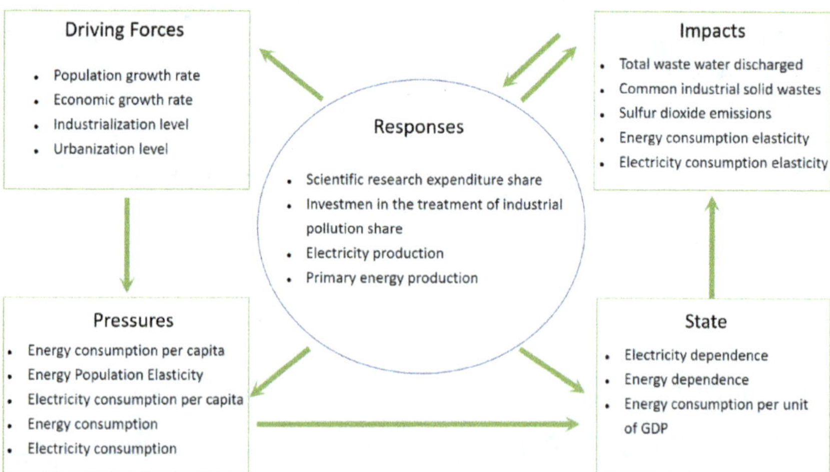

Figure 1: DPSIR framework of energy security evaluation.

Policymakers will make a "response" to the driving forces, pressures, states, and impacts regarding energy security. For example, the government can increase scientific research expenditure to improve the efficiency of energy usage and energy conversion, which can ease the pressures of energy supply and improve the social states. Also, investment in the treatment of industrial pollution can be increased to mitigate its negative impacts on the environment and human health. An example of a response to driving forces is increasing the energy production capacity in terms of electricity and fossil fuels, which can help to meet the need for the increasing demand of energy consumption activities.

To eliminate the impacts caused by various units of indicators and the negative value problem, a dimensionless treatment method was first adopted, see Equation (1) (Zhu and Wei, 2015). In this study, a positive dimension was used to treat the indicators that can enhance energy security, such as urbanization level, scientific research expenditure, and primary energy production. In contrast, a negative dimension was adopted to treat the indicators that may threaten the energy security of a region, such as increasing population, electricity consumption, and sulfur dioxide emissions.

$$y_{i,j} \begin{cases} 0.9 \times \frac{x_{i,j} - \min_j(x_{i,j})}{\max_j(x_{i,j}) - \min_j(x_{i,j})} + 0.1, & \textit{Positive dimension} \\ 0.9 \times \frac{\max_j(x_{i,j}) - x_{i,j}}{\max_j(x_{i,j}) - \min_j(x_{i,j})} + 0.1, & \textit{Negative dimension} \end{cases}, \tag{1}$$

where i and j indicate i province and j indicator, respectively. $\min_j(x_{i,j})$ means $\min(x_{1j}, x_{2j}, \ldots, x_{nj})$ and $\max_j(x_{i,j})$ means $\max(x_{1j}, x_{2j}, \ldots, x_{nj})$. Following Guo, (1998), the entropy method was adopted to obtain the weight of each indicator, as shown in Equation (2).

$$P_{i,j} = \frac{x_{i,j}}{\sum_{i=1}^{m} x_{i,j}}. \tag{2}$$

The entropy value can be obtained using Equation (3).

$$\begin{aligned} e_j &= -k \sum_{i=1}^{m} (p_{i,j} \times \ln p_{i,j}), \\ k &= \frac{1}{\ln(n)}, n = 30. \end{aligned} \tag{3}$$

In this study, n equals to 30 since 30 provinces are included in the evaluation.

The difference coefficient can be measured with the help of Equation (4).

$$g_j = 1 - e_j. \tag{4}$$

The smaller g_j is, the more important the indicator j is. The weight of each indicator can be obtained using Equation (5).

$$w_i = \frac{g_i}{\sum_{j=1}^{n} gj}. \tag{5}$$

Finally, the scores of each component (driving forces, pressure, state, impact, and response) regarding energy security evaluation can be obtained with Equation (6).

$$C_s = \sum_{j=1}^{k} w_j \times y_{i,j}, \quad i = 1, 2, \ldots, 30.\ s = 1, 2, \ldots, 5, \tag{6}$$

where C_s indicates the scores of s components and k means the number of indicators within each component. In this study, $k = 4, 5, 3, 5,$ and 5 for driving forces, pressures, state, impacts, and responses, respectively.

The energy security degree of each province can be calculated using Equation (7).

$$Energy\ security\ degree = \frac{1}{5} \times \sum_{s=1}^{5} C_S. \tag{7}$$

2.2. *Data*

Table 1 presents the indicators of each dimension and their corresponding weights. The driving forces of energy security come from economic development and an increasing population. Also, the industrialization level and urbanization level can affect the driving forces. The industrialization level is the proportion of the output value of the non-agricultural industry in total GDP. The urbanization level is the proportion of the urban population. The "pressures" of energy security mainly come from some indicators that are relevant to fossil fuel consumption and electricity consumption. Energy population elasticity is the growth rate of energy consumption divided by

Table 1: The weight and units of each indicator in 2017.

Dimensions	Indicators	Unit	Weight
Driving forces	1. Population growth rate	%	0.2366
	2. Economic growth rate	%	0.2223
	3. Industrialization level	–	0.1517
	4. Urbanization level	–	0.3894
Pressures	1. Energy consumption per capita	tons/capita	0.1463
	2. Energy population elasticity	–	0.3354
	3. Electricity consumption per capita	10000 kWh/capita	0.1379
	4. Energy consumption	10000 TCE	0.1781
	5. Electricity consumption	million kWh	0.2023
State	1. Electricity dependence	–	0.2034
	2. Energy consumption per unit of GDP	tons/10000 Yuan	0.3897
	3. Energy dependence	–	0.4069
Impacts	1. Total wastewater discharged	10000 tons	0.1408
	2. Common industrial solid wastes produced	10000 tons	0.2780
	3. Sulfur dioxide	10000 tons	0.2817
	4. Energy consumption elasticity	–	0.1078
	5. Electricity consumption elasticity	–	0.1917
Responses	1. The share of scientific research expenditure in GDP	%	0.2657
	2. The share of investment completed in the treatment of industrial pollution in GDP	%	0.2236
	3. Electricity production	million kWh	0.1671
	4. Primary energy production	10000 TCE	0.3436

the growth rate of the population. The “state” of energy security is measured by electricity dependence, energy consumption per unit of GDP, and energy dependence. Electricity dependence is calculated by electricity consumption divided by electricity production, which is used to evaluate how much a province’s electricity is reliant on other regions. In terms of “impacts” of energy security, this study included environmental influence and energy influence. Total wastewater discharged includes chemical oxygen demand, ammonia nitrogen, total nitrogen, total phosphorus, petroleum, and volatile phenol. Energy consumption elasticity is energy consumption divided by GDP, while electricity elasticity equals electricity consumption divided by GDP. Lastly, "response" indicated the measures that policymakers implement to tackle the relevant problems caused by energy activities or to meet the need for energy consumption. Primary energy consumption includes coal, natural gas, and crude oil production. All energy-related indicators were converted to standard coal and GDP was converted to 2011 constant price using GDP index.

3. Results

3.1. *Energy consumption analysis*

Coal dominates China's energy consumption and contributes significantly to energy consumption, representing around 60.4% of the total consumption in 2017 (Figure 2). However, Figure 2 shows the continued drop in China's coal consumption during 2013–2017. Coal consumption in China grew by an average of 1.08% per year between 2000–2013 (Figure 2). Coal consumption peaked at 2809.99 Mt in 2013 and declined by an average of 0.88% per year during 2013–2016 (Figure 2). Several research results suggest that changes in the industrial structure reduced China's coal consumption significantly since 2013 and the intrinsic mechanism results in a permanent trend of China's coal consumption reducing (Figure 2) (Tang *et al.*, 2018).

The projected growth in the consumption of oil is modest. Han *et al.* (2000) estimated an annual rate of growth of 4% for crude oil consumption during 2000-2020 (Figure 2). Also, China's oil consumption in the next decade (i.e., from 2017 to 2026) will be increased by 51% (Figure 2) (Wang and Song, 2019). In recent years, China's domestic oil production decline resulted in increasing external dependency, so it has become increasingly important to consider China's oil energy security. In the future, China should grasp the current development situation of oil and speed up the process of internationalization and marketization of the oil industry so as to ensure the safety of the oil situation.

Importantly, the reduction in coal consumption occurred despite the continued growth of total energy consumption by 0.59%, 1.96%,

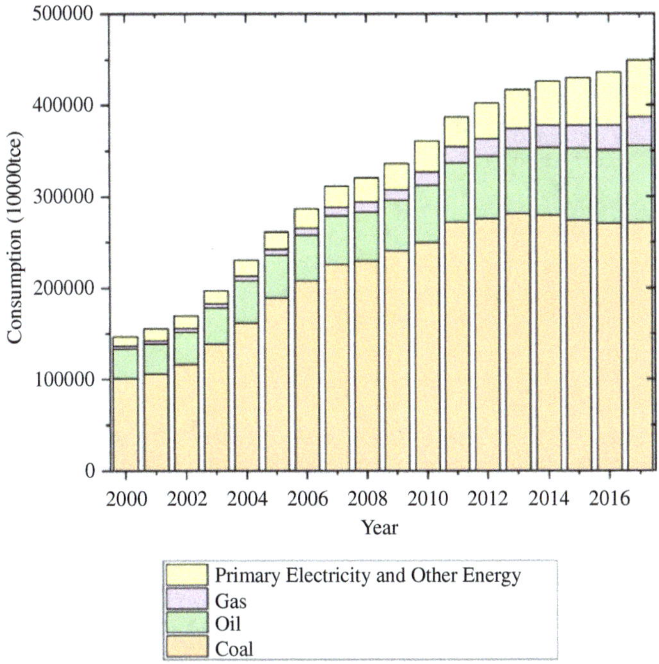

Figure 2: Energy consumption of coal, oil, gas, and other kinds of energy in China from 2000 to 2017.

and 1.33% in 2014, 2015, and 2016, respectively (Figure 2). As coal use decreased, rising energy demand was met by the rapid growth of gas and other kinds of energy supply. Although the consumption of natural gas rose, is not obvious since technical imperfections, low development, and high prices could have led to the reduced rise (Li *et al.*, 2011). In recent years, China has been seeking cleaner energy. Natural gas is a developing form of energy that is cleaner and more efficient than coal, and so natural gas consumption is rapidly increasing. Some studies predict that China's natural gas demand will continue to grow at an average rate of 11% during the period 2014–2020 (Shaikh *et al.*, 2017).

Figure 3 shows the flow between different energy types and sectors of China in 2017. The diagram flows from left to right and is of a Sankey type, wherein the widths of the indicated flows represent their magnitude. For example, a total of 1.9 billion tons of standard coal was produced in China, of which coal accounted for 54.3%, oil

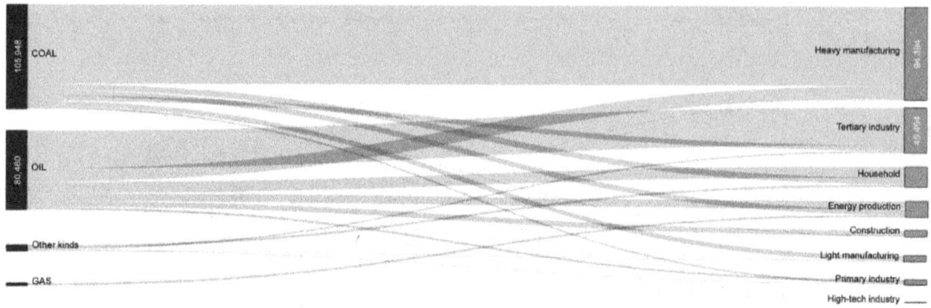

Figure 3: The flow chart showing the links between energy and sectors of China in 2017 (Mt).

41.2%, other energy types 3.1%, and natural gas 1.3% (Figure 3). In terms of its end consumption, 48.4% of the total annual energy consumption went to heavy manufacturing, 23.3% to the tertiary industry, 10.5% to households, 8.5% to energy production, 3.3% to construction, 3.2% to light manufacturing, 2.7% to primary industry, and 0.2% to high-tech industries, respectively (Figure 3).

One major feature of coal that is evident from the figure is that about 76.0% of coal energy flows to the heavy industry (Figure 3). The industrial sector (manufacturing), especially heavy industries, and the steel and cement industries are the main sources of coal consumption and the reason behind its increasing growth in the energy mix in China (Chong *et al.*, 2015). The other feature is that about 47.5% of the oil in China is mainly used for the tertiary industry including transportation, warehousing, and postal services, especially road transportation (Figure 3) (Ma *et al.*, 2012).

3.2. *Energy supply analysis*

Figure 4 shows the national energy production of coal, crude oil, natural gas, and other types of energy from 2000 to 2017. Coal was still the main energy source, representing around 69.6%, in 2017, of total energy production (Figure 4). Crude oil and natural gas accounted for approximately 7.6% and 5.4% of the total energy supply in 2017, respectively (Figure 4). Noticeably, the share of primary electricity and other types of energy experienced an increasing trend, rising from 7.7% in 2000 to 17.4% in 2017 (Figure 4). However, the coal share saw a slight increase from 72.9% in 2000 to 77.8% in 2007, while

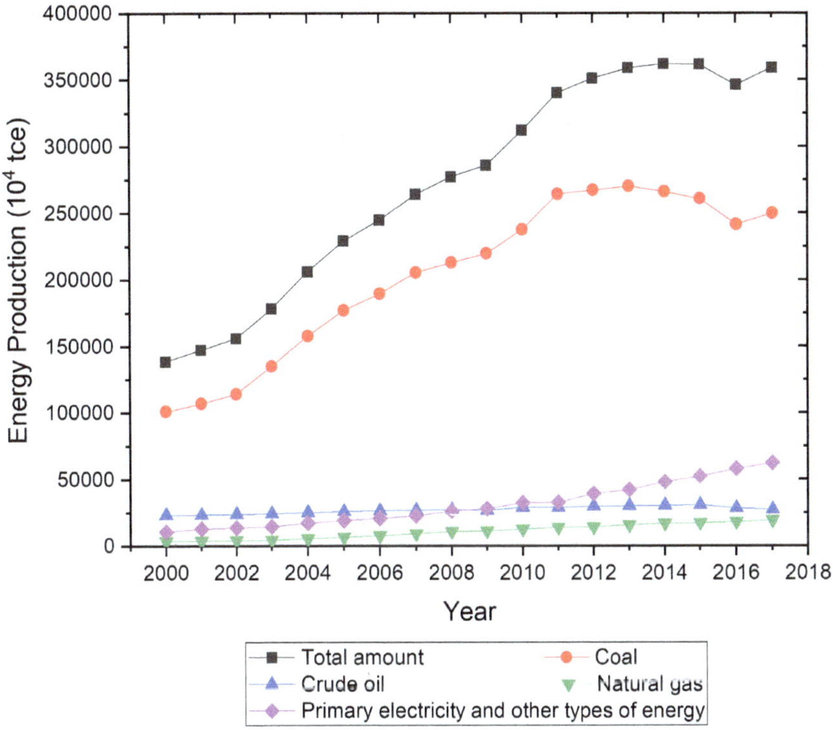

Figure 4: Energy production of coal, crude oil, natural gas, and other types in China from 2000 to 2017.

witnessing a continuous decrease to 69.6% in 2017 (Figure 4). Primary electricity refers to the electricity generated by nuclear power, hydropower, wind power, and solar power. Therefore, China's energy production structure has been optimizing for all these years. The amount of energy production is less than that of energy demand in China (Figures 3 and 4). This is mainly because the majority of China's raw coal, crude oil, and natural gas is imported from other countries; China became a net oil importer in 1993, a net natural gas importer in 2007, and then a net coal importer in 2009. That is to say, China' s primary energy supply depends on other countries' supply to some degree. Therefore, the fluctuation of energy supply in other countries may affect China's energy security. Considering China's large amount of energy consumption, it is of utmost importance to evaluate China's energy security in as much detail as possible.

3.3. *Energy security scores*

Table 2 shows the energy security scores of 30 provinces in China from 2011 to 2017. Energy security scores range from 0 to 1. The greater the score is, the more secure the energy situation of this province will be. The results show that the average energy security scores experienced a slightly decreasing trend during 2011–2017 (Table 2). The energy security degree was 0.61 in 2011, while it decreased to 0.57 in 2017 (Table 2). This indicates that national energy security should be enhanced and that there is much space for this. Tianjin, Liaoning, Heilongjiang, and Jilin are the only provinces that witnessed an increase in 2017, compared with the levels in 2011 (Table 2). Specifically, the energy security degree of Tianjin increased by 0.05, while the figure for Liaoning increased by 0.01 (Table 2). Noticeably, Guizhou, Guangxi, Beijing, Zhejiang, and Jiangxi saw the largest decline over the study period, decreasing by 0.09, 0.08, 0.08, 0.07, and 0.07, respectively (Table 2).

Table 3 presents the results of the provincial energy security performance measurement in 2011. Energy security evaluation is a multi-dimensional process that includes five dimensions, namely "driving forces", "pressures", "state", "impacts", and "responses". The results suggested that Beijing, Shanghai, Tianjin, Shaanxi, and Anhui were the most energy-secure provinces in 2011, with scores of 0.74, 0.71, 0.68, 0.68, and 0.65, respectively (Table 3). Among the five provinces, Beijing, Shanghai, and Tianjin belong to the eastern region and are the most developed provinces in China, with GDP per capita being in the top three in 2011. Take Beijing as an example, its energy security in terms of "driving forces", "pressure", and "impact" was relatively high, at 0.91, 0.82, and 0.94, respectively (Table 3). As for the other two best performers, Shaanxi and Anhui, which belong to western and central regions, respectively, the results were consistent with the results of a previous study (Zhang *et al.*, 2017). However, Sichuan, Xinjiang, Hebei, Ningxia, and Qinghai performed the worst in terms of energy security in 2011, with levels at a mere 0.56, 0.55, 0.53, 0.52, and 0.52, respectively (Table 3). Some of these are energy-based provinces, such as Xinjiang and Ningxia, but this does not necessarily correlate with high energy security. As for the five dimensions, Guizhou, Shandong, Zhejiang, Shandong, and Chongqing had the lowest score in terms of "driving force", "pressure", "state",

Table 2: The energy security scores of 30 provinces in China between 2011 and 2017.

Provinces	2011	2012	2013	2014	2015	2016	2017	Average
Beijing	0.74	0.74	0.67	0.69	0.66	0.64	0.66	0.69
Tianjin	0.68	0.67	0.60	0.64	0.65	0.68	0.73	0.67
Hebei	0.53	0.53	0.48	0.53	0.47	0.48	0.47	0.50
Shanxi	0.64	0.63	0.56	0.61	0.61	0.57	0.57	0.60
Inner Mongolia	0.62	0.60	0.61	0.57	0.55	0.57	0.57	0.58
Liaoning	0.59	0.60	0.61	0.58	0.55	0.58	0.60	0.59
Jilin	0.64	0.62	0.66	0.68	0.68	0.64	0.63	0.65
Heilongjiang	0.64	0.64	0.68	0.65	0.59	0.61	0.64	0.64
Shanghai	0.71	0.72	0.62	0.68	0.61	0.61	0.64	0.66
Jiangsu	0.61	0.60	0.55	0.57	0.55	0.53	0.56	0.57
Zhejiang	0.60	0.63	0.55	0.58	0.53	0.52	0.53	0.56
Anhui	0.65	0.65	0.57	0.61	0.57	0.62	0.60	0.61
Fujian	0.65	0.66	0.56	0.57	0.59	0.59	0.58	0.60
Jiangxi	0.63	0.65	0.54	0.57	0.54	0.57	0.56	0.58
Shandong	0.58	0.57	0.53	0.54	0.49	0.51	0.51	0.53
Henan	0.58	0.59	0.56	0.53	0.51	0.56	0.56	0.55
Hubei	0.59	0.61	0.57	0.57	0.56	0.56	0.55	0.57
Hunan	0.58	0.62	0.57	0.58	0.54	0.57	0.56	0.57
Guangdong	0.63	0.64	0.59	0.56	0.57	0.57	0.57	0.59
Guangxi	0.60	0.61	0.53	0.56	0.52	0.54	0.53	0.56
Hainan	0.59	0.64	0.52	0.56	0.51	0.55	0.55	0.56
Chongqing	0.61	0.62	0.55	0.56	0.55	0.59	0.58	0.58
Sichuan	0.56	0.58	0.55	0.57	0.54	0.56	0.55	0.56
Guizhou	0.60	0.57	0.50	0.53	0.52	0.56	0.51	0.54
Yunnan	0.60	0.59	0.51	0.57	0.55	0.58	0.52	0.56
Shaanxi	0.68	0.66	0.58	0.60	0.60	0.61	0.61	0.62
Gansu	0.62	0.62	0.51	0.56	0.53	0.60	0.56	0.57
Qinghai	0.52	0.53	0.44	0.46	0.47	0.51	0.49	0.49
Ningxia	0.52	0.57	0.50	0.53	0.50	0.53	0.50	0.52
Xinjiang	0.55	0.51	0.41	0.42	0.44	0.44	0.49	0.47
Average	0.61	0.62	0.56	0.57	0.55	0.57	0.57	0.58

"impacts", and "response", respectively, at 0.31, 0.48, 0.58, 0.53, and 0.19 in 2011 (Table 3).

Table 4 shows the provincial energy security scores in 2017. The average score of the 30 provinces in 2017 was 0.57, which is far less than 1, indicating that there is still much improvement needed to

Table 3: Energy security scores and their components for 30 provinces in China in 2011.

Province	Driving Forces	Pressures	State	Impacts	Responses	DPSIR
Beijing	0.91	0.82	0.71	0.94	0.32	0.74
Tianjin	0.57	0.73	0.90	0.86	0.35	0.68
Hebei	0.49	0.54	0.74	0.53	0.32	0.53
Shanxi	0.50	0.64	0.70	0.61	0.72	0.64
Inner Mongolia	0.50	0.49	0.79	0.58	0.75	0.62
Liaoning	0.63	0.60	0.79	0.64	0.29	0.59
Jilin	0.48	0.81	0.86	0.83	0.20	0.64
Heilongjiang	0.55	0.75	0.85	0.80	0.27	0.64
Shanghai	0.95	0.69	0.59	0.93	0.37	0.71
Jiangsu	0.66	0.48	0.83	0.62	0.44	0.61
Zhejiang	0.74	0.60	0.58	0.70	0.39	0.60
Anhui	0.42	0.85	0.92	0.75	0.33	0.65
Fujian	0.57	0.78	0.88	0.74	0.28	0.65
Jiangxi	0.46	0.92	0.91	0.69	0.19	0.63
Shandong	0.57	0.48	0.86	0.53	0.48	0.58
Henan	0.45	0.68	0.86	0.55	0.36	0.58
Hubei	0.46	0.76	0.77	0.70	0.26	0.59
Hunan	0.44	0.78	0.85	0.59	0.24	0.58
Guangdong	0.73	0.52	0.85	0.64	0.41	0.63
Guangxi	0.40	0.87	0.77	0.76	0.22	0.60
Hainan	0.43	0.97	0.61	0.76	0.20	0.59
Chongqing	0.41	0.85	0.84	0.79	0.19	0.61
Sichuan	0.35	0.70	0.84	0.62	0.29	0.56
Guizhou	0.31	0.86	0.71	0.72	0.39	0.60
Yunnan	0.33	0.85	0.82	0.68	0.30	0.60
Shaanxi	0.44	0.83	0.90	0.72	0.48	0.68
Gansu	0.39	0.84	0.77	0.75	0.33	0.62
Qinghai	0.44	0.68	0.60	0.66	0.22	0.52
Ningxia	0.51	0.60	0.60	0.59	0.31	0.52
Xinjiang	0.42	0.77	0.72	0.55	0.32	0.55
Average	0.52	0.72	0.78	0.69	0.34	0.61

increase the national energy security level (Table 4). The imbalance in the energy security scores of different aspects can be the reason for the low level of the overall evaluation of energy security (Table 4). The DPSIR framework considers five aspects, namely driving forces, pressures, states, impacts, and responses. The scores

Table 4: Energy security scores and their components for 30 provinces in China in 2017.

Province	**Driving Forces**	**Pressures**	**State**	**Impacts**	**Responses**	**DPSIR**
Beijing	0.82	0.65	0.64	0.85	0.35	0.66
Tianjin	0.90	0.69	0.89	0.90	0.28	0.73
Hebei	0.45	0.48	0.78	0.38	0.27	0.47
Shanxi	0.50	0.52	0.76	0.37	0.71	0.57
Inner Mongolia	0.63	0.39	0.78	0.38	0.69	0.57
Liaoning	0.76	0.78	0.78	0.48	0.21	0.60
Jilin	0.63	0.71	0.89	0.77	0.17	0.63
Heilongjiang	0.56	0.89	0.84	0.71	0.20	0.64
Shanghai	0.84	0.58	0.53	0.85	0.42	0.64
Jiangsu	0.65	0.36	0.79	0.56	0.43	0.56
Zhejiang	0.56	0.46	0.54	0.69	0.39	0.53
Anhui	0.35	0.65	0.92	0.67	0.43	0.60
Fujian	0.46	0.59	0.85	0.74	0.25	0.58
Jiangxi	0.36	0.69	0.84	0.67	0.23	0.56
Shandong	0.43	0.38	0.88	0.40	0.47	0.51
Henan	0.38	0.58	0.88	0.61	0.32	0.56
Hubei	0.46	0.62	0.66	0.70	0.33	0.55
Hunan	0.41	0.65	0.85	0.73	0.17	0.56
Guangdong	0.54	0.39	0.84	0.60	0.49	0.57
Guangxi	0.30	0.67	0.76	0.73	0.17	0.53
Hainan	0.35	0.73	0.70	0.85	0.14	0.55
Chongqing	0.51	0.65	0.83	0.74	0.15	0.58
Sichuan	0.40	0.59	0.90	0.59	0.25	0.55
Guizhou	0.22	0.65	0.87	0.54	0.27	0.51
Yunnan	0.26	0.65	0.89	0.60	0.21	0.52
Shaanxi	0.46	0.62	0.91	0.66	0.42	0.61
Gansu	0.46	0.66	0.81	0.65	0.23	0.56
Qinghai	0.38	0.56	0.63	0.73	0.14	0.49
Ningxia	0.41	0.40	0.63	0.68	0.36	0.50
Xinjiang	0.25	0.48	0.69	0.73	0.32	0.49
Average	0.49	0.59	0.79	0.65	0.32	0.57

of these five aspects varied significantly. For example, states and impacts had relatively high scores, reaching 0.79 and 0.65 in 2017, respectively (Table 4). In contrast, the scores of driving forces and responses were a mere 0.49 and 0.32 in 2017, respectively (Table 4). In terms of specific provinces, the top five highest levels of energy security in 2017 were seen in Tianjin (0.73), Beijing (0.66), Shanghai (0.64), Heilongjiang (0.64), and Jilin (0.63) (Table 4). Heilongjiang and Jilin achieved moderate energy security performance in 2011, ranked seventh and eighth, respectively, while both of their rankings increased after 5 years (Table 4). This is not because of the increase of Heilongjiang and Jilin's performance but the decrease of other provinces' energy security degree (Table 4).

It should be noted that Guizhou, Ningxia, Xinjiang, Qinghai, and Hebei had the lowest level of energy security in 2017, at 0.51, 0.50, 0.49, 0.49, and 0.47, respectively (Table 4). Many reasons can be the cause of the low energy security of these five provinces. For example, Guizhou and Xinjiang had a low level of energy security in terms of driving forces because the economic and social development was far from sufficient. The energy pressure in Ningxia was pretty high, resulting in a low score (0.40) in terms of energy security pressure (Table 4). Noticeably, the "response" of Qinghai and Guizhou were far from satisfactory, at 0.18 and 0.28 in 2017, respectively (Table 4). Qinghai and Guizhou's policymakers should carry out more effective measures to meet the energy demand of social development and reduce the negative impacts on the environment.

4. Conclusions and Policy Implications

As the world's largest energy consumer since 2010, China, requires a high level of energy security to support the development of the economy and industry. Considering that there is great disparity among Chinese provinces, it is of great importance to evaluate provincial energy security. Therefore, this study adopted the DPSIR model to measure the energy security of China's 30 provinces from 2011 to 2015. Twenty-one indicators were considered in terms of energy security's driving forces, pressure, state, impacts, and responses. The main conclusions reached are as follows.

First, the average provincial energy security is relatively low and experienced a slight decrease from 2011 to 2017. The energy security degree was 0.61 in 2011, while it decreased to 0.57 in 2017. There is still much room for improvement of energy security performance. The imbalance in the energy security scores of the five dimensions can be the reason for the low level of the overall evaluation of energy security, especially the low level of "response" in terms of energy security. More effective policies should be implemented to enhance energy security.

Second, in terms of provincial-level data, the top five highest levels of energy security in 2017 were seen in Tianjin (0.73), Beijing (0.66), Shanghai (0.64), Heilongjiang (0.64), and Jilin (0.63). Tianjin, Liaoning, Heilongjiang, and Jilin were the only provinces that witnessed an increase in 2017, compared with the level in 2011. It is to be noted that Guizhou, Ningxia, Xinjiang, Qinghai, and Hebei had the lowest level of energy security in 2017, at 0.51, 0.50, 0.49, 0.49, and 0.47, respectively. Prompt actions should be taken in those areas with poor or decreasing performance provinces in energy security.

Third, energy-abundant provinces are not necessarily the best performers in terms of energy security. Energy security performance measurement is a multidimensional evaluation. High-level and stable energy supply should be accompanied by environmentally friendly production activities and high-quality social development. Some energy-abundant provinces, such as Guizhou, Ningxia, and Xinjiang, perform poorly in terms of energy security. It can be interpreted that energy-intensive activities in these provinces may lead to high pollution emissions, which destroy the living environment and human health. On the other hand, the development level of these areas is not satisfactory enough to handle the fluctuation of external shocks in energy.

Acknowledgment

The authors would like to express their sincere thanks to the Research Committee of The Hong Kong Polytechnic University for the financial support of the project through a PhD studentship (project account code: RK2K).

References

Bambawale, M. J. and Sovacool, B. K. 2011. China's energy security: The perspective of energy users. *Applied Energy*, 88, 1949–1956.

Bao, C. and Fang, C. 2013. Geographical and environmental perspectives for the sustainable development of renewable energy in urbanizing China. *Renewable and Sustainable Energy Reviews*, 27, 464–474.

British Petroleum (BP) 2019. BP Statistical Review of World Energy.

Chen, W., Li, H. and Wu, Z. 2010. Western China energy development and west to east energy transfer: Application of the Western China sustainable energy development model. *Energy Policy, Energy Efficiency Policies and Strategies* with regular papers. 38, 7106–7120.

Chong, C., Ma, L., Li, Z., Ni, W. and Song, S. 2015. Logarithmic mean divisia index (LMDI) decomposition of coal consumption in China based on the energy allocation diagram of coal flows. *Energy,* 85, 366–378.

Crompton, P. and Wu, Y. 2005. Energy consumption in China: Past trends and future directions. *Energy Economics*, 27, 195–208.

Geng, J.-B. and Ji, Q. 2014. Multi-perspective analysis of China's energy supply security. *Energy*, 64, 541–550.

Guo, X. 1998. Application of improved entropy method in evaluation of economic result. *Systems Engineering Theory and Practice*, 18, 98–102.

Han, W., Liu, X. and Zhu, X. 2000. Analysis on China's supply of and demand for oil and gas. In *Natural Gas Policy Seminar Beijing.*

Hoogeveen, F. and Perlot, W. 2007. The EU's policies of security of energy supply towards the Middle East and Caspian region: Major power politics? *Perspectives on Global Development and Technology*, 6, 485–507.

Kasman, A. and Duman, Y. S. 2015. CO_2 emissions, economic growth, energy consumption, trade and urbanization in new EU member and candidate countries: A panel data analysis. *Economic Modelling*, 44, 97–103.

Li, J., Dong, X., Shangguan, J. and Hook, M. 2011. Forecasting the growth of China's natural gas consumption. *Energy*, 36, 1380–1385.

Liu, G. 2014. Development of a general sustainability indicator for renewable energy systems: A review. *Renewable and Sustainable Energy Reviews*, 31, 611–621.

Ma, L., Fu, F., Li, Z. and Liu, P. 2012. Oil development in China: Current status and future trends. *Energy Policy*, 45, 43–53.

Ren, J. and Sovacool, B. K. 2014. Quantifying, measuring, and strategizing energy security: Determining the most meaningful dimensions and metrics. *Energy,* 76, 838–849.

Shaikh, F., Ji, Q., Shaikh, P.H., Mirjat, N.H. and Uqaili, M.A. 2017. Forecasting China's natural gas demand based on optimised nonlinear grey models. *Energy*, 140, 941–951.

Tang, X., Jin, Y., McLellan, B.C., Wang, J. and Li, S. 2018. China's coal consumption declining—Impermanent or permanent? *Resources, Conservation and Recycling*, 129, 307–313.

Wang, Q. and Song, X. 2019. Forecasting China's oil consumption: A comparison of novel nonlinear-dynamic grey model (GM), linear GM, nonlinear GM and metabolism GM. *Energy* 183, 160–171.

Wu, G., Liu, L.-C., Han, Z.-Y. and Wei, Y.-M. 2012. Climate protection and China's energy security: Win-win or tradeoff. *Applied Energy*, 97, 157–163.

Yang, J. and Chen, B. 2015. Measuring energy security of China, In Reddy, B.S. and Ulgiati, S. (eds.), *Energy Security and Development: The Global Context and Indian Perspectives*. Springer, India, New Delhi, pp. 57–67.

Yao, L. and Chang, Y. 2014. Energy security in China: A quantitative analysis and policy implications. *Energy Policy*, 67, 595–604.

Zhang, L., Yu, J., Sovacool, B. K. and Ren, J. 2017. Measuring energy security performance within China: Toward an inter-provincial prospective. *Energy*, 125, 825–836.

Zhang, Y., Zhang, J., Yang, Z. and Li, J. 2012. Analysis of the distribution and evolution of energy supply and demand centers of gravity in China. Energy Policy, Special Section: Fuel Poverty Comes of Age: Commemorating 21 Years of Research and Policy 49, 695–706.

Zhu, X. and Wei, G. 2015. Discussion on excellent standard of dimensionless method in entropy method. *Statistics & Decision*, 2, 12–15.

https://doi.org/10.1142/9781786349224_0006

Chapter 6

Developing a Composite Energy Security Index for Measuring China's Integrated Energy Security Performances from 2002 to 2016

Di Xu[*,§], Weichen Li[†], Lichun Dong[†,¶], and Yingkui Yang[‡,||]

[*]School of Chemistry and Chemical Engineering, Chongqing University of Science & Technology, Chongqing, China

[†]School of Chemistry and Chemical Engineering, Chongqing University, Chongqing, China

[‡]Department of Sociology, Environmental and Business Economics, University of Southern Denmark, Niels Bohrs Vej 9, DK-6700 Esbjerg, Denmark

[§]xdcq86@163.com

[¶]lcdong72@cqu.edu.cn

[||]yya@sam.sdu.dk

Abstract

Energy security plays a critical role in the development of China. Therefore, this chapter aims at examining how China's energy security performances have changed over a certain period by proposing a composite energy security index, which uses 18 indicators from six dimensions. Subsequently, the method of CRITIC (Criteria Importance Through Inter-criteria Correlation) is suggested to determine the indicators' weights for synthesizing the composite index, where the numerical data of the indicators can be fully utilized for determining their relative importance. After that, a fusion aggregation method is introduced to integrate the weighted indicators into the composite index by combining three well-practiced MCDM (multi-criteria decision-making) approaches, and this offers a reliable way for measuring China's historical energy security. On the basis of the proposed index, an empirical study of China's energy security was conducted, which demonstrated that the performances in 2013, 2012, and 2002 might be the top three best, while the performance in 2008 could be the worst. A sensitivity analysis was also carried out to test how China's energy security has changed in the past years.

Keywords: China's energy security; Energy security index; CRITIC; Multi-criteria decision-making.

1. Introduction

With the progress of society and the continuous improvement of industrialization, the use of various kinds of energy resources has been a hot trend, which is also associated with social stability and national security (Onat and Bayar, 2010). Accordingly, energy security has become a critical concern for all nations in the world as they consider problems like the reliability of supply of energy and access to cheap energy. Meanwhile, with the depletion of non-renewable energy resources and the associated environmental pollution, the definition of energy security additionally seeks an energy sector that is low-carbon emitting, clean, safe, and efficient (Sovacool, 2011). China, as the largest primary energy user on earth, consumed 24% of global energy and contributed 34% to the global energy demand growth in 2018 (BP, 2019). For meeting the vast domestic demand of energy, the import of coal, oil, and natural gas in China continued to grow, with the import dependency on oil and natural gas, respectively, increasing to 72% and 43% , while the coal imports also expanded in 2018 (BP, 2019). One of the most critical consequences of the consumption of fossil fuels is CO_2 emissions, and the corresponding figure in China increased by 2.2% in the same year. For addressing this issue, developing and harnessing low-carbon energy (such as wind, solar, hydropower, biomass, and nuclear energy) remains the leading solution according to the judgments of the policymakers in China, which results in this country being dominated by renewables and nuclear energy growth. For instance, in 2018, China's consumptions of solar, wind, biomass and geothermal, and hydropower respectively, increased by 51%, 24%, 14%, and 32%, contributing over 40% of the growth of the renewables in the whole world, while the nuclear power generation grew by 19%, accounting for 74% of the global nuclear energy power increment (BP, 2019).

The situation of China's energy system would be grim if relying heavily on the import of primary energy and not developing renewables and nuclear power. Meanwhile, the energy security of this country is severely threatened by various issues like fossil fuel exhaustion, geopolitical risk, decarbonization pressure, and renewable energy abandonment (Anwar, 2016; Cox, 2018; Fang *et al.*, 2018). Accordingly, much has been paid to the research of energy security in China. For instance, a quantitative analysis was conducted to investigate how China's energy security has changed over the past 30 years, and suggestions were offered for enhancing the security via developing renewable energy resources and reducing carbon emissions (Yao and Chang, 2014). Ren and Sovacool (Ren and Sovacool, 2014b) clarified the interrelationships among energy security metrics and recommended actionable strategies for policymakers in China. Zhang *et al.* (2017) evaluated the energy security in 30 Chinese provinces, implying that energy availability and diversity would be the most severe threat. An aggregate indicator was developed recently for evaluating the energy security of China, by considering the dimensions of energy supply, economic-technical performance, and environmental impacts, demonstrating that China's best energy security performance was in 2000 while the worst was in 2010 (Song *et al.*, 2019).

According to existing works, for measuring the energy security accurately and comprehensively, a well-rounded evaluation system that consists of suitable metrics from divergent concerns is required (Dale *et al.*, 2015; Fang *et al.*, 2018). However, as stated by Narula and Reddy (2015), the research in energy security could be "three blind people touching an elephant," which means that different, and even opposite, results could be offered by using different analytic tools or considering different decision-makers with divergent perspectives. Therefore, this chapter aims at presenting an energy security index that could contribute to systematically and reliably measure China's historical energy security performances.

2. Literature Review of Energy Security Indicators

Energy security is a rapidly evolving and ever-changing concept, where different definitions would be given by different stakeholders via using divergent assessment indicators (Valdes, 2018). In the early studies, most works focused on energy security research by studying the risk of oil supply chain disruption (Anwar, 2016); accordingly, plenty of evaluation indicators were used to describe the performance of oil energy (Stougie *et al.*, 2018). Nowadays, as the global energy scene needs to meet the rising energy demand while reducing carbon emissions, the energy security concerns should be in line with the coexistence of multiple energy systems and simultaneously meet the requirements of multi-objectivity and multi-dimensionality. For instance, (Ang *et al.*, 2015), believed that energy security is a multidimensional and interdependent concept that embraces measurements from technological, economic, social, political, environmental, and geopolitical aspects. The definition of energy security offered by Narula *et al.* (2017) suggested a combination of energy security and economic development, energy diplomatic security, climate security, ecological security, social security, and so on. For providing a broad view, the dimensions of energy supply and use, quantity and quality, and time and space were included in the energy security (Kiriyama and Kajikawa, 2014). A five-dimensional energy security index was created by measuring availability, affordability, efficiency, sustainability, and governance after taking "demand-side" and "governance" into consideration (Sovacool, 2013a,b), while an energy security index that included the seven dimensions of energy availability, energy prices, waste management, social impact, energy infrastructure, the environment, and energy conversion efficiency is also available (Martchamadol and Kumar, 2013). Since sustainability plays an important role in energy systems, it is suggested that the energy security index should incorporate the concerns from the sustainability perspective (Fang *et al.*, 2018). Bambawale and Sovacool (2011) also held the notion that energy security might be closely related to economic, environmental, and social aspects — the triple-bottom-line of sustainability. In general, the energy security index should be adjusted according to specific countries or regions in different periods because of the different development models, specific strategic priorities, and political objectives (Cabalu, 2010).

3. Multi-Dimensional Energy Security Indicators

The multi-dimensional nature of energy security has been confirmed in previous works; for instance, the "5 Ss" (Kleber), the "4 As" (APERC), and the "4 Rs" (Hughes, 2009) could be applied for offering a multitude definition of energy security. After conducting

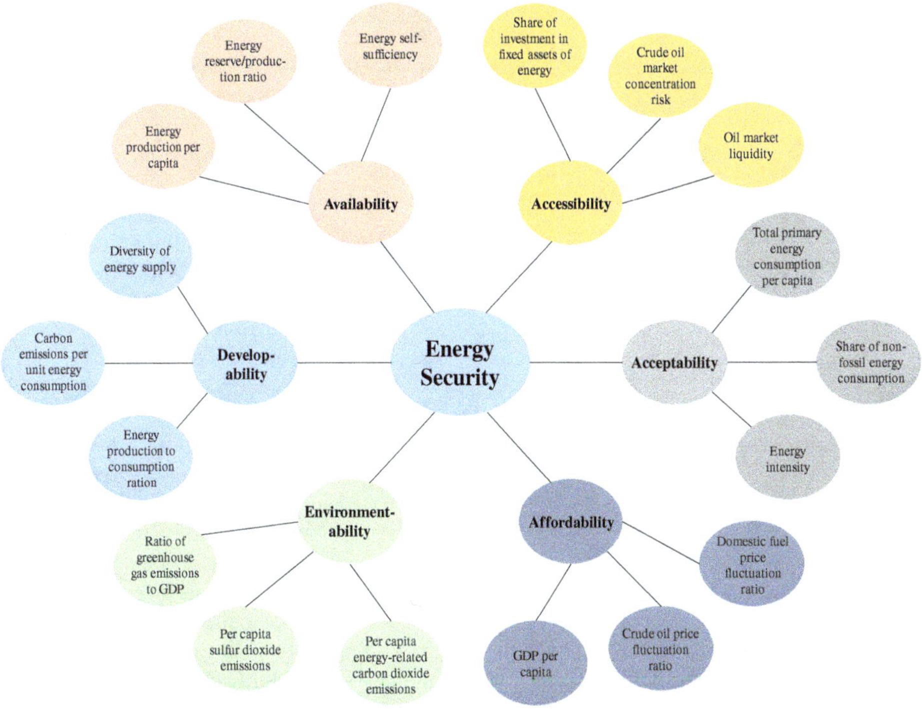

Figure 1: Overview of the multi-dimensional energy security indicators.

an extensive literature review, this work identifies six key dimensions of energy security, including availability, accessibility, acceptability, affordability, environment-ability, and develop-ability; meanwhile, each dimension has three indicators for representing the categorized performances of energy security, as depicted in Figure 1.

3.1. *Availability*

The term of availability in the context of energy security can reflect the possibility of energy supply on geographical or other theoretical objective conditions. Therefore, indicators in the dimension of availability have been frequently used to show whether energy can be applied, or if there are other factors that need to be paid attention to in the process from energy extraction to application, including concerns about functional infrastructures of transportation, conversion, transmission, and utilization. In this study, three proper indicators were selected to represent the concerns of availability, and they are

Table 1: Three indicators in the dimension of availability (Erahman *et al.*, 2016; Wu *et al.*, 2012; Sovacool, 2013b).

Indicator	Description
Energy production per captia $= \frac{\text{Total primary energy production}}{\text{Population}}$	It represents the per capita primary energy ownership of a country, which also implies the equality of resources, and a higher value of C_1 refers to a better performance (being categorized into the positive type).
Energy reserve-to-production ratio $= \sum_i \text{share of energy } i \times \frac{\text{Reserved energy } i}{\text{Produced energy}}$ *where i is a certain type of primary energy.*	It stands for the primary energy available (like oil, coal, and natural gas) over a period of time, and a higher value of C_2 refers to a better performance.
Energy self-sufficiency $= \sum_i \text{share of energy } i \times \frac{\text{Domestic supply of energy } i}{\text{Total supply of energy } i}$ *where i is a certain type of primary energy.*	It measures the self-sufficiency of the primary energy resources (like oil, coal, and natural gas) and primary electricity power, and a higher value of C_3 refers to a better performance.

energy production per capita (C_1) (Erahman *et al.*, 2016), energy reserve-to-production ratio (C_2) (Wu *et al.*, 2012), and energy self-sufficiency (C_3) (Sovacool, 2013b), as given in Table 1.

3.2. *Accessibility*

The dimension of accessibility in energy security generally reflects the availability of energy under subjective and/or objective conditions; for instance, the possibility of being influenced by the subjective conditions of geopolitical or local policies, or by the objective conditions of transport channels, in terms of energy supply. Therefore, accessibility mainly considers whether energy supply and transportation infrastructure meet the energy needs of the investigated country or region; besides, it also evaluates the relationship between local energy supply and political/economic conditions. Since very few countries can achieve energy self-sufficiency, the concern of energy imports would play a significant role in the dimension of accessibility regarding energy security. By referring to the literature (Fang *et al.*, 2018), three critical indicators were employed to describe the performance of energy security-related accessibility in China, and they are share of investment in fixed assets of energy (C_4), crude oil market concentration risk (C_5), and oil market liquidity (C_6), as summarized in Table 2.

3.3. *Acceptability*

In the context of energy security, the dimension of acceptability measures the impacts of the generation and application of energy on economic and environmental concerns. There is no doubt that fossil fuels will run out in the future depending upon the consumption rate; meanwhile, the production and utilization of fossil fuels have been linked to climate change and environmental pollution. Accordingly, the world needs an energy sector that is low-carbon, clean, safe, and efficient. For selecting adequate indicators to address the concerns regarding the acceptability in energy security, the relationships among energy, economy, and environment must be considered. Therefore, by referring to the work of Sovacool (2013b), three indicators, i.e., total primary energy consumption per capita (C_7), share of non-fossil fuel consumption (C_8), and energy intensity (C_9) were used here to represent the acceptability of energy systems in China, as given in Table 3.

3.4. *Affordability*

Since energy prices have impacts on the energy supply, the related indicators could be categorized into the dimension of affordability in energy security. Considering that "adequate and uninterrupted supply of energy at reasonable prices" always plays a significant role in evaluating the energy security, two price-related indicators are

Table 2: Three indicators in the dimension of energy accessibility (Fang *et al.*, 2018).

Indicator	Description
Share of investment in find assets of energy = $\frac{\text{Investment in fixed assets of energy industry}}{\text{Total investment in fixed assets}}$	It represents the proportion of fixed assets investment in the energy-related industry to the total fixed assets investment in the whole country. Since a higher proportion of this indicator implies better infrastructure and higher capacities regarding the energy system, it belongs to the positive type.
Crude oil market concentration risk = $\sum_j \text{Risk coefficient } j \times \left(\frac{\text{Crude oil imports } j}{\text{Total Crude oil imports}}\right)^2$ *where j is a country that exports crude oil to China, and the risk coefficient can be calculated by following the method of International Energy Agency (IEA, 2007).*	The geopolitical risk associated with energy security could be measured by the indicator of crude oil market concentration risk. It belongs to the negative type, i.e., a lower value of the indicator indicates a better performance regarding the investigated objective.
Oil market liquidity = $\frac{\text{Global oil exports}}{\text{China's oil imports}}$	It measures the relationship between a country's energy import status and the world's energy flow, which also reflects the geopolitical risk regarding energy security. This indicator belongs to the positive type, since good liquidity can lower the risk of market concentration.

Table 3: Three indicators in the dimension of acceptability (Sovacool, 2013b).

Indicator	Description
Total primary energy consumption per capita $= \frac{\text{Total primary energy consumption}}{\text{Population}}$	It measures individual energy consumption. Considering that the population in China is considerably large, if the value in per capita energy consumption goes up, the risk of energy security would rise; therefore, this indicator belongs to the negative type.
Share of non-fossil energy consumption $= \frac{\text{Total non-fossil energy consumption}}{\text{Total prime energy consumption}}$	It measures the ratio of low-carbon energy (like solar, wind, hydropower, geothermal, biomass, and nuclear energy) consumption in total primary energy supply, representing the status of the development of renewable energy and the abandonment of fossil fuels. Therefore, it is a positive indicator.
Energy intensity $= \frac{\text{Total primary energy consumption}}{\text{Gross domestic product (GDP)}}$	It reflects the relationship between energy consumption and economic situation. In energy security, a lower energy intensity refers to the ratio of energy consumption to GDP being smaller. Therefore, it is a negative indicator.

selected, and they are domestic fuel price fluctuation ratio (C_{10}), and crude oil price fluctuation ratio (C_{11}) (Wu *et al.*, 2012); besides, the relationship between the individual affordability regarding the purchase of energy products would be another indicator for evaluating the affordability of energy supplies, and therefore GDP per capita (C_{12}) (Wang and Zhou, 2017) is incorporated into this dimension.

Table 4: Three indicators in the dimension of affordability (Wu *et al.*, 2012; Wang and Zhou, 2017).

Indicator	Description
Domestic fuel price fluctuation ratio $= \|1 - \text{Retail price index of fuel}\|$	It measures the stability of fuel commodities in a country or region, which is calculated by the retail price of domestic fuel obtained from the database of National Bureau Statistics (NBS). Since a higher value of this indicator implies lower stability of the domestic fuel market, it belongs to the negative type.
Crude oil price fluctuation ratio $= \frac{\sum_k \text{Crude oil price } k}{4}$ *where k refers to four main resources including Brent, Dubai, Nigerian Forcados, and West Texas Intermediate.*	It measures the fluctuation in world crude oil prices, based on the average price among four main resources (Brent, Dubai, Nigerian Forcados, and West Texas Intermediate). This indicator is also a negative one for having side effects on the stability of energy security.
GDP per captia $= \frac{\text{Gross domestic product (GDP)}}{\text{Population}}$	It reflects the individual affordability regarding the purchase of energy product; meanwhile, it also represents the tolerance of people toward the energy price fluctuations. Since a higher per-capita GDP implies stronger affordability and better tolerance, it is a positive indicator.

For more detailed information regarding the three indicators in affordability, please see Table 4.

3.5. *Environment-ability*

Environmental concerns are closely associated with energy security since carbon and other emissions would contribute to global warming and other forms of pollution. Therefore, an increasing number of works have highlighted the environmental dimension as the area for achievement of efficiency and improvement of energy supply from

Table 5: Three indicators in the dimension of environment-ability (Sovacool, 2013b; Wu *et al.*, 2012).

Indicator	Description
Per capita energy-related carbon dioxide emissions $= \frac{\text{Total energy} - \text{related CO}_2 \text{ emissions}}{\text{Population}}$	This indicator could be dependent on several factors such as energy mix, energy efficiency, economic growth, and individual energy consumption patterns. In general, this indicator is highly correlated with per capita energy consumption, and it also belongs to the negative type.
Per capita sulfur dioxide emissions $= \frac{\text{Total energy} - \text{related SO}_2 \text{ emissions}}{\text{Population}}$	It measures the sulfur dioxide-based air pollutants arising from human activity regarding energy production and consumption. Since SO_2 emissions are a critical air pollutant in terms of its adverse impact on human health and other environmental issues, it is a negative indicator.
Ratio of greenhouse gas emissions to GDP $= \frac{\text{Carbon dioxide emissions}}{\text{Gross domestic product (GDP)}}$	It is the ratio of CO_2 emissions to GDP, implying the relationships among energy use, environmental concern, and economic prospect. Since CO_2 emissions stand for the utilization of fossil fuels and have side effects on climate change, this indicator belongs to the negative type.

low-carbon and clean energy. In this study, the environment-ability is considered as the index of energy security by incorporating three emission-related indicators, and these are per capita energy-related carbon dioxide emissions (C_{13}) (Sovacool, 2013b), per capita sulfur dioxide emissions (C_{14}) (Wu *et al.*, 2012), and the ratio of greenhouse gas emission to GDP (C_{15}); see Table 5.

3.6. *Develop-ability*

Develop-ability in terms of energy or energy security generally refers to the ability of the energy system to be low-carbon, clean, and

Table 6: Three indicators in the dimension of develop-ability (Wang and Zhou, 2017; Wu *et al.*, 2012).

Indicator	Description
Energy production-to-energy consumption $= \frac{\text{Total energy production}}{\text{Total energy consumption}}$	It is the ratio of the produced energy to the consumed energy, which measures the statues of total energy production and consumption. Since producing more energy while reducing energy consumption helps improve energy self-sufficiency, this indicator belongs to the positive type.
Carbon emissions per unit energy consumption $= \frac{\text{Total carbon emissions}}{\text{Total primary energy consumption}}$	It evaluates the sustainability of both patterns of energy consumption and carbon emissions. Lowering fossil fuel consumption would be beneficial to CO_2 emission issues since a large amount of carbon emission is contributed by the primary energy consumption. Therefore, a lower value of this indicator implies a more desirable performance.
Diversity of energy supply $= \sum_i \text{share of } i \times \ln(\text{Share of } i)$ *It is calculated by using the Shannon–Wiener index, and i is an option of energy resource including coal, natural gas, oil, and primary electricity power in the total energy consumption.*	It reflects the diversity of energy resources for a country or region, where the main fossil fuels of coal, natural gas, oil, and primary electricity power consumption are considered. Since an energy system that relies heavily on a single energy option is inflexible and unsafe, diversity in the available energy resources can enhance the robustness and security of the energy scene. Therefore, this indicator belongs to the positive type.

sustainable. In other words, the develop-ability dimension should include indicators that reflect the sustainability of the energy system and consider the compatibility with the current energy situation. To build a clean, low-carbon, and efficient energy system for China, incorporating the concept of sustainability into energy security becomes increasingly important, since unsustainable energy systems are bound to cause certain energy security problems. Therefore, three indicators in the dimension of develop-ability are used to measure the energy security, and these are energy production-to-energy consumption ratio (C_{16}) (Wang and Zhou, 2017), carbon emission per unit energy consumption (C_{17}) (Wu *et al.*, 2012), and diversity of energy supply (C_{18}) (Wang and Zhou, 2017); see Table 6.

It is worth pointing out that although a well-rounded index is created by incorporating the above-mentioned 18 indicators from divergent dimensions, some other indicators could also be considered for certain purposes. For instance, energy production security index for measuring the degree of energy production security (Wu *et al.*, 2012), power distribution losses for calculating the efficiency (Erahman *et al.*, 2016), cost of energy imports/exports in relation to GDP for assessing the economic-based energy security (Jewell *et al.*, 2014), and patents owned by the state for representing the technological innovations (Yao and Chang, 2014). Besides, in this energy security index, some indicators could be categorized into more than one dimension according to the cognition of the decision-makers/stakeholders. For instance, the primary energy consumption per capita was regarded as an affordability indicator in the work of Yao and Chang (2014), and a develop-ability indicator in the work of Fang *et al.* (2018); while share of non-fossil energy consumption could be either an acceptability indicator (Fang *et al.*, 2018) or an availability indicator (Sovacool, 2013b). Therefore, the suggested energy security index could be modified according to the actual situation of the investigated systems and the subjective preferences of the users.

4. Energy Security Index

Since a hierarchical structure for energy security assessment can be found in Section 3, an energy security index was proposed in this study to aggregate the multi-dimensional indicators into a composite

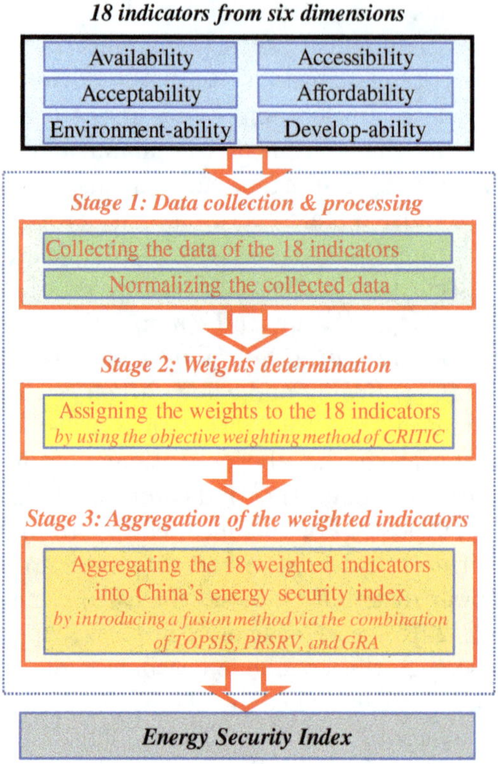

Figure 2: Framework for the calculation of energy security index.

index for measuring China's historical energy security performances, which embraces three main stages including data collection and processing, weights determination of the indicators, and aggregation of the weighted indicators, as depicted in Figure 2.

4.1. *Data collection and processing*

As stated in Section 3, 18 indicators in six dimensions were used to measure China's energy security performances, resulting in the data of each indicator being collected from different literature resources or calculated by specific methodological procedures. It should be noted that the data with respect to different indicators have different physical units and scales and that both positive and negative ones can be found, with the positive implying that a higher value would make that indicator more desirable (like energy self-sufficiency), while the negative ones indicate that a lower value would be better (like per capita energy-related carbon dioxide emissions). Hence, it is a prerequisite for the historical analysis to normalize the data with respect to all the indicators into dimensionless and unitary data according to the associated positive or negative type. Here, Equation (1) is employed for processing the data.

$$\begin{cases} x_k(i) = \dfrac{r_k(i)}{\sqrt{\sum\limits_k r_k(i)^2}} \text{ for the positive indicator} \\ x_k(i) = 1 - \dfrac{r_k(i)}{\sqrt{\sum\limits_k r_k(i)^2}} \text{ for the negative indicator,} \end{cases} \tag{1}$$

where $r_k(i)$ is the collected data of for the k-th year with respect to the i-th indicator, and $x_k(i)$ represents the normalized data of for the k-th year with respect to the i-th indicator, which ranges from 0 to 1.

4.2. *Weights determination for the indicators*

The relative importance of each indicator in the energy security assessment should be different from one another because they usually play different roles for energy security, and the relative importance (weight) is usually determined by using the subjective weighting methods or the objective weighting methods Xu *et al.* (2018). To be specific, subjective methods such as AHP (analytic hierarchy process) and BWM (best-worst method) determine the weight of each indicator based on the subjective judgments of the experts. However, subjective weighting methods usually result in an overestimated weighting result due to the lack of experience and imprecise information (Xu *et al.*, 2018). Moreover, it is also very difficult for the experts to compare multiple indicators for energy security analysis simultaneously. Therefore, recent works employed objective methods such as entropy weighting method, rather than the subjective ones, to determine the weights according to dispersion analysis of the collected data of indicators (Fang *et al.*, 2018), where the greater the degree of disorder of the data of an investigated indicator, the greater the discrimination power of the indicator in the final ranking

(Xu and Dong, 2020). In this chapter, an objective weighting method, the so-called "CRITIC (Criteria Importance Through Inter-criteria Correlation) indicator," was employed to calculate the weights of the indicators for synthesizing the composite energy security index, since this method can provide an insight into the nature of the dilemmas created by the existence of conflicting indicators and even incorporates the interdependencies among the indicators in the weighting process (Diakoulaki *et al.*, 1995). Herein, the weight of each indicator can be obtained by using Equations (2)–(5).

$$\sigma(i) = \sqrt{\frac{\sum_k \left(x_k(i) - \overline{x_k(i)}\right)^2}{K}}, \tag{2}$$

$$\rho(i\,|j) = \frac{\sum_k (x_k(i) - \overline{x(i)})(x_k(j) - \overline{x(j)})}{\sqrt{\sum_k \left(x_k(i) - \overline{x_k(i)}\right)^2}\sqrt{\sum_k \left(x_k(j) - \overline{x_k(j)}\right)^2}}, \tag{3}$$

$$f(i) = \sigma(i)\left[K - \sum_j \rho(i\,|j)\right], \tag{4}$$

$$w(i) = \frac{f(i)}{\sum_i f(i)}. \tag{5}$$

Here, Equation (2) is the standard derivation of the i-th indicator, and $\overline{x(i)} = \sum_k x_k(i)$ is the average performance of all years regarding the i-th indicator; $\rho(i\,|j)$ in Equation (3) is the correlation coefficient between the i-th and j-th indicators; $f(i)$ in Equation (4) indicates the amount of information associated with the i-th indicator; the higher the value of $f(i)$, the greater the weight of the i-th indicator; and, $w(i)$ in Equation (5) offers the final weight after the normalization.

4.3. *Aggregation of the weighted indicators*

As for the aggregation of the weighted indicators into a composite index for measuring the overall energy security, various MCDM techniques could be employed, i.e., AHP (analytic hierarchy process) (Ren and Sovacool, 2014a), DEMATEL (decision-making trial and evaluation laboratory) (Ren and Sovacool, 2014a), DEA (data envelopment analysis) (Gokgoz and Guvercin, 2018), TOPSIS (technique for order preference by similarity to an ideal solution) (Fang *et al.*, 2018), PROMETHEE (preference ranking organization method for enrichment evaluations) (Zhang *et al.*, 2017), etc. However, different merits and shortcomings exist for the different MCDM alternatives, and there is no such thing as a superior approach that must be applied over another (Mulliner *et al.*, 2016; Xu and Dong, 2019); more importantly, in any investigated case, different–even opposite ranking–sequences could be generated by using different MCDM techniques (Peng *et al.*, 2011). Consequently, some contributions have been made to enhance the reliability of the prioritization result by aggregating the rankings generated by more than one MCDM technique (Peng *et al.*, 2011; Xu and Dong, 2019).

In this work, a fusion method is introduced for developing the composite energy security index, by reconciling the mathematical mechanisms of TOPSIS, PRSRV (projection ranking by similarity to referencing vector), and GRA (grey relation analysis). Compared with some other MCDM approaches, the selected three methods have the following three advantages: (1) They are compensatory ranking methods that can offer complete ranking results by using the aggregation function of the weighted indicators (Mulliner *et al.*, 2016); (2) They fully utilize the data of the weighted indicators by resorting to the consideration of both best and worst referencing solutions, which would generate more rational results (Guan *et al.*, 2018; Ren and Sovacool, 2015; Xu *et al.*, 2018); (3) They are easy to conduct since similar operational procedures can be used in a generic way (specified in what follows). Table 7 summarizes the optimal functions of the adopted TOPSIS, PRSRV, and GRA methodologies, and further detailed information regarding these methods can be found in the work of Ren and Sovacool (2015), Xu *et al.* (2018), and Guan *et al.* (2018), respectively. Notably, the crisp value-based version of GRA is used in this study. The procedures for aggregating the weighted indicators are given in what follows:

- **Creating the weighted decision-making matrix:** The data of the weighted indicators can be obtained using Equation (6); subsequently, the weighted decision-making matrix can be created as presented in Table 8, and the performance regarding a certain

Table 7: Optimal functions of TOPSIS, PRSRV, and GRA.

MCDM	Optimal Function
TOPSIS (Ren and Sovacool, 2015)	The best option should have the nearest distance to the ideal scenario and the farthest distance to the nadir scenario.
PRSRV (Xu *et al.*, 2018)	The best option should have the highest similarity to the ideal scenario and the lowest similarity to the nadir scenario.
GRA (Guan *et al.*, 2018)	The best option should have the biggest closeness to the ideal scenario and the smallest closeness to the nadir scenario.

Table 8: The weighted decision-making matrix.

		A_1	A_2	...	A_k	...	A_m
Availability	C_1	$y_1(1)$	$y_2(1)$	...	$y_k(1)$	...	$y_m(1)$
	C_2	$y_1(2)$	$y_2(2)$	...	$y_k(2)$	...	$y_m(2)$
	C_3	$y_1(3)$	$y_2(3)$	...	$y_k(3)$	...	$y_m(3)$
Accessibility	C_4	$y_1(4)$	$y_2(4)$	...	$y_k(4)$	...	$y_m(4)$
	C_5	$y_1(5)$	$y_2(5)$	...	$y_k(5)$	...	$y_m(5)$
	C_6	$y_1(6)$	$y_2(6)$	...	$y_k(6)$	...	$y_m(6)$
Acceptability	C_7	$y_1(7)$	$y_2(7)$	...	$y_k(7)$	...	$y_m(7)$
	C_8	$y_1(8)$	$y_2(8)$	...	$y_k(8)$	...	$y_m(8)$
	C_9	$y_1(9)$	$y_2(9)$	...	$y_k(9)$	...	$y_m(9)$
Affordability	C_{10}	$y_1(10)$	$y_2(10)$	...	$y_k(10)$	...	$y_m(10)$
	C_{11}	$y_1(11)$	$y_2(11)$	...	$y_k(11)$	...	$y_m(11)$
	C_{12}	$y_1(12)$	$y_2(12)$	...	$y_k(12)$	...	$y_m(12)$
Environment-ability	C_{13}	$y_1(13)$	$y_2(13)$	...	$y_k(13)$	...	$y_m(13)$
	C_{14}	$y_1(14)$	$y_2(14)$	...	$y_k(14)$	...	$y_m(14)$
	C_{15}	$y_1(15)$	$y_2(15)$	...	$y_k(15)$	...	$y_m(15)$
Develop-ability	C_{16}	$y_1(16)$	$y_2(16)$	...	$y_k(16)$	...	$y_m(16)$
	C_{17}	$y_1(17)$	$y_2(17)$	...	$y_k(17)$	...	$y_m(17)$
	C_{18}	$y_1(18)$	$y_2(18)$	...	$y_k(18)$	...	$y_m(18)$

year (i.e., the k-th year) can be obtained by using Equation (7).

$$y_k(i) = w_i \times x_k(i), \tag{6}$$

$$A_k = \{y_k(1), y_k(2), \ldots, y_k(18)\}. \tag{7}$$

- **Using the computational mechanisms of the three MCDM techniques:** (1) The ideal reference solution and the nadir one should be determined by using Equations (8) and (9), respectively. From the computational mechanism of each ranking method, the corresponding deviation between the alternative and the ideal/nadir reference solutions can be determined; the distance measurement (Equation (10)) in TOPSIS (Ren and Sovacool, 2015), the vector similarity (Equation (11) in PRVSR (Xu *et al.*, 2018), and the grey relational degree (Equation (12) in GRA (Guan *et al.*, 2018) are used to depict the three types of deviations. Subsequently, the ideal and nadir deviations in each MCDM technique should be integrated into the combined coefficient (CC), as given in Equation (13), which can then be used to determine the corresponding ranking set of a certain method. A larger value of CC implies a higher priority of the corresponding historical year.

$$\begin{aligned} A^{+} &= \left\{ \max_{j=1,2,\ldots,m} y_j(1), \max_{j=1,2,\ldots,m} y_j(2), \ldots, \max_{j=1,2,\ldots,m} y_j(18) \right\} \\ &= \left\{ y^{+}(1), y^{+}(2), \ldots, y^{+}(18) \right\}, \end{aligned} \tag{8}$$

$$\begin{aligned} A^{-} &= \left\{ \min_{j=1,2,\ldots,m} y_j(1), \min_{j=1,2,\ldots,m} y_j(2), \ldots, \min_{j=1,2,\ldots,m} y_j(18) \right\} \\ &= \left\{ y^{-}(1), y^{-}(2), \ldots, y^{-}(18) \right\}, \end{aligned} \tag{9}$$

$$\begin{cases} d_j^{+}(\text{TOPSIS}) = \sqrt{\sum_{i=1}^{18} \left[y_j(i) - y^{+}(i) \right]^2} \\ d_i^{-}(\text{TOPSIS}) = \sqrt{\sum_{i=1}^{18} \left[y_j(i) - y^{-}(i) \right]^2} \end{cases}, \tag{10}$$

$$\begin{cases} d_j^{+}(\text{PRSRV}) = \dfrac{\sum_{i=1}^{18} \left[y_j(i) \times y^{+}(i) \right]}{\sum_{i=1}^{18} \left(y^{+}(i) \right)^2} \\ d_j^{-}(\text{PRSRV}) = \dfrac{\sum_{i=1}^{18} \left[y_j(i) \times y^{-}(i) \right]}{\sum_{i=1}^{18} \left(y_j(i) \right)^2} \end{cases}, \tag{11}$$

$$\begin{cases} d_i^+(\text{GRA}) = \displaystyle\sum_{i=1}^{18} \frac{\min\limits_j \min\limits_i |y_j(i) - y^+(i)| + 0.5\max\limits_j \max\limits_i |y_j(i) - y^+(i)|}{|y_j(i) - y^+(i)| + 0.5\max\limits_j \max\limits_i |y_j(i) - y^+(i)|} \\ d_i^-(\text{GRA}) = \displaystyle\sum_{i=1}^{18} \frac{\min\limits_j \min\limits_i |y_j(i) - y^-(i)| + 0.5\max\limits_j \max\limits_i |y_j(i) - y^-(i)|}{|y_j(i) - y^-(i)| + 0.5\max\limits_j \max\limits_i |y_j(i) - y^-(i)|} \end{cases}, \tag{12}$$

$$\begin{cases} CC(\text{TOPSIS}) = \dfrac{d_j^-(\text{TOPSIS})}{d_j^+(\text{TOPSIS}) + d_j^-(\text{TOPSIS})} \\ CC(\text{PRSRV}) = \dfrac{d_j^+(\text{PRSRV})}{d_j^+(\text{PRSRV}) + d_j^-(\text{PRSRV})} \\ CC(\text{GRA}) = \dfrac{d_j^+(\text{GRA})}{d_j^+(\text{GRA}) + d_j^-(\text{GRA})} \end{cases}. \tag{13}$$

- **Obtaining the reconciled ranking:** Based on the value of CC, the rankings generated by the three MCDM techniques can be given, which would be different from each other. Therefore, a Spearman's rho-based Borda Count (Xu and Dong, 2019) must be adopted to determine the final sequence. To be specific, Equation (14) offers the similarity between a pair of data sets regarding the sequences determined by two MCDM methods. In which, $S(t|t')$ ranges from -1 to 1, and 1 refers to a complete positive linear correlation, 0 implies no correlation, -1 represents a complete negative correlation. After running Equation (15), the Spearman's rho of an individual MCDM method can be obtained, and a larger value of $S(t)$ implies that the sequence determined by this method is closer to the ideal ranking than the sequences determined by the others, which results in greater voting power in the Borda Count (BC). Finally, as shown in Equation (16), for ranking the performances of different years, a smaller value of BC refers to better performance (or higher ranking) of the investigated year.

$$S(t|t') = 1 - \frac{6\sum_{k=1}^{K}\left[R_k(t) - R_k(t')\right]^2}{K(K^2-1)}, \quad t \neq t' \text{ (TOPSIS, PRSRV, GRA)} \tag{14}$$

$$S(t) = \frac{\sum_{t'} S(t|\, t')}{T-1}, \; t \neq t', \; T = 3$$

(is the number of sets of sequences) (15)

$$BC_i = \sum_{t=\text{TOPSIS, PRSRV, GRA}} [R_i(t) \times S(t)], \qquad (16)$$

where K is the number of investigated years, $R_k(t)$ is the sequence of the k-th year calculated using the MCDM technique of t (among TOPSIS, PRSRV, and GRA), and $S(t|t')$ measures the similarity between the sets of sequences determined by the methods of t and t'.

5. Historical Analysis and Discussion

Based on the 18 indicators that were created (explained in Section 3) and the developed energy security index (explained in Section 4), China's historical energy security during the period 2002–2016 can be measured.

5.1. *Data collection and processing in the historical analysis*

The majority of data regarding the 18 indicators for 2002–2016 were taken from "China Energy Statistical Yearbook" and "BP Statistical Review of World Energy", including the amount of energy production and consumption, population and GDP, share of fossil fuels or non-fossil fuels, and the CO_2 and SO_2 emissions. Meanwhile, some necessary and supplementary information was needed for calculating specific indicators, such as the risk coefficient (IEA, 2007) for determining the crude oil concentration risk. Table 9 summarizes the collected data concerning each indicator in the energy security index. It is worth noting that all the GDP values in Table 9 refer to the real gross domestic products at constant 2010 prices.

After normalizing the data in Table 6 with the help of Equation (1), the normalized value of each indicator from 2002 to 2016 can be obtained, as given in Table 10.

Table 9: Collected data of each indicator (2002–2016).

	C_1 ton/ person	C_2 (%)	C_3 (%)	C_4 (%)	C_5 (%)	C_6 (%)	C_7 ton/ person	C_8 (%)	C_9 ton/ 10^4RMB
2002	1.1235	44.193	99.0	6.04	0.41	32.009	1.320	8.2	1.401
2003	1.2824	43.318	98.0	5.18	0.43	25.580	1.525	7.4	1.443
2004	1.4718	44.525	95.0	5.17	0.51	20.002	1.772	7.6	1.433
2005	1.6284	46.371	94.0	5.37	0.57	20.098	1.999	7.4	1.406
2006	1.7746	43.561	93.0	5.17	0.68	18.723	2.179	7.4	1.306
2007	1.9055	40.588	93.0	4.89	0.71	17.516	2.357	7.5	1.153
2008	1.9803	37.398	94.0	4.59	0.99	15.746	2.414	8.4	1.003
2009	2.0312	34.726	91.0	4.45	1	13.283	2.519	8.5	0.963
2010	2.1986	32.133	88.1	4.03	1.04	11.596	2.690	9.4	0.873
2011	2.3976	30.672	89.0	3.68	1.05	11.003	2.873	8.4	0.791
2012	2.4387	29.033	87.0	3.31	1.17	10.304	2.970	9.7	0.744
2013	2.4726	29.087	86.0	3.14	1.16	10.389	3.064	10.2	0.700
2014	2.4576	28.021	85.0	3.01	1.14	9.581	3.113	11.3	0.661
2015	2.4262	28.902	84.0	2.74	1.05	9.280	3.127	12.1	0.624
2016	2.2791	64.563	79.8	1.94	1.18	8.695	3.152	13.3	0.586

	C_{10} (%)	C_{11} (%)	C_{12} 10^4 RMB/ person	C_{13} ton/ person	C_{14} ton/ person	C_{15} ton/ 10^4 RMB	C_{16} (%)	C_{17} ton/ ton	C_{18}
2002	16.1	2.618	0.942	2.985	0.015	3.169	92.221	2.261	0.879
2003	10.2	15.376	1.057	3.500	0.0167	3.312	102.519	2.295	0.850
2004	4.9	31.388	1.236	4.095	0.0173	3.312	89.477	2.312	0.852
2005	15.4	42.645	1.422	4.653	0.0195	3.273	87.631	2.328	0.823
2006	12.4	20.171	1.669	5.068	0.0197	3.036	85.446	2.325	0.829
2007	4.2	10.591	2.045	5.467	0.0187	2.673	84.850	2.320	0.834
2008	16	36.841	2.406	5.544	0.0175	2.304	86.529	2.296	0.862
2009	7.3	36.826	2.616	5.764	0.0166	2.204	85.109	2.289	0.863
2010	12.3	28.080	3.080	6.055	0.0163	1.966	88.984	2.251	0.910
2011	11.1	33.978	3.632	6.536	0.0165	1.800	87.882	2.275	0.898
2012	2.9	0.669	3.991	6.632	0.0156	1.662	87.303	2.233	0.933
2013	0.1	1.145	4.375	6.775	0.015	1.549	86.063	2.211	0.956
2014	0.8	7.881	4.708	6.744	0.0144	1.432	84.973	2.166	0.991
2015	12.3	47.086	5.013	6.667	0.0135	1.330	84.083	2.132	1.021
2016	5.8	16.405	5.382	6.598	0.008	1.226	79.405	2.093	1.049

Table 10: Normalized data of each indicator (2002–2016).

	C_1	C_2	C_3	C_4	C_5	C_6	C_7	C_8	C_9
2002	0.142	0.288	0.282	0.360	0.444	0.489	0.432	0.228	0.160
2003	0.162	0.282	0.279	0.309	0.424	0.391	0.374	0.206	0.155
2004	0.186	0.290	0.271	0.308	0.357	0.305	0.322	0.211	0.156
2005	0.206	0.302	0.268	0.320	0.320	0.307	0.285	0.206	0.159
2006	0.225	0.284	0.265	0.308	0.268	0.286	0.262	0.206	0.172
2007	0.241	0.264	0.265	0.292	0.257	0.267	0.242	0.208	0.194
2008	0.251	0.244	0.268	0.274	0.184	0.240	0.236	0.233	0.223
2009	0.257	0.226	0.259	0.265	0.182	0.203	0.226	0.236	0.233
2010	0.279	0.209	0.251	0.240	0.175	0.177	0.212	0.261	0.257
2011	0.304	0.200	0.254	0.219	0.173	0.168	0.198	0.233	0.283
2012	0.309	0.189	0.248	0.197	0.156	0.157	0.192	0.269	0.301
2013	0.313	0.189	0.245	0.187	0.157	0.159	0.186	0.283	0.320
2014	0.311	0.183	0.242	0.179	0.160	0.146	0.183	0.314	0.339
2015	0.307	0.188	0.240	0.163	0.173	0.142	0.182	0.336	0.359
2016	0.289	0.421	0.228	0.116	0.154	0.133	0.181	0.369	0.383
	C_{10}	C_{11}	C_{12}	C_{13}	C_{14}	C_{15}	C_{16}	C_{17}	C_{18}
2002	0.006	0.214	0.075	0.433	0.255	0.156	0.272	0.257	0.250
2003	0.010	0.036	0.084	0.370	0.229	0.149	0.302	0.253	0.242
2004	0.020	0.018	0.098	0.316	0.221	0.149	0.264	0.251	0.243
2005	0.006	0.013	0.113	0.278	0.196	0.151	0.258	0.249	0.235
2006	0.008	0.028	0.132	0.255	0.194	0.163	0.252	0.250	0.236
2007	0.024	0.053	0.162	0.237	0.205	0.185	0.250	0.250	0.238
2008	0.006	0.015	0.191	0.233	0.219	0.215	0.255	0.253	0.246
2009	0.014	0.015	0.207	0.224	0.231	0.225	0.251	0.254	0.246
2010	0.008	0.020	0.244	0.214	0.235	0.252	0.262	0.258	0.259
2011	0.009	0.016	0.288	0.198	0.232	0.275	0.259	0.255	0.256
2012	0.034	0.838	0.316	0.195	0.245	0.298	0.257	0.260	0.266
2013	0.991	0.489	0.347	0.191	0.255	0.320	0.254	0.263	0.273
2014	0.124	0.071	0.373	0.192	0.266	0.346	0.250	0.268	0.282
2015	0.008	0.012	0.397	0.194	0.284	0.372	0.248	0.272	0.291
2016	0.017	0.034	0.427	0.196	0.478	0.404	0.234	0.277	0.299

5.2. *Weights determination of the indicators in the historical analysis*

The objective weighting method of CRITIC (see Equations (2)–(5)) was utilized to calculate the relative importance of the 18 indicators. Table 11 summarized the key parameters and result of the CRITIC, indicating that two indicators, C_{10} and C_{11}, had much higher weights

Table 11: The parameters and results of the CRITIC weighting method in the historical analysis.

	$\mathbf{C_1}$	$\mathbf{C_2}$	$\mathbf{C_3}$	$\mathbf{C_4}$	$\mathbf{C_5}$	$\mathbf{C_6}$	$\mathbf{C_7}$	$\mathbf{C_8}$	$\mathbf{C_9}$
$\sigma(i)$	0.055	0.062	0.015	0.067	0.098	0.100	0.073	0.050	0.078
$f(i)$	0.839	0.844	0.243	1.144	1.471	1.523	1.038	0.655	1.021
$w(i)$	0.042	0.042	0.012	0.057	0.073	0.076	0.052	0.033	0.051
	$\mathbf{C_{10}}$	$\mathbf{C_{11}}$	$\mathbf{C_{12}}$	$\mathbf{C_{13}}$	$\mathbf{C_{14}}$	$\mathbf{C_{15}}$	$\mathbf{C_{16}}$	$\mathbf{C_{17}}$	$\mathbf{C_{18}}$
$\sigma(i)$	0.244	0.226	0.117	0.070	0.066	0.085	0.014	0.008	0.020
$f(i)$	3.319	3.046	1.509	0.969	0.768	1.098	0.208	0.098	0.098
$w(i)$	0.166	0.152	0.075	0.048	0.038	0.055	0.010	0.005	0.012

than the others since the historical data in this regard have changed dramatically during the investigated period; on the contrary, the indicators C_{17} and C_{16} had much fewer impacts on the overall performance since their historical values were relatively stable. Moreover, it could be concluded that the dimension of affordability (C_{10-12}) is the most critical one for improving the energy security of China, while the dimension of develop-ability (C_{16-18}) may play an insignificant role in determining China's historical energy security performance.

5.3. *Aggregation of the weighted indicators in the historical analysis*

The fusion method, via the integration of TOPSIS, PRSRV, and GRA, was applied to aggregate the weighted indicators into the energy security index. That is, the weighted decision-making matrix was first created, as given in Table 12 by using Equation (6), and the performance for each year can then be observed.

Subsequently, the ranking methods of TOPSIS, PRSRV, and GRA were, respectively, used for determining the corresponding ranking sets by calculating the deviations from the ideal/nadir referencing solutions (D^+/D^-) as well as the combined coefficient (CC). Table 13 lists the key parameters, while Figure 4 depicts the sequences of the historical analysis determined by the three MCDM techniques.

As can be observed in Figure 3, on the one hand, the three MCDM techniques offered the same ranking results in the top three historical performances (2013, 2012, and 2002) and shared relatively similar trends regarding the overall energy security, demonstrating the feasibility of the three techniques; on the other hand, the detailed sequences derived from the three MCDM techniques were quite different from each other, verifying the necessity of using the fusion method for offering a more reliable ranking result. Subsequently, by conducting the Spearman's rho-based Borda Count (see Equations (14)–(16)), the compromised ranking regarding China's historical energy security performances from 2002 to 2016 can be offered, and the result is given in Figure 4, indicating that the energy security performances in 2013, 2012, and 2002 were the top three best, while the year 2008 could be the worst one.

Table 12: The weighted decision-making matrix in the historical analysis.

	C_1	C_2	C_3	C_4	C_5	C_6	C_7	C_8	C_9
2002	5.96E-03	1.21E-02	3.42E-03	2.06E-02	3.26E-02	3.72E-02	2.24E-02	7.44E-03	8.15E-03
2003	6.80E-03	1.19E-02	3.39E-03	1.76E-02	3.11E-02	2.97E-02	1.94E-02	6.72E-03	7.91E-03
2004	7.81E-03	1.22E-02	3.29E-03	1.76E-02	2.62E-02	2.32E-02	1.67E-02	6.90E-03	7.97E-03
2005	8.64E-03	1.27E-02	3.25E-03	1.83E-02	2.35E-02	2.33E-02	1.48E-02	6.72E-03	8.12E-03
2006	9.41E-03	1.20E-02	3.22E-03	1.76E-02	1.97E-02	2.17E-02	1.36E-02	6.72E-03	8.75E-03
2007	1.01E-02	1.11E-02	3.22E-03	1.67E-02	1.88E-02	2.03E-02	1.25E-02	6.81E-03	9.91E-03
2008	1.05E-02	1.03E-02	3.25E-03	1.56E-02	1.35E-02	1.83E-02	1.22E-02	7.62E-03	1.14E-02
2009	1.08E-02	9.53E-03	3.15E-03	1.52E-02	1.34E-02	1.54E-02	1.17E-02	7.71E-03	1.19E-02
2010	1.17E-02	8.82E-03	3.05E-03	1.37E-02	1.29E-02	1.35E-02	1.10E-02	8.53E-03	1.31E-02
2011	1.27E-02	8.42E-03	3.08E-03	1.25E-02	1.27E-02	1.28E-02	1.03E-02	7.62E-03	1.44E-02
2012	1.29E-02	7.97E-03	3.01E-03	1.13E-02	1.14E-02	1.20E-02	9.95E-03	8.80E-03	1.53E-02
2013	1.31E-02	7.98E-03	2.97E-03	1.07E-02	1.15E-02	1.21E-02	9.64E-03	9.26E-03	1.63E-02
2014	1.30E-02	7.69E-03	2.94E-03	1.03E-02	1.17E-02	1.11E-02	9.49E-03	1.03E-02	1.73E-02
2015	1.29E-02	7.93E-03	2.91E-03	9.33E-03	1.27E-02	1.08E-02	9.45E-03	1.10E-02	1.83E-02
2016	1.21E-02	1.77E-02	2.76E-03	6.61E-03	1.13E-02	1.01E-02	9.37E-03	1.21E-02	1.95E-02
Max	1.31E-02	1.77E-02	3.42E-03	2.06E-02	3.26E-02	3.72E-02	2.24E-02	1.21E-02	1.95E-02
Min	5.96E-03	7.69E-03	2.76E-03	6.61E-03	1.13E-02	1.01E-02	9.37E-03	6.72E-03	7.91E-03

	C_{10}	C_{11}	C_{12}	C_{13}	C_{14}	C_{15}	C_{16}	C_{17}	C_{18}
2002	1.02E-03	3.25E-02	5.63E-03	2.10E-02	9.78E-03	8.56E-03	2.82E-03	1.26E-03	2.97E-03
2003	1.61E-03	5.54E-03	6.31E-03	1.79E-02	8.79E-03	8.19E-03	3.13E-03	1.24E-03	2.87E-03
2004	3.35E-03	2.71E-03	7.38E-03	1.53E-02	8.48E-03	8.19E-03	2.73E-03	1.23E-03	2.88E-03
2005	1.07E-03	2.00E-03	8.49E-03	1.35E-02	7.53E-03	8.29E-03	2.68E-03	1.22E-03	2.78E-03
2006	1.32E-03	4.22E-03	9.97E-03	1.24E-02	7.45E-03	8.94E-03	2.61E-03	1.22E-03	2.80E-03
2007	3.91E-03	8.04E-03	1.22E-02	1.14E-02	7.85E-03	1.01E-02	2.59E-03	1.23E-03	2.82E-03
2008	1.03E-03	2.31E-03	1.44E-02	1.13E-02	8.39E-03	1.18E-02	2.64E-03	1.24E-03	2.91E-03
2009	2.25E-03	2.31E-03	1.56E-02	1.09E-02	8.84E-03	1.23E-02	2.60E-03	1.24E-03	2.92E-03
2010	1.33E-03	3.03E-03	1.84E-02	1.03E-02	9.00E-03	1.38E-02	2.72E-03	1.26E-03	3.08E-03
2011	1.48E-03	2.51E-03	2.17E-02	9.58E-03	8.89E-03	1.51E-02	2.69E-03	1.25E-03	3.04E-03
2012	5.66E-03	1.27E-01	2.38E-02	9.44E-03	9.41E-03	1.63E-02	2.67E-03	1.27E-03	3.15E-03
2013	1.64E-01	7.44E-02	2.61E-02	9.24E-03	9.78E-03	1.75E-02	2.63E-03	1.29E-03	3.23E-03
2014	2.05E-02	1.08E-02	2.81E-02	9.28E-03	1.02E-02	1.89E-02	2.60E-03	1.31E-03	3.35E-03
2015	1.33E-03	1.81E-03	2.99E-02	9.39E-03	1.09E-02	2.04E-02	2.57E-03	1.33E-03	3.45E-03
2016	2.83E-03	5.19E-03	3.21E-02	9.49E-03	1.83E-02	2.21E-02	2.43E-03	1.36E-03	3.55E-03
Max	1.64E-01	1.27E-01	3.21E-02	2.10E-02	1.83E-02	2.21E-02	3.13E-03	1.36E-03	3.55E-03
Min	1.02E-03	1.81E-03	5.63E-03	9.24E-03	7.45E-03	8.19E-03	2.43E-03	1.22E-03	2.78E-03

Table 13: The key parameters and result of the three MCDM techniques.

	TOPSIS			PRSRV			GRA		
	D^+	D^-	CC	D^+	D^-	CC	D^+	D^-	CC
2002	0.192	0.052	0.212	0.185	0.331	0.359	15.98	16.75	0.488
2003	0.206	0.033	0.139	0.108	0.459	0.190	15.70	17.13	0.478
2004	0.207	0.025	0.109	0.097	0.537	0.153	15.54	17.28	0.474
2005	0.209	0.023	0.101	0.085	0.559	0.132	15.49	17.35	0.472
2006	0.208	0.020	0.089	0.088	0.598	0.129	15.43	17.38	0.470
2007	0.204	0.020	0.090	0.106	0.600	0.150	15.44	17.30	0.472
2008	0.209	0.017	0.076	0.079	0.641	0.110	15.40	17.42	0.469
2009	0.209	0.017	0.074	0.082	0.652	0.111	15.39	17.43	0.469
2010	0.209	0.018	0.080	0.081	0.634	0.113	15.41	17.42	0.469
2011	0.209	0.021	0.091	0.081	0.597	0.120	15.43	17.41	0.470
2012	0.164	0.128	0.438	0.414	0.078	0.842	16.07	16.75	0.490
2013	0.067	0.180	0.728	0.803	0.044	0.948	16.39	16.23	0.502
2014	0.190	0.035	0.157	0.170	0.429	0.283	15.60	17.04	0.478
2015	0.210	0.031	0.127	0.086	0.480	0.152	15.62	17.28	0.475
2016	0.207	0.037	0.150	0.106	0.425	0.200	15.84	17.05	0.482

As can be seen from Figure 4, there are three trends regarding China's historical energy security performances that are visible, and they are as follows: (1) the energy security in the period 2002–2007 presented a downward trend; (2) the most unsatisfactory performance can be found in 2008, and the level of energy security had recovered slowly from 2009 to 2011; (3) the best situation for China's energy security was observed in 2013 and 2012, followed by an acceptable downward trend in the next three years.

5.4. *Sensitivity analysis*

To investigate the effects of weights on prioritization, a sensitivity analysis was conducted by assigning different sets of weights to the indicators. To be specific, equal weight ($w_i = 1/18$) was used in case EW; while for case D_j, a dominant weight was assigned to the three indicators in the j-th dimension, for instance, in case D_1, $w_1 = w_2 = w_3 = 1/6$, while the others were deemed as equal with a weight of 1/30. After conducting the same ranking procedure methodologies, the overall energy security of China in different cases was determined,

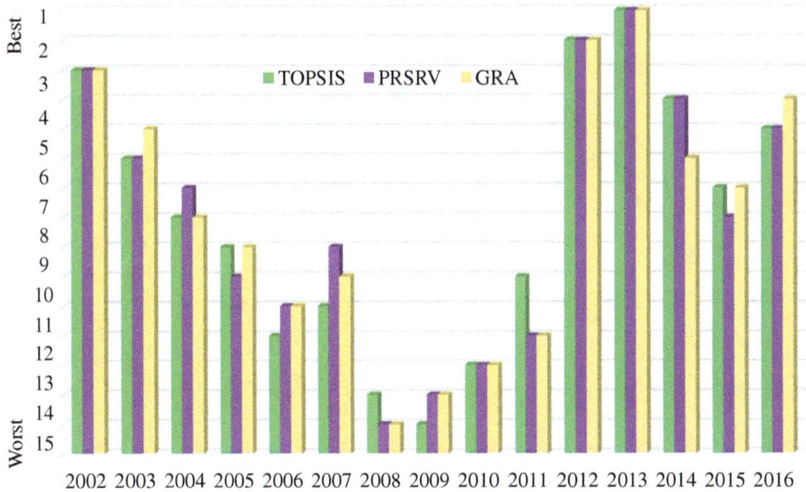

Figure 3: The sequence sets determined by the three MCDM techniques.

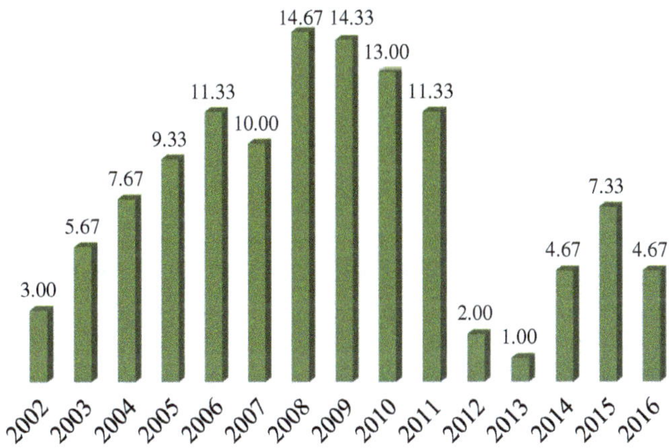

Figure 4: The combined coefficient for each year.

as shown in Figure 5; for the comparison, the original result (denoted as OW) is also given.

It can be noticed that relatively similar trends can be found in most of the cases, except for the case of D_2 (accessibility) and D_3 (acceptability). Therefore, it could be deduced that (1) the ranking result determined by the fusion method were relatively

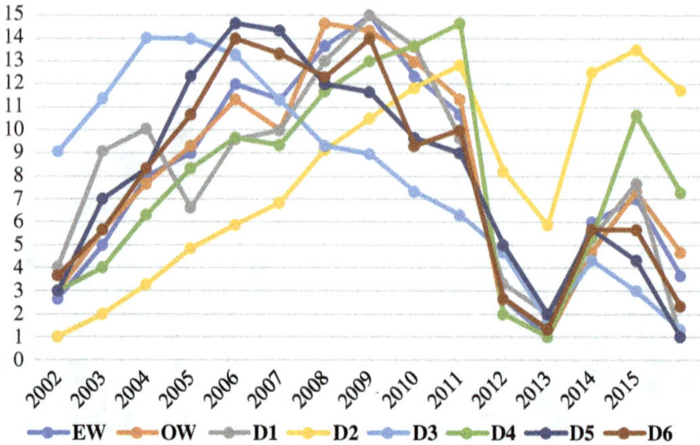

Figure 5: The result of the sensitivity analysis.

robust and that, to some extent, the objective weighting method, CRITIC was suitable for application in synthesizing the energy security index. Consequently, the most preferable energy security performances regarding the investigated period were seen in 2013. (2) However, weights regarding the indicators still had impacts on the prioritization results, especially the indicators from the perspectives of accessibility and acceptability.

6. Conclusions

For measuring China's historical energy security performances systematically, this work proposed a methodological-based energy security index in which 18 indicators from the fields of availability, accessibility, affordability, acceptability, environment-ability, and develop-ability were considered; the objective weighting method–CRITI–was applied to determine the relative importance of each indicator; and a fusion method that incorporated TOPSIS, PRISRV, and GRA was introduced to aggregate the weighted indicators into a composite energy security index. The main advantages of the index are threefold: (1) divergent concerns with the quantifiable 18 indicators are included, which results in the proposed energy security index providing a well-rounded and objective evaluation result regarding China's historical performances; (2) the objective method of CRITIC assigns the weights by looking at the degree of disorder of the data of an investigated indicator, which offers an easy yet rational way for the determination of the weights; and (3) the fusion aggregation method via the combination of TOPSIS, PRSRV, and GRA is used to integrate the weighed indicators into the composite index, which improves the reliability of the assessment result by reconciling the conflicting sequences derived from different MCDM techniques. By applying the energy security index in the historical analysis from 2002 to 2016, the best performing and the worst performing year can be, respectively, identified as 2013 and 2008. After conducting the sensitivity analysis, the obtained trends regarding China's energy security performances were confirmed, while the rationality of the proposed energy security index was also verified.

Acknowledgments

The authors are grateful to the support provided by the Science and Technology Research Program of Chongqing Municipal Education Commission (Grant No. KJQN201901512), Foundation of Chongqing University of Science & Technology (Grant No. 2019001).

References

Ang, B. W., Choong, W. L. and Ng, T. S. 2015. Energy security: Definitions, dimensions and indexes. *Renewable and Sustainable Energy Reviews,* 42, 1077–1093.

Anwar, J. 2016. Analysis of energy security, environmental emission and fuel import costs under energy import reduction targets: A case of Pakistan. *Renewable and Sustainable Energy Reviews,* 65, 1065–1078.

APERC 2007. A quest for energy security in the 21st century–resources and constraints. Tokyo: APERC.

Bambawale, M. J. and Sovacool, B. K. 2011. China's energy security: The perspective of energy users. *Applied Energy,* 88, 1949–1956.

BP 2019. BP Statistical Review 2019. https://www.bp.com/content/dam/bp/business-sites/en/global/corporate/pdfs/energy-economics/statistical-review/bp-stats-review-2019-china-insights.pdf.

Cabalu, H. 2010. Indicators of security of natural gas supply in Asia. *Energy Policy,* 38, 218–225.

Cox, E. 2018. Assessing long-term energy security: The case of electricity in the United Kingdom. *Renewable and Sustainable Energy Reviews,* 82, 2287–2299.

Dale, V. H., Efroymson, R. A., Kline, K. L. and Davitt, M. S. 2015. A framework for selecting indicators of bioenergy sustainability. *Biofuels, Bioproducts and Biorefining,* 9, 435–446.

Diakoulaki, D., Mavrotas, G. and Papayannakis, L. 1995. Determining objective weights in multiple criteria problems–the critic method. *Computers and Operations Research*, 22, 763–770.

Erahman, Q. F., Purwanto, W. W., Sudibandriyo, M. and Hidayatno, A. 2016. An assessment of Indonesia's energy security index and comparison with seventy countries. *Energy*, 111, 364–376.

Fang, D., Shi, S. and Yu, Q. 2018. Evaluation of sustainable energy security and an empirical analysis of China. *Sustainability*, 10.

Gokgoz, F. and Guvercin, M. T. 2018. Energy security and renewable energy efficiency in EU. *Renewable and Sustainable Energy Reviews*, 96, 226–239.

Guan, X., Sun, G. D., Yi, X. and Zhao, J. 2018. Grey relational analysis for hesitant fuzzy sets and its applications to multiattribute decision-making. *Mathematical Problems in Engineering.* https://doi.org/10.1155/2018/7436054.

Hughes, L. 2009. The four "R"s of energy security. *Energy Policy,* 37, 2459–2461.

International Energy Agency (IEA). 2007. Energy Security and Climate Policy-Assessing Interactions. OECD Publishing: Paris, France.

Jewell, J., Cherp, A. and Riahi, K. 2014. Energy security under decarbonization scenarios: An assessment framework and evaluation under different technology and policy choices. *Energy Policy*, 69, 647–648.

Kiriyama, E. and Kajikawa, Y. 2014. A multilayered analysis of energy security research and the energy supply process. *Applied Energy,* 123, 415–423.

Kleber, D. 2009. The U.S. Department of defense: Valuing energy security. *Journal of Energy Security*, 12–22.

Martchamadol, J. and Kumar, S. 2013. An aggregated energy security performance indicator. *Applied Energy*, 103, 653–670.

Mulliner, E., Malys, N. and Maliene, V. 2016. Comparative analysis of MCDM methods for the assessment of sustainable housing affordability. *Omega–The International Journal of Management Science*, 59, 146–156.

Narula, K. and Reddy, B. S. 2015. Three blind men and an elephant: The case of energy indices to measure energy security and energy sustainability. *Energy*, 80, 148–158.

Narula, K., Sudhakara Reddy, B. and Pachauri, S. 2017. Sustainable energy security for India: An assessment of energy demand sub-system. *Applied Energy*, 186, 126–139.

Onat, N. and Bayar, H. 2010. The sustainability indicators of power production systems. *Renewable and Sustainable Energy Reviews*, 14, 3108–3115.

Peng, Y., Kou, G., Wang, G. X. and Shi, Y., 2011. FAMCDM: A fusion approach of MCDM methods to rank multiclass classification algorithms. *Omega–The International Journal of Management Science*, 39, 677–689.

Ren, J. Z. and Sovacool, B. K. 2014a. Enhancing China's energy security: Determining influential factors and effective strategic measures. *Energy Conversion and Management*, 88, 589–597.

Ren, J. Z. and Sovacool, B. K. 2014b. Quantifying, measuring, and strategizing energy security: Determining the most meaningful dimensions and metrics. *Energy*, 76, 838–849.

Ren, J. Z. and Sovacool, B. K. 2015. Prioritizing low-carbon energy sources to enhance China's energy security. *Energy Conversion and Management*, 92, 129–136.

Song, Y., Zhang, M. and Sun, R. F. 2019. Using a new aggregated indicator to evaluate China's energy security. *Energy Policy*, 132, 167–174.

Sovacool, B. K. 2011. Evaluating energy security in the Asia pacific: Towards a more comprehensive approach. *Energy Policy*, 39, 7472–7479.

Sovacool, B. K. 2013a. Assessing energy security performance in the Asia Pacific, 1990–2010. *Renewable and Sustainable Energy Reviews*, 17, 228–247.

Sovacool, B. K. 2013b. An international assessment of energy security performance. *Ecological Economics,* 88, 148–158.

Stougie, L., Tsalidis, G. A., van der Kooi, H. J. and Korevaar, G. 2018. Environmental and exergetic sustainability assessment of power generation from biomass. *Renewable Energy*, 128, 520–528.

Valdes, J. 2018. Arbitrariness in multidimensional energy security indicators. *Ecological Economics*, 145, 263–273.

Wang, Q. and Zhou, K. 2017. A framework for evaluating global national energy security. *Applied Energy,* 188, 19–31.

Wu, G., Liu, L. C., Han, Z. Y. and Wei, Y. M. 2012. Climate protection and China's energy security: Win-win or tradeoff. *Applied Energy*, 97, 157–163.

Xu, D. and Dong, L. 2019. Strategic diagnosis of China's modern coal-to-chemical industry using an integrated SWOT-MCDM framework. *Clean Technologies and Environmental Policy*, 21, 517–532.

Xu, D. and Dong, L. 2020. Comprehensive evaluation of sustainable ammonia production systems based on fuzzy multi-attribute decision making under hybrid information. *Energy Science & Engineering*, 6, 1902–1923.

Xu, D., Lv, L. P., Ren, X. S., Ren, J. Z. and Dong, L. C. 2018. Route selection for low-carbon ammonia production: A sustainability prioritization framework based-on the combined weights and projection ranking by similarity to referencing vector method. *Journal of Cleaner Production*, 193, 26–276.

Yao, L. X. and Chang, Y. H. 2014. Energy security in China: A quantitative analysis and policy implications. *Energy Policy,* 67, 595–604.

Zhang, L., Yu, J., Sovacool, B. K. and Ren, J. Z. 2017. Measuring energy security performance within China: Toward an inter-provincial prospective. *Energy*, 125, 825–836.

https://doi.org/10.1142/9781786349224_0007

Chapter 7

Measuring China's Oil Import Security with a Multi-Dimensional Approach from the Perspective of External Suppliers

Long Zhang[*,‡], Wuliyasu Bai[*,§], and Jingzheng Ren[†,¶]

[*]School of Business, Xinyang Normal University,
No. 237 Nanhu Road, Xinyang, 464000, China

[†]Department of Industrial and Systems Engineering,
The Hong Kong Polytechnic University,
Hong Kong SAR, China

[‡]hbzhanglong876@163.com

[§]wuliyasu666@163.com

[¶]jzhren@polyu.edu.hk

Abstract

China has been the world's second largest oil consumer and importer for several years; though many studies have focused on China's energy security, few have examined it from the perspective of external suppliers. This study provides a group of indicators to assess the reliability of China's 37 oil-importing sources over the period 1995–2018 based on the perspective of external suppliers. These indicators are made up of four dimensions: energy availability, political status, economic status, and energy transportation. Then, an index was created based on the reliability of the oil-importing sources and their corresponding shares in China's total oil imports, to evaluate China's oil import security. The results show that, for China, the members of Commonwealth of Independent States, the Asia-Pacific region, and American countries are more reliable oil suppliers than Europe, Africa, and the Middle East. Besides, energy availability and energy transportation are the main threats to China's oil import security. Based on these conclusions, this study suggests that China should increase its internal energy supply and control the growth of energy consumption to reduce its dependence on oil imports, diversify its energy importing sources and transportation routes, and implement energy-focused diplomatic policies and activities to enhance its oil import security.

Keywords: China; Crude oil; Import security; Importing sources.

1. Introduction

Since oil is the main energy source that drives economy development, secure supply of oil products is vital to sustain the normal social and economic development (Kokwaro, 1993). However, there are plenty of factors affecting oil supply security. First, oil is the largest contributor to the world's energy mix, taking up 33.6% of the world's total primary energy supply in 2017, despite this share having dropped by 19% in the past four decades (British Petroleum, 2019a). Second, the world's oil reserves demonstrated a concentrated distribution. In fact, about half of the world's proven oil reserves were located in the Middle East (British Petroleum, 2019a), and even more than 80% of reserves were hold by the Organization of Petroleum Exporting Countries (OPEC) members, namely Venezuela, Saudi Arabia, Iran, Iraq, Kuwait, United Arab Emirates, Libya, Nigeria, Qatar, Algeria, Angola, Congo, and Ecuador (OPEC, 2019). Third, there arose a fierce international competition in securing crude oil supplies around the world. The major economic entities of the world have considerable demand for oil. In particular, the traditional economies, namely the United States, the European Union, and Japan, need a large amount of oil to sustain its development, while the emerging competitors, e.g., the BRICS (Brazil, Russia, India, China, and South Africa), also have shown a sharp increase in demand for oil, which put great pressure on the competition for global oil supply (Wabiri and Amusa, 2010).

Due to the global disparity between oil supply and demand, a large amount of oil was traded every year. For instance, the Middle East contributed the most to the world's oil production, or one-third of the world total, while it only consumed about 30% of their production, which is less than 10% of world's oil consumption, and exported the rest (British Petroleum, 2019a). However, the Asia-Pacific region only accounted for less than 10% of

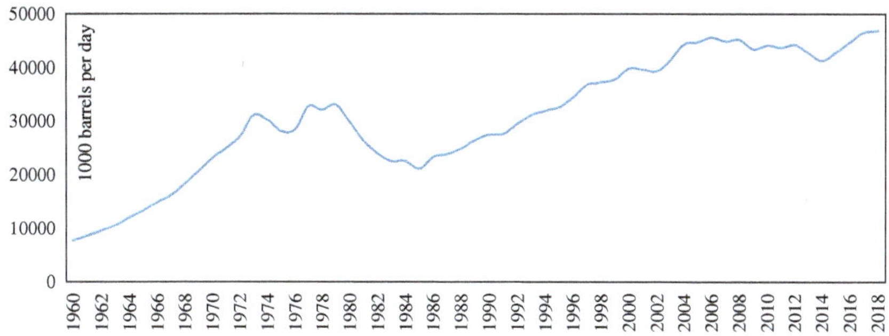

Figure 1: World imports of crude oil, 1960–2018.
Source: 2019 OPEC Annual Statistics Bulletin.

world's oil production yet contributed 34% of the total consumption (British Petroleum, 2019a). Due to the fast-growing economy and great resource disparity, the world oil trade climbed rapidly over the past several decades, as shown in Figure 1, and more than half of the crude was exported from the OPEC (OPEC, 2019). However, most of the world's oil exporting regions are prone to geopolitical instability as well as religious and ethnic conflicts, and even terrorist attacks, which is a special barrier for ensuring energy security (Toft *et al.*, 2010).

As the world's largest developing country, China has taken over the United States as the world's largest energy consumer in 2010, with a share of 20.3% of world's total energy consumption that year (British Petroleum, 2019a). Although China's energy mix is chronically dominated by coal, oil consumption and imports have been growing dramatically during the past two decades, as shown in Figure 2. In fact, China has been a net oil importer since the early 1990s. Compared with the level of 1995, China consumed almost three times more oil in 2018, and the net oil imports sharply rose from 12 million tons to 460 million tons. Consequently, its oil dependence witnessed a rapid increase from 7.6% to more than 70%. It is estimated that China would overtake the United States as the world's largest oil consumer by around 2030, and the dependence on imported oil would reach 76% by 2040, which is much higher than the historical record of the United States in 2005 (British Petroleum, 2019b).

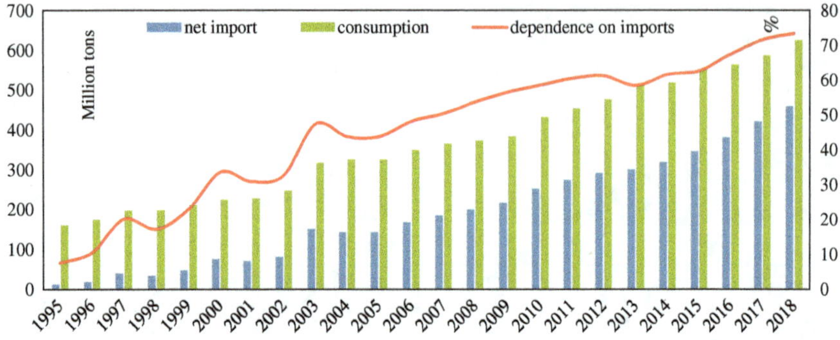

Figure 2: China's oil consumption, net imports, and dependence, 1995–2018. *Source*: China Energy Statistics Yearbook.

Moreover, China is increasingly depending on the oil from the OPEC members, whose share in China's oil imports rose from 20% in 1995 to more than 60% in early 2010s, and then dropped back to 53% in 2018, as shown in Figure 3. With regard to the importing sources, the Middle East was the largest source where China's oil imports came from, and took up a share of about 50%. Africa contributed the second largest share of 25%, and the Latin American counties and the Commonwealth of Independent States accounted for about 10%, respectively. It is obvious that China has highly concentrated oil-importing sources, which is a great threat to its energy security. Furthermore, more than half of China's oil imports come from the Middle East, where the most number of religious conflicts and terrorist attacks happen, and 25% came from the Africa, which is extremely politically and economically unstable. All of these factors have posed great threats to China's oil import security.

Thus, considering these issues, the Chinese decision-makers are confronted with the following questions:

- What are the factors that affect China's oil import security?
- How can we measure China's oil import security?
- Who are the reliable oil-importing sources for China?
- What trends has China's oil import security shown during the past two decades?
- How should China manage its high oil dependence to ensure oil supply security?

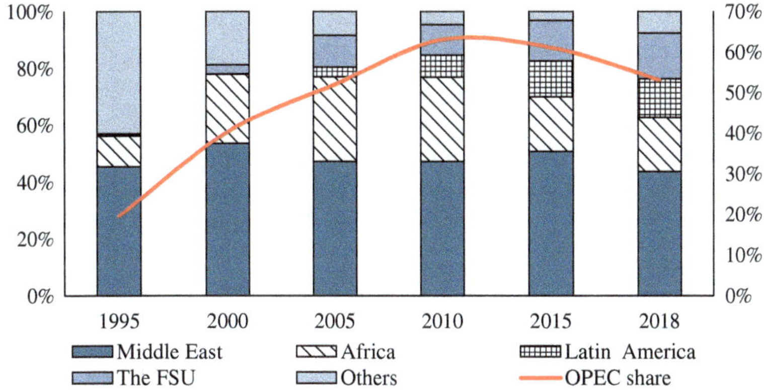

Figure 3: Sources of China's oil imports by region, 1995–2018.
Source: Author's calculation based on data from UN Comtrade Database.

To answers these questions, this chapter first reviewed the literature on energy supply and import security as well as risks, proposed a systematic analytic framework for measuring the reliability of oil-importing sources, and created an index for evaluating oil import security based on reliability investigation. Then, taking China as an example, this framework was tested and its oil import security investigated over the period 1995–2018. Finally, some major conclusions are drawn and policy implications provided for policymakers to ensure its external oil supply security.

2. Indicators for Measuring Oil Import Security

2.1. *Literature review*

At present, many studies have investigated national energy security. Among them, some were concerned with the theoretical framework and measuring tools. For instance, Blyth and Lefevre-Marton (2005) developed the Energy Security Index, APERC (2007) proposed the 4A framework of energy security, Kruyt *et al.* (2009) reviewed the indicators and index that can be used to measure energy security, and Chester (2010), Winzer (2012), and Ang *et al.* (2015) conceptualized energy security. In particular, an international survey about people's attitudes and perceptions on energy security was conducted (Sovacool and Mukherjee, 2011; Sovacool *et al.*, 2012;

Knox-Hayes *et al.*, 2013). Narula (2016) proposed a multidimensional Sustainable Energy Security Index composed of 23 metrics. Kisel *et al.* (2016) presented a novel Energy Security Matrix that structures relevant energy security indicators from the aspects of technical resilience and vulnerability, economic dependence, and political affectability for the electricity, heat, and transport fuel sectors. Radovanović *et al.* (2017) designed an Energy Security Index that included environmental and social aspects, and even proposed a new geo-economic concept of energy security which took into account the basic energy security indicators as well as economic, financial, and political stability (Radovanović *et al.*, 2018). Garciagusano *et al.* (2017) developed the Renewable Energy Security Index, which combined environmental life cycle assessment and techno-economic energy systems modelling. Bompard *et al.* (2017) outlined a methodology that considered and integrated external and internal dimensions about national energy security. Martisauskas *et al.* (2018) proposed a methodology for energy security assessment in terms of energy system resilience based on the analysis of emerging threats, disruptions, and associated consequences to energy systems.

In addition, many national and regional energy security evaluation were conducted for US (Greene, 2010), France, and the UK (Lefevre, 2010); Sri Lanka, Thailand, and Vietnam (Selvakkumaran and Limmeechokchai, 2013; Kamsamrong and Sorapipatana, 2014); Taiwan (Chuang and Ma, 2013); China (Yao and Chang, 2014; Zhang, *et al.*, 2017; Lu *et al.*, 2019); India (Narula *et al.*, 2017); Pakistan (Nawaz and Alvi, 2018); Japan (Matsumoto and Shiraki, 2018); and Finland (Jaaskelainen *et al.*, 2019). Furthermore, some international energy security assessments were also undertaken, such as for the Asia–Pacific region (Vivoda, 2010), Northeast Asia (Von Hippel *et al.*, 2011), ASEAN (Sovacool, 2011; Tongsopit *et al.*, 2016), OECD countries (Sovacool and Brown, 2010; Cohen *et al.*, 2011), Baltic States (Zeng *et al.*, 2017; Augutis *et al.*, 2017), and the European Union (Radovanović *et al.*, 2017, 2018), even international and global comparison and assessments were made (Umbach, 2010; Sovacool, 2013; Jewell, 2014).

Besides, scholars have paid great attention to measuring energy supply security, which considered internal and external energy supply. Jansen *et al.* (2004) designed a set of indicators for long-term energy supply security. Some specific indices were developed for assessing the security of energy supply in the EU (Egenhofer *et al.*, 2004; Scheepers *et al.*, 2006; Chalvatzis and Ioannidis, 2017a). Correljé and van der Linde (2006) and Costantini *et al.* (2007) reviewed European energy security from the aspects of energy reserves, market structure, and political stability. Le Coq and Paltseva (2009) designed a Risky External Energy Supply Index for EU members. Badea *et al.* (2011) used an ordered weighted averaging method to composite six indicators and energy supply security for 27 EU members. Chalvatzis and Ioannidis (2017b) discussed energy supply security for five European countries from the perspective of financial wealth. Ruble (2017) described the benefits of natural gas imports from the Eastern Mediterranean for improving EU's energy supply security. Saldarriagac and Salazar (2016) discussed the significance of gas regasification terminals for Colombian energy supply security. Wu *et al.* (2012) and Geng and Ji (2014) measured China's energy supply security by aggregating several indicators. Li *et al.* (2018) measured China's energy supply security based on the "4A" framework by using a dynamic model. Narula *et al.* (2017) assessed energy security in India from an energy supply perspective.

In the field of oil import security and risks, portfolio theory and diversification index were frequently used to measure energy security risks. Lesbirel (2004) explored the relationship between diversification and energy security risks and used portfolio theory to measure the systematic and specific risks associated with Japanese energy imports over the period 1970–1999. Wu *et al.* (2007, 2008, 2009) and Wabiri and Amusa (2010) also used a similar method and quantified oil import risks for China and South Africa, respectively. Moreover, Stern (2004) analyzed the systemic risk of UK's gas supply security. Gupta (2008) assessed the relative oil vulnerability of 26 net oil-importing countries for the year 2004 based on various indicators. Vivoda (2009) examined the importance of diversification policy for oil importers. Doukas *et al.* (2011) identified and analyzed seven risks for EU oil and gas supply security. Zhang *et al.* (2013) established an evaluation framework and a two-phase DEA-like model to evaluate China's oil import security during 1993–2011 from the perspective of supply chain process. In fact, geopolitical dimensions have been proven to be of significance to national oil security (Krane and Medlock, 2018). Thus, Ji and Fan (2016) evaluated the impact of oil exports from GCC countries on China's oil security.

Ji *et al.* (2019) also analyzed the impact OPEC on oil import security in East Asia.

There is no shortage of research in the fields of energy security, and some even focus on energy import security. However, very few of them have investigated the issue of oil import security from the perspective of external suppliers. Thus, this study focuses on national oil imports security evaluation based on an external perspective.

2.2. *Dimensions and indicators*

Based on the previous literature on energy supply security and import security as well as our workshop discussion, this chapter puts forward some specific indicators for measuring national oil import security from the perspective of external suppliers. To be specific, we selected indicators for oil import security from the aspects of external availability, political status, economic status, and energy transportation, as shown in Table 1.

2.2.1. *External availability*

Energy availability is the basic element to sustain energy supply, and two indicators were selected in this paper to reflect energy availability: reserves/production index and production/demand index.

(1) Reserves/production index indicates oil potential of importing sources.

$$RPI = POR/OP, \tag{1}$$

where RPI is the reserve/production index, POR is the proved oil reserves, and OP refers to oil production.

(2) Production/consumption index implies the export capacity of importing sources.

$$PCI = OP/OC, \tag{2}$$

where PCI is the production/consumption index, and OP and OC are oil production and consumption of importing sources, respectively.

2.2.2. *Political status*

Political factors have a significant effect on oil production and trade flow on importing sources. For instance, the several oil crises during

Table 1: Dimensions and indicators for measuring oil import security.

Dimension	Indicator	Description	Data Source
External availability	I_1: Reserves/ production index	Proven recoverable oil reserves of exporter divided by its oil production	BP Statistical review
	I_2: Production/ demand index	Oil production of exporter divided by its production	BP Statistical review
Political status	I_3: Political stability	Worldwide Governance Indicators	World Bank
	I_4: Political relations	The political communication and conflicts between exporter and importer	Chinese embassies
Economic status	I_5: Economic stability	The Consumer Price Index of exporter	Federal Reserve Bank of St. Louis
	I_6: Economic relations	The share of trade volume between exporter and importer in the total foreign trade volume of exporter	UN Comtrade Database
	I_7: Oil importing price	The oil price traded between exporter and importer	UN Comtrade Database
Energy transportation	I_8: Transport route distance	The shortest shipping distance from port to port between exporter and importer, land transport not included	SEA-DISTANCES.ORG
	I_9: Transport risk	The share of piracy attacks along the shipping route in the world's total piracy attacks	Annual IMB Piracy Report

the 1970s were mainly induced by the political conflict between oil exporters and western countries, as well as internal political instability (Ikenberry, 1986). This study thus used political stability of oil exporters and political relations between oil exporters and importers to reflect on the political status.

(1) *Political stability*:
The political stability of oil exporters can affect its oil production and trade, and the Worldwide Governance Index of World Bank was used here to indicate political stability.

(2) *Political relations*:
The political relations between oil exporters and importers can exert influence on their economic communication. The political communication and conflicts between countries can dictate their political relations. In this study, we relied on workshop discussions to rate the political relations between China and its oil importers.

2.2.3. *Economic status*

International oil trade can be affected by the economic status of oil exporters. Here, economic stability, economic relations, and oil export prices were used to dictate the economic factors.

(1) *Economic stability*:
The economic stability reflects the economic development of importing sources, which can be reflected by the inflation rate. Usually, the Consumer Price Index is the best indicator for inflation rate, and economists have found an optimal quantitative inflation target, which is typically 2% per year (Svensson, 1997).

(2) *Economic relations*:
Economic relations explain the economic dependency of oil exporters on importers, which can be represented by the share of trade volume between exporters and importers in the total foreign trade volume of the exporter.

$$ER = TEI/TTE, \tag{3}$$

where ER is the economic relations, TEI is the trade volume between oil exporters and importers, and TTE is the total trade volume of the exporter.

Table 2: Shipping route of China.

Region	Transport Route
Asia Pacific	Asia Pacific region–Malacca Strait–South China Sea–China
Middle East	Middle East–Hormuz Strait–Indian Ocean–Malacca Strait–South China Sea–China
North Africa	North Africa–Mediterranean–Suez Canal–Mand Strait–Malacca Strait–South China Sea–China
Europe	Europe–Atlantic Ocean–Mediterranean–Suez Canal–Mand Strait–Malacca Strait–South China Sea–China
South and West Africa	South and West Africa–Cape of Good Hope–Indian Ocean–Malacca Strait–South China Sea–China
Central and South America	Central & South America–Caribbean Sea–Panama Canal–Pacific Ocean–China
	Central & South America–Atlantic Ocean–Cape of Good Hope–Indian Ocean–Malacca Strait–South China Sea–China

(3) *Oil export price*:
Oil export price reflects the average price at which the exporters sold their crude oil to the importers, since different oil exporters may sell their oil at different prices.

2.2.4. *Energy transportation*

Since a country may import oil from countries and regions around the world, which needs to pass through a number of chokepoints and dangerous waters, these differences in the transport distance and risks also affect the transport security.

(1) *Transport distance*:
Usually, longer transport distance can result in the higher cost and risks. With respect to China, most of its oil imports are transported by shipping through six shipping routes for oil imports (see Table 2), except the imports from the Commonwealth of Independent States, which are conveyed through land transport or pipelines.

(2) *Transport risk*:
China's oil imports face different risks as they follow different shipping routes, and the global piracy attacks are focused in some specific

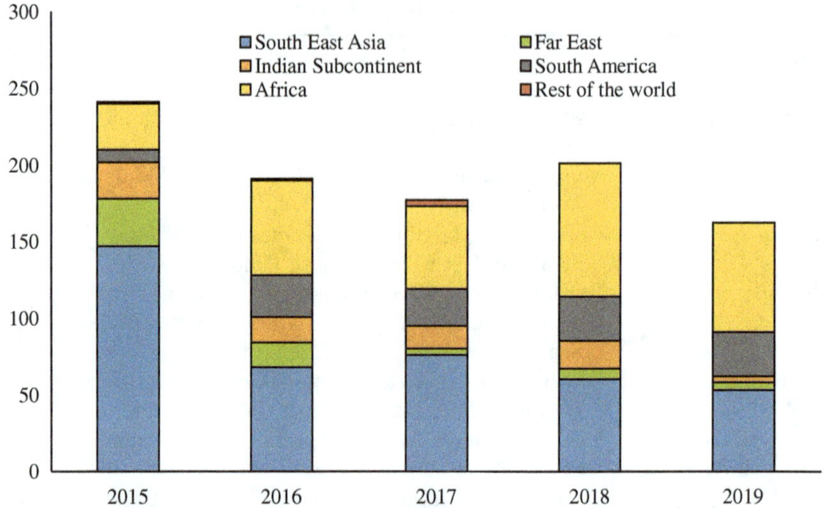

Figure 4: Piracy attacks around the world in 2015–2019.

areas along the route like Malacca Straits, Somalia's waters, Gulf of Aden, Persian Gulf, Gulf of Guinea, and Caribbean Sea (Wu *et al.*, 2009), as shown in Figure 4. The transportation risk can be represented with Equation (4).

$$TR = PAR/WPA, \tag{4}$$

where TR is the transport risk, PAR indicates the piracy attacks along the shipping route, and WPA is the total piracy attacks in the world.

3. Data and Methodology

With the dimensions and indicators determined, we then collected data on them. Then we assessed the reliability of 37 external oil suppliers of China as well as made an Oil Import Security Index to evaluate the oil import security for China over the period 1995–2018.

3.1. *Data collection*

During the past decades, China used to import crude oil from more than 70 countries and areas around the world. After rejecting these irregular oil exporters, 37 countries are thought to be China's regular oil-importing sources, making up 99% of China's oil imports, as shown in Table 3.

A total of nine indicators are selected in this study, and the data on them were from different sources (see Table 1). The data for the nine indicators with respect to the 37 countries were collected for the period 1995–2018 in five-year increments, which means China's oil import security with respect to years 1995, 2000, 2005, 2010, 2015, and 2018 were assessed in this study.

3.2. *Methodology*

Rather than using some type of complex Multi-Criteria Decision-Making or mathematical methods to measure oil import security, we created an Oil Import Security Index by aggregating these indicators.

Among the nine indicators, five are benefit-type, which means the larger, the better; three are cost-type, which means the smaller, the better; and one is medium-type, which means the closer it is to a specific value in the mid-range, the better. In particular, reserves/production index (I_1), production/demand index (I_2), political stability (I_3), political relations (I_4), and economic relations (I_6) are benefit-type indicators; while oil importing price (I_7), transport route distance (I_8), and transport risk (I_9) are cost-type indicators; and economic stability (I_5) is a medium-type indicator.

The procedure for creating Oil Import Security Index is as follows:

Step 1: The raw data for the benefit-type, cost-type, and medium-type indicators were normalized using Equations (5)–(7), respectively.

$$p_{ij} = (x_{ij} - \min x)/(\max x_j - \min x_j), \tag{5}$$

$$p_{ij} = (\max x - x_{ij})/(\max x_j - \min x_j), \tag{6}$$

$$p_{ij} = 1 - \frac{|x_{ij} - x_j^*|}{\max x_j - \min x_j}, \tag{7}$$

where p_{ij} is the normalized value of the ith importing source with respect to the jth indicator x_{ij} represents the original value of the ith importing source with respect to the jth indicator, x_j^* is the optimal

Table 3: China's oil-importing sources and the corresponding shares, 1995–2018 (%).

Importing Sources	1995	2000	2005	2010	2015	2018	Importing Sources	1995	2000	2005	2010	2015	2018
Algeria	0.76	—	0.65	0.73	0.29	0.14	Kuwait	—	0.62	1.30	4.11	3.44	5.03
Angola	5.84	12.29	13.77	16.46	13.18	10.26	Libya	1.22	0.18	1.78	3.08	0.31	1.86
Argentina	—	—	0.72	0.47	0.10	0.24	Malaysia	3.44	1.06	0.27	0.87	0.07	1.92
Australia	0.38	1.58	0.18	1.20	0.88	0.28	Mexico	—	—	—	0.47	0.22	0.15
Azerbaijan	—	—	0.00	0.05	0.07	0.12	Nigeria	2.28	1.78	1.03	0.54	0.65	0.10
Brazil	—	0.32	1.06	3.36	2.28	6.85	Norway	—	2.10	0.41	0.03	0.05	0.19
Brunei	—	0.39	0.40	0.43	0.03	—	Oman	21.38	22.29	8.54	6.63	9.65	7.12
Canada	—	—	0.00	0.13	0.07	0.26	Papua New Guinea	1.96	0.56	—	0.07	0.03	—
Chad	—	—	0.43	0.40	0.05	0.04	Qatar	—	2.28	0.27	0.23	0.12	2.92
Colombia	—	—	—	0.84	3.27	2.33	Russian	0.21	2.10	10.08	6.37	10.74	15.48
Congo	0.15	2.07	4.36	2.11	2.29	2.72	Saudi Arabia	1.98	8.16	17.49	18.66	16.11	12.28
Ecuador	—	—	0.07	0.34	0.24	0.41	Sudan*	—	4.72	5.22	5.26	2.66	0.93
Egypt	—	0.17	0.06	0.29	0.31	—	Thailand	—	0.41	0.94	0.10	0.00	0.14
Equatorial Guinea	—	1.74	2.92	0.34	1.05	0.54	United Arab Emirates	2.15	0.61	2.02	2.21	3.78	2.64
Gabon	0.51	0.65	—	0.18	0.50	0.78	United Kingdom	1.65	1.48	0.00	0.03	0.40	1.67
Indonesia	30.89	6.51	3.22	0.58	0.12	0.10	Venezuela	—	—	1.52	3.15	4.47	3.60
Iran	5.45	9.96	11.25	8.91	8.91	6.34	Viet Nam	4.45	4.50	2.52	0.29	0.48	0.26
Iraq	—	4.53	0.92	4.70	9.27	9.75	Yemen	14.47	5.14	5.39	1.68	0.81	0.27
Kazakhstan	—	1.03	1.02	4.20	1.84	0.50							

Note: *Including the South Sudan established in 2011.
Source: Author's calculation based on data of UN Comtrade Database.

value of the medium-type indicator, $\max x_j$ and $\min x_j$ are the maximum and minimum values of all the importing sources with respect to the jth indicator, respectively.

Step 2: The reliability of the ith importing source with respect to the kth year can be calculated with Equation (8).

$$RE_{ik} = \frac{\sum_{j=1}^{9} p_{ij}}{9}, \tag{8}$$

where RE_{ik} is the reliability of the ith importing source with respect to the kth year, and $k = 1995, 2000, 2005, 2010, 2015$, and 2018.

Step 3: Oil Import Security Index can be created using Equation (9).

$$OISI_k = \frac{\sum_i RE_{ik}^* S_{ik}}{\sum_i S_{ik}}, \tag{9}$$

where $OISI_{ik}$ is the Oil Import Security Index of the ith importing source with respect to the kth year and S_{ik} is the share of the ith importing source in China's oil imports with respect to the kth year.

4. Measuring China's Oil Import Security

With the data and procedures determined, the next phase was to assess the reliability of China's 37 oil-importing sources and calculate the score of China's oil import security. Several results are offered here to help policymakers and scholars understand the fact of China's oil import security.

First, the reliability of China's 37 oil-importing sources has been evaluated in this study. By calculating the mean score for each year and indicator, and aggregating them, the reliability for each importing sources can be obtained, and these results are shown in Figure 5. The best and worst possible score for any importing source within this period were six and zero, respectively, which would happen only in rather occasional cases. It is obvious that Kazakhstan, Russia, Canada, Vietnam, and Brunei were the top five reliable oil-importing sources for China during the past two decades, while Nigeria, the United Kingdom, Angola, Algeria, and Chad were the five least reliable importing sources.

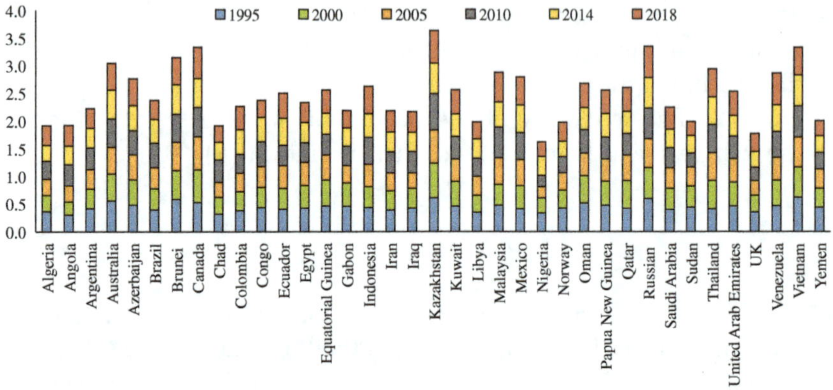

Figure 5: National reliability of China's oil-importing sources.

Second, if we take a regional perspective, these oil-importing sources can be divided into six regions according to their geographical and cultural situation, namely the Commonwealth of Independent States (CIS), Asia-Pacific countries, American countries, the Middle East and North Africa (MENA), West Africa, and Europe. The regional reliability of China's oil-importing sources is demonstrated in Figure 6. It can be concluded that the members of the Commonwealth of Independent States are the most reliable oil-importing sources for China, followed by the Asia-Pacific countries. An obvious reason for this is that these countries are very close to China, thus leading to a reduction in the shipping costs and risks significantly. Also, the Commonwealth of Independent States has close relations with China, and yet another added bonus is that the oil shipment can be completed through land transport and pipelines. In addition, the CIS members and Asian Pacific countries are more politically and economically stable than the countries in the Middle East, Africa, and Latin America. However, their reliability is compromised because of their less oil availability compared with other regions. American countries are the third most reliable region for China's oil imports. Although countries in this region are far away from China, and have bad economic and political situations, their shipping routes mean no the reliance on the Strait of Malacca and the ASEAN waters, where most of world piracy incidents happen. Besides, considerable oil availability has been proved here, which makes it a highly reliable oil-importing source for China. Although

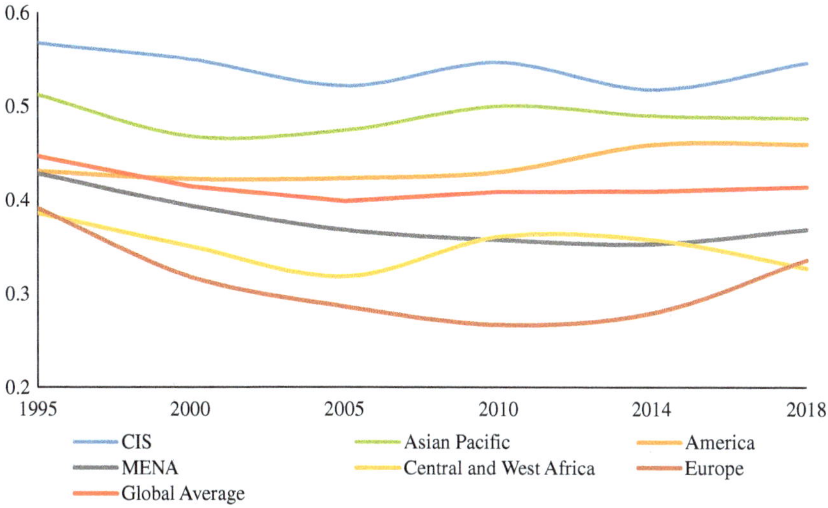

Figure 6: Regional reliability of China's oil-importing sources.

MENA and West Africa are the major oil-importing sources of China currently, they are not as reliable as people think. The main reason for this is their extremely terrible political and economic situation. It has to be admitted that countries in these regions do have close economic relations with China, as well as owing the world's highest amount of oil reserves and production. However, they are also the place where world's most military conflicts and terrorist attacks, which compromises their reliability. Besides, oil shipment from these places to China has to pass through most of world's chokepoints, e.g., Suez Canal, Gulf of Aden, the Cape of Good Hope, Hormuz Strait, Malacca Strait, and South China Sea, which made it very long and dangerous shipping routes. Europe is the least reliable oil-importing source because it does not have any advantage in oil availability and has a long and dangerous shipping route.

Third, the reliability of China's oil-importing sources can also be analyzed from a dimensional perspective. When calculating the average score with respect to each indicator for all the sources, followed by the average score with respect to each dimension, the dimensional score of reliability can be obtained, as shown in Figure 7. Obviously, the dimension of energy availability gets a much less score than

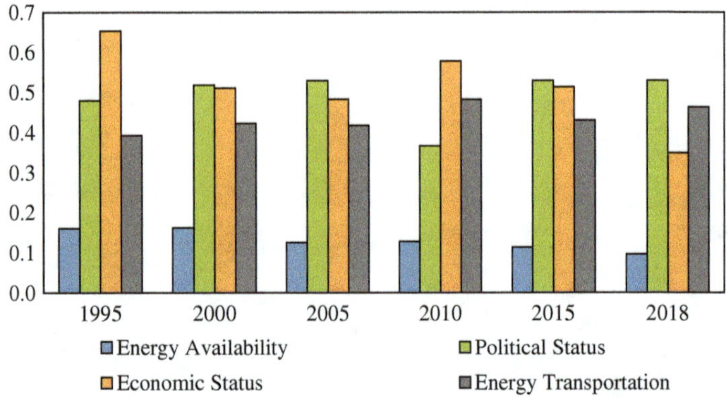

Figure 7: Dimensional reliability of China's oil-importing sources.

others, and has even shown a descending trend over the period 1995–2018, which means it is the main threat for China's oil import security. Since most economic entities of the world need to import large amounts of crude oil from the above-mentioned regions and countries, and these oil exporters also consume increasing oil to sustain their development every year, the global oil reserves are decreasing year by year. Thus, global energy availability is the main threat for national oil import security, not only for China, but also for countries around the world. On the contrary, economic status is the most reliable dimension for China's oil import security. With the Reform and Opening Up, China has become the main trading partner for most countries, and the economic relations have been strengthened in the 21st century. Moreover, political status is another reliable dimension for China. With the dependence on importing oil climbing up, China's diplomatic policy was increasingly focusing on energy, and it has maintained good political relations with most oil exporters. With respect to the dimension of energy transportation, China is geographically far away from most of the oil importing regions and is restricted by chokepoints in the shipping routes e.g., the Malacca Strait and the Cape of Good Hope. Therefore, the dimension of energy transportation gets a relatively low score in China's oil importing security.

Lastly, if one aggregates the reliability score of each importing sources and their corresponding share in China's total oil imports with respect to each year, then China's Oil Import Security Index can be calculated, and the results are shown in Figure 8. Overall,

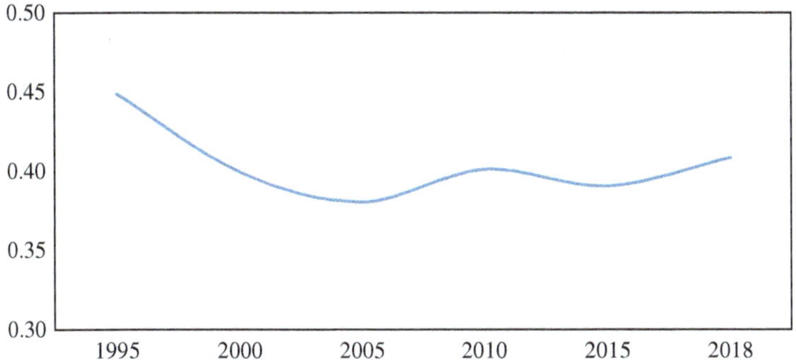

Figure 8: China's oil import security index from 1995 to 2018.

China's oil import security was at a medium to low level, with its security index ranging from 0.38 to 0.45 over the period 1995–2018, and an apparent declining tendency was observed. Year 1995 witnessed the best performance in terms of China's oil import security, with a security score of 0.45 that year. Then, the score dropped dramatically in the following decade, and further dropped to 0.40 in 2000, and then to the lowest record of 0.38 in 2005. Despite this score having slightly increased back to 0.40 in the following decades, the bad oil importing situation of China has not been improved. When considering its high dependence on imported petroleum, this is still a very serious threat for the external energy supply security.

5. Policy Implications

As the second largest oil consumer and importer in the world, China is facing degrading oil import security and increasing risks of external oil supply disruption, which threatens its energy security. China has very limited control over these dimensions and related risks to ensure its oil import security. Therefore, China needs to establish strategies and take effective measures to address the risks from different dimensions and strengthen its ability to resist risks and improve the security of oil imports. This study put forward several policy implications for improving China's oil imports security.

First, China should find more energy sources to increase domestic energy supply and control the growth of its energy consumption, to reduce the dependence on external energy supply and import risks.

China's oil import security is substantially affected by its large volume of energy consumption and over-dependence on importing oil resources. Thus, other energy sources should be fully developed and used. China has great potential in terms of renewable energy, for instance, Western China is rich in solar resources, Northern and Eastern China are gifted with great potential onshore and offshore wind power, and Southwest China has the largest hydropower in the country. Besides, non-conventional fuels like shale oil and gas should also be exploited. All of these renewables could be alternatives to the imported crude oil and give China a promising and secure energy future. However, it may take a very long time and plenty of investments from the time the renewable industry is deployed to its maturity; thus, China is not likely to make any significant achievements in the near future. Furthermore, as the world's largest developing country, China's economy develops with an amazing speed, as does its energy consumption. Although there has been an obvious decline in China's energy intensity since its Reform and Opening Up, China is still among the countries with the world's highest energy intensity (Voigt *et al.*, 2014). Thus, China should pay more efforts to the improvement of energy technology and efficiency, as well as energy saving and management.

Second, seeking diversified and reliable energy importing sources could enhance oil import security. Diversification is a regular strategy for improving import security and was taken as a very effective measure for addressing the high dependence on external oil supply (Lesbirel, 2004; Vivoda, 2009). China has a high dependence on crude oil imported from the Middle East and Africa, and most of these sources have high geopolitical and transportation risks, which makes China vulnerable to disruptions of external oil supply. Therefore, China should increase oil imports from more reliable sources, such as the Central Asian countries, Russia, Asia-Pacific countries, Canada, and the Latin American countries. These regions and countries are more politically and economically stable and are convenient and safe for oil shipment.

Third, actions dealing with transportation risks should be taken, and more reliable transportation routes should be developed. Crude oil pipelines offer a more reliable transportation mode than ocean shipping. Thus, China should develop reliable and friendly relations with its neighbors and establish crude oil pipelines as soon as possible. In fact, China has already established the China–Russia, China–Kazakhstan, and China–Burma crude oil pipelines, and the China–Pakistan crude oil pipelines are under construction. The pipelines between China and Russia and Kazakhstan could guarantee oil imports from the Commonwealth of Independent States, and that between China and Burma and Pakistan contribute to the diversification of China's oil shipping routes and reduce its dependence on the Malacca Straits. Besides, as piracy increases rampantly around the world, China should involve itself in the international cooperation for combating piracy and ensuring ocean transportation security.

Then, more attention should be paid to the overseas oil investment to ensure the stable acquisition of equity oil. Although large volumes of oil are imported to China every year, trade oil contributes the majority of this, and equity oil just contributes a minor supplement. For most oil importers, the overseas equity oil is more critical because it indicates control over the external oil resources and can ensure stability of external oil supply. However, trade oil is frequently affected by some external factors such as trade patterns and oil market. Hence, China should actively yet carefully invest in and cooperate with overseas oilfields after evaluating its risks and benefits.

Lastly, energy acquisition and cooperation should be the focus of national diplomatic policies and activities. Since international oil trade is easily influenced by geopolitical factors, China needs to play an important role in international mediation and form close political and economic relations with these importing sources. In 2013, China proposed the initiative of the Silk Road Economic Belt and the 21st-Century Maritime Silk Road (the Belt and Road), providing a great opportunity for China to conduct international energy cooperation with the Central Asian and Middle Eastern countries. Although some Middle Eastern countries have hostile relations with each other, China should play a role as a mediator and maintain good relations with both sides.

6. Conclusions and Discussions

This study proposed a group of indicators and aggregated them into an Oil Import Security Index from the perspective of external suppliers. With these indicators and index, this study assessed the reliability of China's 37 oil-importing sources, analyzed their regional and dimensional reliability, and evaluated China's oil import security over the period 1995–2018. Lastly, it provided some policy implications for improving China's oil import security. The conclusions of this study are summarized in what follows.

First, from the perspective of external suppliers, the indicators for measuring oil import security were proposed and aggregated in this study. These indicators are categorized into four dimensions: energy availability, political status, economic status, and energy transportation. These dimensions and indicators have almost covered any possible risks and factors that may affect national oil import security, and so can be used for any country for analyzing its oil import security. Although some indicators are hard to qualify, for instance, the political relations between oil importer and exporter, they can still be rated by fact description.

Second, this study investigated the national, regional, and dimensional reliability of China's 37 oil-importing sources for the period 1995–2018. The results indicated that Kazakhstan, Russia, Canada, Vietnam, and Brunei were the top five reliable oil-importing sources for China during the past two decades, while Nigeria, the United Kingdom, Angola, Algeria, and Chad were the five least reliable importing sources. Interestingly, the regional reliability investigation also showed that the Commonwealth of Independent States, Asia-Pacific region, and American countries were the most reliable regions for China to import oil from, while Europe, Africa, and the Middle East are not as reliable as people think. Moreover, the dimensional reliability investigation demonstrated that the dimensions of economic status and political status did much better in ensuring China's oil import security than the other dimensions, energy availability and energy transportation, which were the main threats for China that need to be improved.

Finally, China's oil import security over the period 1995–2018 was assessed based on reliability results, and the results demonstrated that China was at a medium to low level of oil import security. Besides, a downward trend was observed in China's oil import security from 1995 to 2005. Although the security level gradually stabilized, China needs to take some measures to improve its import security. Furthermore, some policy implications, for instance, increasing internal energy supply and controlling the growth of energy consumption, diversifying oil-importing sources and transportation routes, and energy-focused diplomatic policies and activities, were provided in this study.

Based on this study, some areas of research could be further explored. One would be assigning different weights to these indicators, and even dimensions, since they may have different contributions to oil import security. For instance, some scholars believe that political factors may not contribute as much as economic factors do. Besides, the importance of dimensions and indicators may change over time, because a country may face different international situations at different years, as well as transportation risks. Thus, assigning weights to different indicators could test how they alter the oil import security.

Another would be the relationship between our Oil Import Security Index and the diversification index. China has been diversifying its oil-importing sources in the past two decades, since its Herfindahl–Hirschman Index has declined, which indicates that the concentration of oil-importing sources was reducing, while the results in this study showed decreasing oil import security. The game between diversification and reliability of importing sources could be an interesting topic.

Acknowledgments

This research was funded by the Philosophy and Social Science Planning Program in Henan Province, China (2020CJJ094), the Key R&D and Promotion Program (Soft Science Research) in Henan Province, China (202400410068), the Key Scientific Research Program of Colleges and Universities in Henan Province, China (19A790020), Research project of Social Sciences Association in Henan Province, China (SKL-2020-2418), and the Nanhu Scholars Program for Young Scholars of XYNU, China.

References

Ang, B. W., Choong, W. L. and Ng, T. S. 2015. Energy security: Definitions, dimensions and indexes. *Renew. Sustain. Energy Reviews* 42, 1077–1093.

Asia Pacific Energy Research Centre. 2007. A Quest for Energy Security in the 21st century. Institute of energy economics. Japan.

Augutis, J., Krikstolaitis, R., Martisauskas, L., Peciulytė, S. and Žutautaitė, I. 2017. Integrated energy security assessment. *Energy*, 138, 890–901.

Badea, A. C., Tarantola, S. and Bolado, R. 2011. Composite indicators for security of energy supply using ordered weighted averaging. *Reliability Engineering and System Safety*, 96, 651–662.

Blyth, W. and Lefevre-Marton, N. 2005. *Energy Security and Climate Change Policy Interactions: An Assessment Framework*. International Energy Agency, Paris, France.

Bompard, E. F., Carpignano, A., Erriquez, M., Grosso, D., Pession, M. and Profumo, F. 2017. National energy security assessment in a geopolitical perspective. *Energy*, 144–154.

British Petroleum. 2019a. BP Statistical Review of World Energy (68th Edition). Available at: https://www.bp.com/content/dam/bp/business-sites/en/global/corporate/pdfs/energy-economics/statistical-review/bp-stats-review-2019-full-report.pdf (accessed on July 24, 2019).

British Petroleum. 2019b. BP Energy Outlook: Insights from the Evolving transition scenario – China. Available at: https://www.bp.com/content/dam/bp/business-sites/en/global/corporate/pdfs/energy-economics/energy-outlook/bp-energy-outlook-2019-country-insight-china.pdf (accessed on 24 July 2019).

Chalvatzis, K. J. and Ioannidis, A. 2017a. Energy supply security in the EU: Benchmarking diversity and dependence of primary energy. *Applied Energy*, 207, 465–476.

Chalvatzis, K. J. and Ioannidis, A. 2017b. Energy supply security in Southern Europe and Ireland. *Energy Procedia*, 105, 2916–2922.

Chester, L. 2010. Conceptualising energy security and making explicit its polysemic nature. *Energy policy*, 38(2), 887–895.

China National Bureau of Statistics. 2018. *China Energy Statistical Yearbook 2018*. China Statistics Press. Beijing.

Chuang, M. C. and Ma, H. W. 2013. An assessment of Taiwan's energy policy using multi-dimensional energy security indicators. *Renewable and Sustainable Energy Reviews*, 17, 301–311.

Cohen, G., Joutz, F. and Loungani, P. 2011. Measuring energy security: Trends in the diversification of oil and natural gas supplies. *Energy Policy*, 39(9), 4860–4869.

Correljé, A. and van der Linde, C. 2006. Energy supply security and geopolitics: A European perspective. *Energy Policy*, 34, 532–543.

Costantini, V., Gracceva, F., Markandya, A. and Vicini, G. 2007. Security of energy supply: Comparing scenarios from a European perspective. *Energy Policy*, 35, 210–226.

Doukas, H., Flamos, A. and Psarras, J. 2011. Risks on the security of oil and gas supply. *Energy Sources Part B: Economics, Planning and Policy*, 6, 417–425.

Egenhofer, C., *et al.* 2004. Market-based options for security of energy supply. Working Papers from Fondazione Eni Enrico Mattei.

Garciagusano, D., Iribarren, D. and Garrain, D. 2017. Prospective analysis of energy security: A practical life-cycle approach focused on renewable power generation and oriented towards policy-makers. *Applied Energy*, 190, 891–901.

Geng, J. B. and Ji, Q. 2014. Multi-perspective analysis of China's energy supply security. *Energy*, 64, 541–550.

Greene, D. L. 2010. Measuring energy security: Can the United States achieve oil independence? *Energy Policy*, 38(4), 1614–1621.

Gupta, E. 2008. Oil vulnerability index of oil-importing countries. *Energy Policy*, 36, 1195–1211.

Ikenberry, G. J. 1986. The irony of state strength: Comparative responses to the oil shocks in the 1970s. *International Organization*, 40, 105.

International Energy Agency. Key World Energy Statistics. 2018. Available at: https://www.connaissancedesenergies.org/sites/default/files/pdf-actualites/key_world_2018.pdf.

Jaaskelainen, J., Lager, J. and Syri, S. 2019. Development of energy security in Finland and in the Baltic States since 1991. *International Conference on the European Energy Market.*

Jansen, J. C., Van Arkel, W. G. and Boots, M. G. 2004. *Designing Indicators of Long-term Energy Supply Security.* Energy research Centre of the Netherlands.

Jewell. J., Cherp, A. and Riahi, K. 2014. Energy security under de-carbonization scenarios: An assessment framework and evaluation under different technology and policy choices. *Energy Policy*, 65, 743–760.

Ji, Q. and Fan, Y. 2016. Evaluating the impact of oil exports from GCC countries on China's oil security. *Energy Relations and Policy Making in Asia.* Springer, Singapore, pp. 183–202.

Ji, Q., Zhang, H. and Zhang, D. 2019. The impact of OPEC on East Asian oil import security: A multidimensional analysis. *Energy Policy*, 126, 99–107.

Kamsamrong, J. and Sorapipatana, C. 2014. An assessment of energy security in Thailand's power generation. *Sustainable Energy Technologies and Assessment*, 7, 45–54.

Kisel, E., Hamburg, A., Harm, M., Leppiman, A. and Ots, M. 2016. Concept for energy security matrix. *Energy Policy*, 95, 1–9.

Knox-Hayes, J., Brown, M. A. Sovacool, B. K. and Wang, Y. 2013. Understanding attitudes toward energy security: Results of a cross-national survey. *Global Environmental Change*, 23(3), 609–622.

Kokwaro, J. O. 1993. Current status of utilization and conservation of medicinal plants in Africa South of the Sahara. *Acta Horticulturae*, (332), 121–130.

Krane, J. and Medlock K. B. 2018. Geopolitical dimensions of US oil security. *Energy Policy*, 558–565.

Kruyt, B., van Vuuren, D. P., De Vries, H. J. M. and Groenenberg, H. 2009. Indicators for energy security. *Energy Policy*, 37(6), 2166–2181.

Le Coq, C. and Paltseva, E. 2009. Measuring the security of external energy supply in the European Union. *Energy Policy*, 37, 4474–4481.

Lefèvre, N. 2010. Measuring the energy security implications of fossil fuel resource concentration. *Energy policy*, 38(4), 1635–1644.

Lesbirel, S. H. 2004. Diversification and energy security risks: The Japanese case. *Japanese Journal of Political Science*, 5, 1–22.

Li, P., Zhang, J., Xu, J. and Wang, P. 2018. A dynamic approach to measuring China's Provincial energy supply security along "the Belt and Road". *Mathematical Problems in Engineering*, 3605024.

Lu, H., Xu, F., Liu, H., Wang, J., Campbell, D. E. and Ren, H. 2019. Emergy-based analysis of the energy security of China. *Energy*, 181, 123–135.

Martisauskas, L., Augutis, J. and Krikstolaitis, R. 2018. Methodology for energy security assessment considering energy system resilience to disruptions. *Energy Strategy Reviews*, 22, 106–118.

Matsumoto, K. and Shiraki, H. 2018. Energy security performance in Japan under different socioeconomic and energy conditions. *Renewable and Sustainable Energy Reviews*, 90, 391–401.

Narula, K. and Reddy, B. S. 2016. A SES (sustainable energy security) index for developing countries. *Energy*, 94, 326–343.

Narula, K., Reddy, B. S., Pachauri, S. and Dev, S. M. 2017. Sustainable energy security for India: An assessment of the energy supply sub-system. *Energy Policy*, 103, 127–144.

Nawaz, S. M. and Alvi, S. 2018. Energy security for socio-economic and environmental sustainability in Pakistan. *Heliyon*, 4(10), 1–21.

Organization of the Petroleum Exporting Countries. 2019. 2019 OPEC Annual Statistical Bulletin (54th edition). Available at: https://nangs.org/analytics/download/3910_e7f6b1d9f4e4b07605efc424d3d9425b.

Radovanović, M., Filipović, S. and Pavlović, D. 2017. Energy security measurement – A sustainable approach. *Renewable and Sustainable Energy Reviews*, 68, 1022–2032.

Radovanovic, M., Filipovic, S. and Golusin, V. 2018. Geo-economic approach to energy security measurement – Principal component analysis. *Renewable and Sustainable Energy Reviews*, 82(2), 1691–1700.

Ruble, I. 2017. European Union energy supply security: The benefits of natural gas imports from the Eastern Mediterranean. *Energy Policy*, 105, 341–353.

Saldarriagac, C. A. and Salazar, H. 2016. Security of the Colombian energy supply: The need for liquefied natural gas regasification terminals for power and natural gas sectors. *Energy*, 100, 349–362.

Seebregts, A. J., De Jong, J. J. and Maters, J. M. 2006. *EU Standards for Energy Security of Supply*. Energy Research Center of the Netherlands.

Selvakkumaran, S. and Limmeechokchai, B. 2013. Energy security and co-benefits of energy efficiency improvement in three Asian countries. *Renewable and Sustainable Energy Reviews*, 20, 491–503.

Sovacool, B. K. 2013. An international assessment of energy security performance. *Ecological Economies*, 88, 148–158.

Sovacool, B. K. and Brown, M. A. 2010. Competing dimensions of energy security: An international perspective. *Annual Review of Environment and Resources*, 35, 77–108.

Sovacool, B. K. and Mukherjee, I. 2011. Conceptualizing and measuring energy security: A synthesized approach. *Energy*, 36(8), 5343–5355.

Sovacool, B. K., Mukherjee, I., Drupady, I. M. and D'Agostino, A. L. 2011. Evaluating energy security performance from 1990 to 2010 for eighteen countries. *Energy*, 36(10), 5846–5853.

Sovacool, B. K., *et al.* 2012. Exploring propositions about perceptions of energy security: An international survey. *Environmental Science & Policy*, 16, 44–64.

Stern, J. 2004. UK gas security: Time to get serious. *Energy Policy*, 32, 1967–1979.

Svensson, L. E. 1997. Inflation forecast targeting: Implementing and monitoring inflation targets. *European Economic Review*, 41(6), 1111–1146.

Toft, P., Duero, A. and Bieliauskas, A. 2010. Terrorist targeting and energy security. *Energy Policy*, 38, 4411–4421.

Tongsopit, S., Kittner, N., Chang, Y., Aksornkij, A. and Wangjiraniran, W. 2016. Energy security in ASEAN: A quantitative approach for sustainable energy policy. *Energy Policy*, 90, 60–72.

Wabiri, N. and Amusa, H. 2010. Quantifying South Africa's crude oil import risk: A multi-criteria portfolio model. *Economic Model*, 27, 445–453.

Winzer, C. 2012. Conceptualizing energy security. *Energy Policy*, 46, 36–48.

Wu, G., Liu, L. C., Han, Z. Y. and Wei, Y. M. 2012. Climate protection and China's energy security: Win-win or tradeoff. *Applied Energy*, 97, 157–163.

Wu, G., Wei, Y. M., Fan, Y. and Liu, L. C. 2007. An empirical analysis of the risk of crude oil imports in China using improved portfolio approach. *Energy Policy*, 35, 4190–4199.

Wu, G., Wei, Y. M. and Fan, Y. 2008. An empirical analysis for the import risk of China's petroleum products based on the improved portfolio approach. In *Sustainable Energy Technologies, 2008. ICSET 2008.* IEEE International Conference on. IEEE, 57–62.

Wu, G., Liu, L. C. and Wei, Y. M. 2009. Comparison of China's oil import risk: Results based on portfolio theory and a diversification index approach. *Energy Policy*, 37, 3557–3565.

Vivoda, V. 2009. Diversification of oil import sources and energy security: A key strategy or an elusive objective? *Energy Policy*, 37, 4615–4623.

Vivoda, V. 2010. Evaluating energy security in the Asia-Pacific region: A novel methodological approach. *Energy Policy*, 38(9), 5258–5263.

Voigt, S., De Cian E., Schymura, M. and Verdolini, E. 2014. Energy intensity developments in 40 major economies: Structural change or technology improvement? *Energy Economics*, 41, 47–62.

Von Hippel, D., Suzuki, T., Williams, J. H., Savage, T. and Hayes, P. 2011. Energy security and sustainability in North East Asia. *Energy Policy*, 39(11), 6719–6730.

Umbach, F. 2010. Global energy security and the implications for the EU. *Energy Policy*, 38(3), 1229–1240.

Yao, L. and Chang, Y. 2014. Energy security in China: A quantitative analysis and policy implications. *Energy Policy*, 67, 595–604.

Zeng, S., Streimikiene, D. and Baležentis, T. 2017. Review of and comparative assessment of energy security in Baltic States. *Renewable and Sustainable Energy Reviews*, 76, 185–192.

Zhang, H. Y., Ji, Q. and Fan, Y. 2013. An evaluation framework for oil import security based on the supply chain with a case study focused on China. *Energy Economics*, 38, 87–95.

Zhang, L., Yu, J., Sovacool, B. K. and Ren, J. 2017. Measuring energy security performance within China: Toward an inter-provincial prospective. *Energy*, 125, 825–836.

https://doi.org/10.1142/9781786349224_0008

Chapter 8

China's Energy-Supply Security in the Multi-Energy Transition Period from Fossil Fuels to Renewable Energy

Volkan Ş. Ediger*,‡, John V. Bowlus*,§, and Ahmet Faruk Dursun†,¶

*Center for Energy and Sustainable Development (CESD), Kadir Has University, Cibali 34083 İstanbul, Turkey

†Energy and Sustainable Development Graduate Program, Kadir Has University, Cibali 34083 İstanbul, Turkey

‡volkanediger@gmail.com

§johnbowlus@gmail.com

¶ahmetfdursun@gmail.com

Abstract

The rise of China as an economic superpower after the 2008 global financial crisis has attracted increasing worldwide attention. Securing access to ample and affordable energy supplies — energy-supply security — has underpinned its rise and will continue to contribute to its economic prosperity. This chapter examines China's energy-security challenge with respect to its policies. The global energy system is currently undergoing a multi-energy transition away from fossil fuels: the powers will take different paths, creating competition between one another and thus between energy sources. The development of China's energy-security policies and challenges as well as climate change, both at home and abroad, will therefore shape this competition and the global energy transition in the coming decades.

Keywords: Energy-supply security; China; Multi-energy transition; Fossil fuels; Renewable energy.

1. Introduction

China is the newest member of the "economic superpower club" — even if it is not yet as powerful as the United States and the European Union (EU) — due to its incredible growth and deep integration into the global economy since 2008 (Bergsten, 2008). China's hard economic and military power is notable, but so is its soft power, as it now plays a significantly important role in world peace and global economic growth. It also provides great economic contributions and has cultural influences in Europe, Africa, and South America.

Energy has underpinned China's rise as a globally influential country. It overtook the EU in 2006 and the USA in 2008 to become the world's largest energy consumer (Figure 1). In 2019, it consumed 3.273 billion tons-of-oil equivalent (BToe) of total primary energy (Lee and Zhang, 2012; Song *et al.*, 2019; BP, 2019). Since China is rapidly industrializing and urbanizing, its consumption continues to rise; its per-capita consumption, however, is still considerably lower than that of developed countries (Bai *et al.*, 2014; Song *et al.*, 2019).

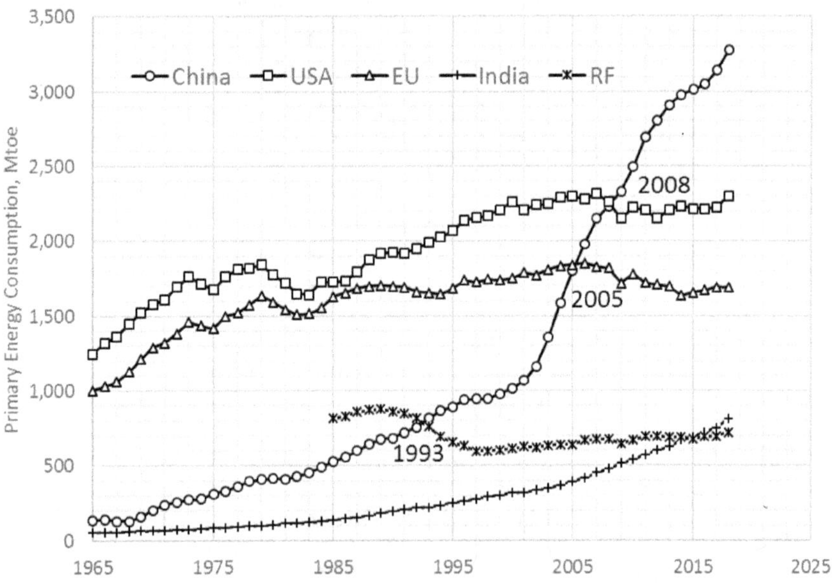

Figure 1: Primary energy consumption of China, USA, EU, India, and Russia, 1965–2018.

Source: BP (2019).

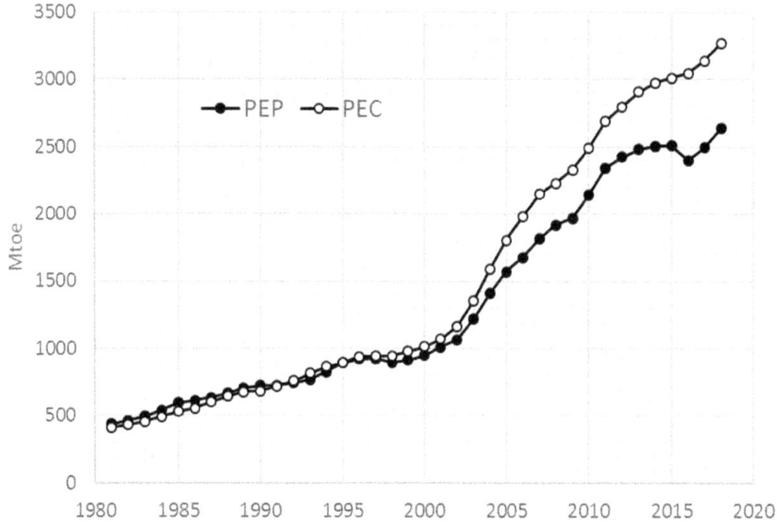

Figure 2: Primary energy production (PEP) and consumption (PEC) of China, 1980–2018.
Source: BP (2019).

China's domestic energy production, however, can no longer meet its consumption needs (Figure 2). The share of domestic production in consumption has declined from 100% in 1995 to 80% in 2018, and the gap is now met by imports, which reached 634.4 MToe in 2018. China's fossil fuel reserves are also below the world average (Zhao *et al.*, 2013; Liu, 2019). The exploitation duration ratios (reserve-to-production ratios) of coal, oil, and natural gas resources are estimated at 38 years, 18.7 years, and 37.6 years, respectively (BP, 2019). China's lack of sufficient domestic energy supplies to sustain its energy-based growth has been the most important driver of its foreign and energy policies (Cáceres and Ear, 2012).

China has also become the largest greenhouse gas (GHG) emitter, overtaking Russia in 1989, the EU in 2003, and the USA in 2005 (Figure 3). In 2019, its CO_2 emissions reached approximately 9.428 billion tons (BTon). Since 2005, it has faced more pressing challenges in climate change and energy security than any other country (Duan and Wang, 2018). Although per-capita emissions are still lower than those in developed countries, they grew 8.5% on average from 2001 to 2013.

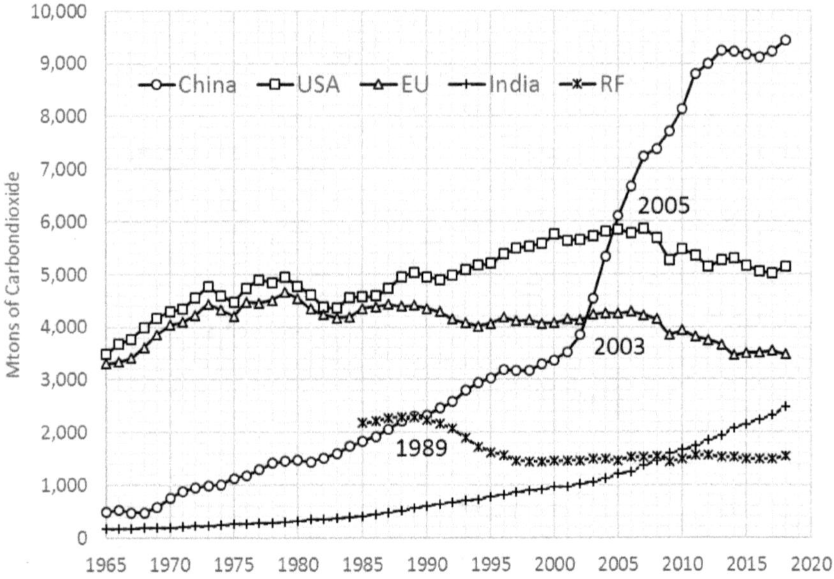

Figure 3: CO_2 emissions of China, USA, EU, India, and Russia, 1965–2018. *Source*: BP (2019).

Energy-supply security and climate change are, thus, the two largest problems facing China's energy system. In order to lower GHGs emissions, the Chinese government has taken various measures to vigorously develop renewable energy (Zhang *et al.*, 2019). It has also persistently sought to secure its foreign gas and oil supplies through strategic bilateral relations with key energy producers and resource-rich countries (Cáceres and Ear, 2012). In addition, China's import of energy resources is changing global geopolitics (Broedsgaard and Heurlin, 2002; Marketos, 2010; Cáceres and Ear, 2012). Its energy plans and strategies will therefore increase competition in world energy markets (Song *et al.*, 2019).

Meanwhile, domestic and international conditions have changed drastically in recent years and are reshaping China's energy policy (Yatsui, 2017). The Chinese economy has slowed and its structure has shifted from an industry focus to services, causing a substantial decrease in the rate of primary energy consumption, from 16.5% in 2003, 17.0% in 2004, and 13.6% in 2005 to 1.2% in 2016, 3.0% in 2017, and 4.3% in 2018 (Figure 2). Moreover, air pollution caused by fine particulate matter has become a serious domestic problem, and the government is attempting to curb coal production and expand clean energy to combat it. At the same time, China has benefited from the decline in oil prices, from \$111.26 per barrel in 2011 to \$45.76 in 2016, \$55.52 in 2017, and \$71.31 in 2018.

In this chapter, we examine China's energy-supply security problem with respect to its policies. The second section chronologically summarizes China's past energy policies. The third section argues that the major changes in the global energy system should be viewed through the concept of a multi-energy transition concept. The fourth section summarizes the findings and places them in the context of current energy transition and geopolitical dynamics.

2. The Shifting Global Energy Scene

Since the Industrial Revolution, humans have been substituting fossil fuel energy sources (Ediger, 2011a, 2011b, 2019a, 2019b). Coal, the dominant energy source from 1881 to 1965, was first replaced by oil and then natural gas (Figure 4). Oil peaked as the dominant energy source in 1973 before it began declining after the 1970s oil crises (Ediger and Berk, 2018). In 1973, the shares of oil, coal, and natural gas were 47.4%, 25.5%, and 16.6%, respectively. Since then, oil has declined to 32.5%, whereas coal increased to 26.4% and gas to 23.1%. Assuming that past trends would continue, energy experts had expected that while oil would continue to decline, gas would increase its share and cut the coal curve to become the second most used energy source. The gas and coal curves converged twice, first around 1977 and then in 1999–2000, but gas never caught up with coal, as its rise slowed.

China's energy-security policies, especially its increased domestic production of coal and renewables, were the main reasons for this trend reversal. China has 138.819 BTons of coal reserves, ranking fourth after the USA, Russia, and Australia, with a global share of 13.2%. It ranks first both in coal production and consumption. Domestic coal production increased first from 310.8 MToe in 1981 to 800.3 MToe in 2002, with an average annual growth rate of 4.7%, and then from 945.3 MToe in 2003 to 1894.6 MToe in 2013 with an average annual growth rate of 8.3% (Figure 5). Notably, production

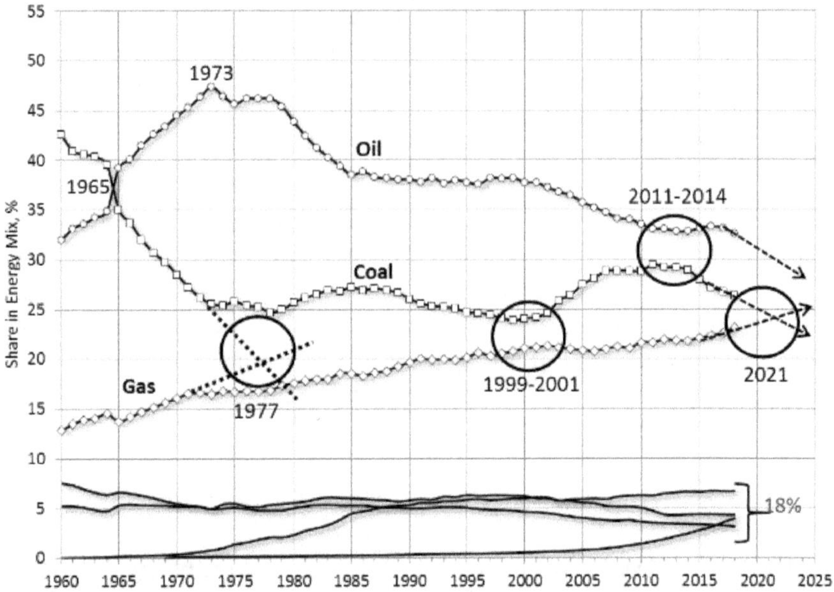

Figure 4: Trend reversal in world energy mix, 1960–2018.
Source: BP (2019).

has declined from 1864.2 MToe in 2014 to 1828.8 MToe in 2018, with an average annual growth rate of −0.6%. During the first period, production generally met demand, but in the second and third periods, consumption outpaced production. The difference between production and consumption reached 197.7 MToe in 2016 and 143.8 MToe in 2017. In 2018, China was responsible for 46.7% of world coal production and 50.5% of world coal consumption.

Renewable energy production (excluding hydro) started slowly in the 1990s, but increased rapidly after 2005. China overtook India and Japan in 2008, Germany in 2011, and the USA in 2016 to become the world's largest renewable energy producer. From 2005 to 2018, its average annual growth rate of 45.3% was, by far, the highest in the world (Figure 6). In 2018, its total renewable energy production was 634.2 TWh (143.5 MToe), accounting for a 25.6% share of the global total, followed by the USA (18.5%) and Germany (8.4%). Of this amount 57.7% was wind, 28.0% solar, and 14.3% others. China was the leader in wind energy, with 366.0 TWh (82.8 MToe) and a

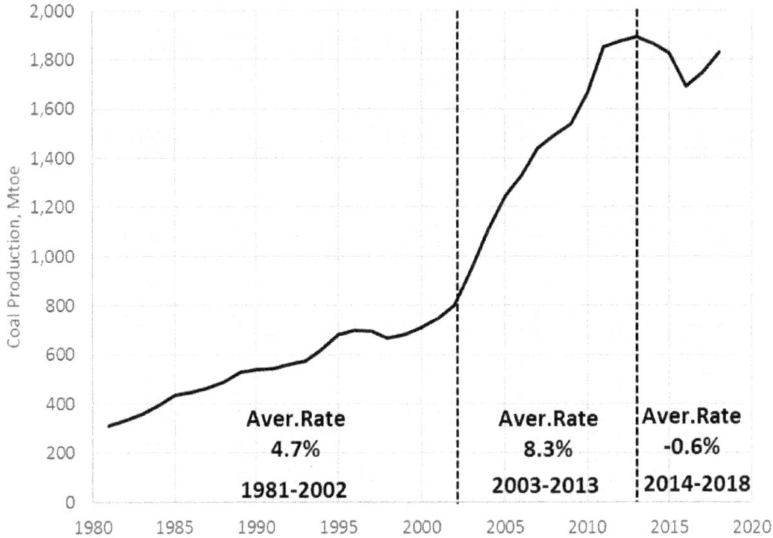

Figure 5: Coal production in China, 1981–2018.
Source: BP (2019).

28.8% share of the global total, and solar power, with 177.7 TWh (40.2 MToe) and a 30.4% share of the global total.

China's energy-security strategy not only reversed the trend of substituting fossil fuel sources but also affected the energy geopolitics of the powers (Ediger 2019a, 2019b). Power has grown steadily more diffuse, as world order became more multipolar, where China appears to be one of four centers of relative geopolitical autonomy (Bergsten, 2008; Haass, 2008; Wallerstein, 2010).

However it is defined, this new world order causes a divergence of fossil fuel consumption paths among the powers. To explain this dynamic, Ediger (2019a) suggested the concept of "multi-energy transition," which means that different countries will follow different paths for a transition from fossil fuels to renewables, resulting in different energy regimes. In our multipolar world order, the four powers are, in other words, expected to follow four different energy paths. China will continue to rely on coal while attempting to mitigate its negative environmental effects through a renewable energy revolution. Russia will continue to base its energy system on gas and produce and consume conventional oil and gas. The USA will continue to diversify its energy mix by using science and technology for

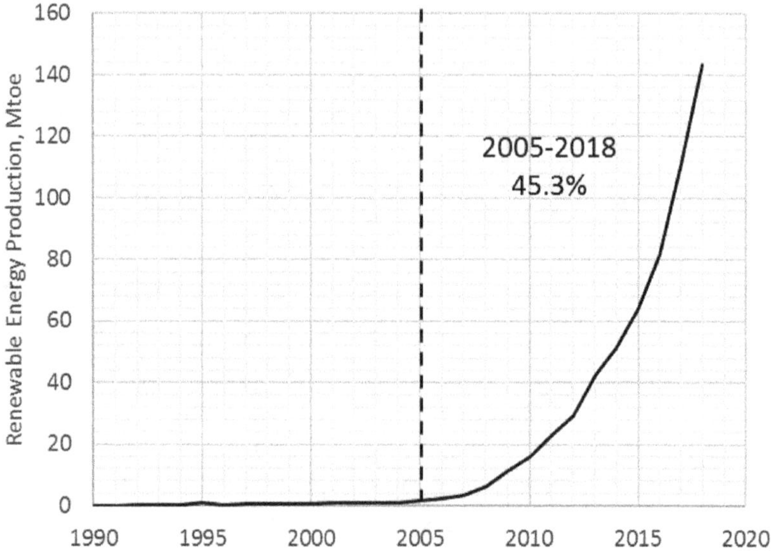

Figure 6: Renewable energy production in China, 1981–2018.
Source: BP (2019).

the development of its fossil fuel resources, especially unconventionals, most notably its shale oil and gas, and renewable energy sources. The EU's high ratio of fossil fuel import dependency and its current energy transition policies mean that it will continue to improve energy efficiency and increase domestic renewable energy usage.

3. China's Energy Policies

Ensuring adequate energy supplies to sustain economic growth has been a primary concern of the Chinese government since 1949 (Andrews-Speed, 2014). The First Five-Year Plan (1953–1957) aimed at developing strategies for the social and economic development of China was shaped. In this plan, China adopted the Soviet model, based on state ownership and centralized planning. Coal dominated this process, as primary energy consumption rose from 24 million tonnes-of-coal-equivalent (MTCE) to 500 MTCE from 1949 to 1976. China also made significant advances in energy exploration and extraction, becoming self-sufficient. During the second half of the 1970s and throughout the 1980s, China's energy policies became increasingly diversified and complicated, especially as the country took tentative steps to engage with the world economy (Meidan, 2016).

In the period of rapid economic growth, opening up to the world, reform, and modernization, China tried to ensure stable and sustained economic growth during the Eighth Five-Year Plan between 1991 and 1995 (UNDP China, 2012). In 2004, the National Development Research Center (NDRC) published the "China National Energy Strategy and Policy 2020 (NESP)" (Sinton *et al.*, 2005). This report included recommendations to China's government on energy security, economic growth, equity, and well-being, with specific changes in energy investment, supply, and efficiency. Subtitle 6 of the report, "Energy, Environment and Its Public Health Impact," outlined the energy-related environmental challenges that China would face in the coming two decades. These were described as environmental constraints and included environmental capacity, environmental management constraints, and global climate change (Jinnan *et al.*, 2004, p. 6). Chapter 7 of the report, "Renewable Energy Strategy and Policy," provided targets for 2020 for renewable energy development: an installed capacity of 90 gigawatts (GW)-100 GW and consumption of 400–500 MTCE. According to this chapter, there were four reasons to encourage renewable energy development in China: (1) the inevitability of executing sustainable energy strategies, (2) the need to speed up the development of rural economies and increase the income of farmers, (3) the creation of new job opportunities and promotion of economic growth, and (4) environmental protection and greenhouse gas abatement (pp. 8–12). The main barriers for the development of renewable energy in China were also enumerated: cost, market share, and policy (pp. 12–14). The chapter suggested a four-phase strategy for renewable energy development in China: (1) creating a nucleus of renewable energy technologies by 2010, (2) commercializing large numbers of renewable energy technologies by 2020, (3) realizing renewable energy commercialization in an all-round way and substituting fossil fuels at a large scale, and (4) bringing renewable energy consumption to 50% by 2100 (pp. 15–16).

Annex 1 of Subtitle 7 of the report, entitled "Global Climate Change: Challenges, Opportunities, and Strategy Faced by China," explained the central challenges relating to global climate change: (1) developed countries would continue to urge China to limit and control its GHG emissions, (2) climate change would undermine China's current development and consumption model, and (3) global climate change would present great challenges to China's coal-dominated energy mix (Huaqing *et al.*, 2004; pp. 7–8). On the other hand, climate change also offered opportunities for China's energy development. It would encourage China to carry out its sustainable development strategy and to obtain more advanced energy conservation technologies as well as new energy technologies, which would facilitate energy mix adjustment. The adoption of GHG emissions mitigation policies and measures, moreover, would help reduce air pollution (pp. 8–9).

During the 11th Five-Year Plan (2006–2010), the country transitioned from a communist economy to a socialist market economy, and the term "plan" was replaced by "guideline" (Andrews-Speed, 2014). In this guideline, the main targets for 2010 were to increase the rate of GDP growth to 7.5% and per capita GDP growth to 6.6% annually and to decrease the rate of energy intensity to 20%. In 2007, China became the first developing country to publish a national strategy on global warming, entitled "The First National Action Plan on Climate Change," which targeted to reduce annual GHG emissions by 1.5 BTons of carbon dioxide equivalent by 2010. It also sought to increase the share of electricity generation from renewable energy sources and nuclear power, increase the efficiency of coal-fired power stations, use cogeneration, and develop coal-bed and coal-mine methane.

Since the start of the 11th Five-Year Plan, China's policymakers have increasingly emphasized control of the country's rising energy demand and emissions and proposed targets for energy intensity and renewable energy, including in the 12th Five-Year Plan (2011–2015) (Qi *et al.*, 2019). In 2012, a report entitled "12th Five-Year Plan on Greenhouse Emission Control" set goals to reduce carbon intensity by 17% and to raise energy-consumption intensity by 16% by 2015. China also planned to meet 11.4% of its primary energy demand from non-fossil sources by 2015. Furthermore, the plan targeted the construction of a number of low-carbon development zones and low-carbon residential communities. In November 2014, President Xi Jinping announced that China would reduce carbon dioxide emissions and increase the use of non-fossil fuels as a percentage of primary energy consumption by 20% in 2030 (Sahu, 2018). China set national energy-intensity reduction targets of 20% and 16% in the 11th and 12th Five-Year Plans, respectively (Li *et al.*, 2016). In addition, the central government directed provincial governments to meet specific targets for the reduction in energy intensity (Zhang and Wu, 2018).

China is currently implementing its 13th Five-Year Plan (2016–2020), which was one of the most expected official documents in the world at the time, since it would significantly affect the growth of GHG emissions of the world's largest emitter (Tianjie, 2016). The plan aimed to switch from coal to natural gas and from fossil fuels to non-fossil fuels by championing policies such as "everyone is an entrepreneur," "creativity of the masses," and "made in China 2025" (Yatsui, 2017). The plan targeted to reduce energy consumption and carbon emissions per unit of GDP by 15% and 18%, respectively, as well as coal dependence more broadly. It also promoted clean energy developments, notably through a commitment to increasing nuclear energy capacity to 58 GW by 2020, with an additional 30 GW under construction. This would mean commissioning between six and eight nuclear reactors every year (Sahu, 2018). In December 2016, China also issued the "Energy Production and Consumption Reform Strategy (2016–2030)," which aimed to limit total energy consumption and energy intensity and revise the country's energy mix (NDRC, 2016). For example, energy consumption in 2020 and 2030 should not exceed 5 BTCE and 6 BTCE, respectively, while the share of non-fossil energy in primary energy consumption should increase to 20% by 2030 (Wang and Zhang, 2017; Duan *et al.*, 2018).

Recently, Song *et al.* (2019) revealed that the change in China's energy security index (CESI) has resembled an "N" curve. The country's best energy-security performance came in 2000; its worst was in 2010. The main strengths of China's energy security are its installed capacity to generate renewable energy and thermal power; its main weaknesses are indigenous energy availability and energy dependence.

4. Transition Towards Clean, Domestic Energy

To a large extent, China's energy-supply security will hinge on how rapidly it transitions to renewable energies, which do not depend on imports and access to the seas. The more renewable energy that China produces domestically, and even exports, the less it will pay for fossil fuel imports, increase export revenues, and decrease domestic pollution. China has long understood these dynamics, and President Xi Jinping underscored them at the 19th National Congress of the Communist Party in October 2017: "We will promote a revolution in energy production and consumption, and build an energy sector that is clean, low-carbon, safe, and efficient ... What we are doing today to build an ecological civilization will benefit generations to come. We should have a strong commitment to socialist ecological civilization and work to develop a new model of modernization with humans developing in harmony with nature. We must do our generation's share to protect the environment" 2017 (CNREC, 2018).

According to the China Renewable Energy Outlook 2018 (CNREC, 2018, p. 32): "The single most important step now is to reduce coal consumption in China ... The decisions and targets for coal reduction must be enforced strictly to avoid stranded investments and reduce vested interests in a continuation of high coal consumption."

China's coal-dominated energy consumption structure has resulted in many serious environmental problems (Zhen *et al.*, 2016). China aims, through its own development and joint efforts, to achieve clean and low-carbon energy goals that will optimize industrial structure, limit total energy consumption, and improve its energy consumption structure. On the other hand, according to Zhen *et al.* (2017, p. 305), in view of China's resource endowments and consumption levels, the clean-and-low-carbon utilization of coal is a realistic choice; to develop non-fossil energy sources vigorously is a strategic choice; as a dominant source of transportation fuel, oil will remain critical in the short and medium term, while gas will play an important role as a bridge to achieving clean and low-carbon energy goals.

Wang *et al.* (2014, p. 542) showed that China's ultimate recoverable coal reserves equaled 223.6×10^9 MT and that its production will peak between 2025 and 2030 at approximately 3.9×10^9 MT. According to them, the extent to which China can import coal in the future is uncertain. With rising coal demand, this combination is likely to complicate China's future economic development.

Before the 1990s, the main purpose of the development and utilization of renewable energy in China was to supplement the shortage of agricultural fuels. The relevant guidelines at that time were, thus, rural energy construction policies. From the 1990s to 2005, specialized policies and laws for renewable energy were gradually released that approached the issue of air pollution in addition to rural energy. The most important legal paper was the Renewable Energy Law (REL), which came into being in 2005 and was amended in 2009 (Schuman and Lin, 2012). Thus far, China has formed a comprehensive renewable energy legal system essentially based on the REL and supplemented by other related laws and policies (Liu, 2019). Currently, nearly 20% of China's electricity comes from renewables. Under the business-as-usual scenario, this is expected to rise to 30% by 2030 and, under the RE Map 2030 options, it approaches 40% (Sahu, 2018).

Wind and solar power-installed capacities have grown faster than that seen in any country in the world (Shen, 2017). The 11th Five-Year Plan stimulated high growth in wind energy, from 1.3 GW in 2005 to 44.7 GW in 2010, which was eight times higher than the original target of 5 GW. The National Energy Administration (NEA) revealed that China's renewable energy capacity and consumption have increased significantly since the 12th Five-Year Plan (Liu, 2019). China set the record for wind investment in 2015 with USD 102.9 billion, which represented a produced capacity growth of 17% and 36% of global investment that year (Sahu, 2018). Most of China's coastal belts have excellent wind energy resources, and the government has been introducing attractive subsidies for local and foreign manufacturers to enter the industry. Both pricing and non-pricing policies have played key roles for the developments of wind energy capacities (Sahu, 2018).

The legal framework of renewable energy in China has greatly contributed to past achievements, but limitations may impede further development. It is still, moreover, insufficient to integrate renewable energy into the national energy system (Liu, 2019). Binz *et al.* (2017, p. 418) summed up the challenges as follows: "We find that traditional top-down catching-up policies played a decisive role in the development of China's wind industry, but were of limited importance in the early solar PV industry, and resulted only in a limited period of rapid growth in the biomass power plant industry. The relative progress achieved in these three industries is not related to top-down policy guidance alone, but also to private sector initiative, international interdependencies, and flexibility in adapting policy mixes to each industry's technological characteristics. These results suggest that policy makers in newly industrializing countries (NICs) should avoid drafting generic sector plans, but should tailor plans to individual industries, and respond to changing policy support needs as technological capacities and global competitiveness develop."

5. Conclusion

China is the center of global supply chains and the world's largest importer of oil, but the uncertainties of the novel coronavirus have raised further questions about the future of China's energy-supply security and necessitate a reassessment of the themes and developments outlined in this chapter. The habits and practices undertaken by China's energy suppliers and consumers of its renewable energy technologies, as well as those of its energy suppliers, will shift, some more systematically than others. It is too early to predict what forms these shifts will take, but the current international environment and the international relationships could challenge China's energy-supply security.

Amid the global outbreak of COVID-19, Russia and Saudi Arabia launched an oil-price war that added uncertainty for China's oil-supply security. Lower prices will help China recover from COVID-19 and reduce the cost of oil and gas imports, but the price war will also create greater price volatility. China might well revert to more fossil fuel-friendly policies in light of lower prices, but it will prolong its own fight against environmental degradation, most notably pollution, and accelerate global climate change, if it chooses to do so. The energy-security decisions that China faces will involve trade-offs, as China is still a large developing country with around 1.4 billion people. Energy security will be one of the most critical factors for lifting the people in China's remote areas out of poverty. Regardless of how these developments play out, China's energy-supply security will remain a central story of the 2020s and beyond.

References

Andrews-Speed, P. 2014. China's energy policymaking processes and their consequences, the National Bureau of Asian Research (NBR), Special Report No. 47.

Bai, X., Shi, P. and Liu, Y. 2014. Society: Realizing China's Urban Dream, Nature, 509(7499), pp. 158–160.

Bergsten, C. F. 2008. A partnership of equals: How Washington should respond to china's economic challenge. *Foreign Affairs*, 87(4), 57–69.

Binz, C., Gosens, J., Hansen, T. and Hansen, U. E. 2017. Toward technology-sensitive catching-up policies: Insights from renewable energy in China. *World Development*, 96, 418–437.

BP 2019. Statistical review of world energy. https://www.bp.com/en/global/corporate/energy-economics/statistical-review-of-world-energy.html. [Accessed 19 Jan. 2020].

Broedsgaard, K. E. and Heurlin, B. 2002. China's place in global geopolitics: International, regional and domestic challenges, Routledge, London.

Cáceres, S. B. and Ear, S. 2012. The geopolitics of china's global resources quest. *Geopolitics*, 17(1), 47–79.

CNREC (China National Renewable Energy Centre). 2018. China renewable energy outlook 2018, *Energy Research Institute of Academy of Macroeconomic Research/NDRC China National Renewable Energy Centre.* http://boostre.cnrec.org.cn/wp-content/uploads/2018/12/CNREC_China-Renewable-Energy-Outlook-2018_Executive-Summary_ENG.pdf. [Accessed 10 Jan. 2020].

Duan, H. and Wang, S. 2018. Potential impacts of china's climate policies on energy security. *Environmental Impact Assessment Review*, 71, 94–101.

Duan, H., Mo, J., Fan, Y. and Wang, S. 2018. Achieving china's energy and climate policy targets in 2030 Under Multiple Uncertainties. *Energy Economics*, 70, 46–60.

Ediger, V. Ş. 2011a. New world order in energy and Turkey, Akademi Forumu No. 67, TÜBA-Turkish Academy of Sciences, Ankara, 62.

Ediger, V. Ş. 2011b. Energy transition periods: Lessons Learnt from the Past, in The Oil Era: Emerging Challenges, ECSSR (The Emirates Center for Strategic Studies and Research) Publications, Abu Dhabi, pp. 175–202.

Ediger, V. Ş. 2019a. An integrated review and analysis of multi-energy transition from fossil fuels to renewables. *Energy Procedia*, 156, 2–6.

Ediger, V. Ş. 2019b. Geopolitical considerations of the global energy transition to renewable energies, Keynote Speaker, Global Transitions 2019, 14–16 October 2019, Beijing.

Ediger, V. Ş. and Berk, İ. 2018. Geostrategic challenges in the oil and gas sectors, in Dorsman, A., Ediger, V.Ş., and Karan, M.B. (eds), *Energy Economics, Finance, and Geostrategy*, Springer International Publishing, Cham, 173–197.

EIA (US Energy Information Administration). 2012. Annual Energy Outlook 2012 with Projections to 2035. US EIA, Washington, USA. https://www.eia.gov/outlooks/aeo/pdf/0383(2012).pdf. [Accessed 25 Sep. 2019].

Haass, R. N. 2008. The age of nonpolarity: What will follow U.S. dominance. *Foreign Affairs*, 87(3), 44–56.

Huaqing, X., Yuan, G., Shuang, Z., Shiyuan, Q. and Shengmin, Y. 2004. China national energy strategy and Policy 2020, Subtitle 7: Global Climate Change: Challenges, Opportunities, and Strategy Faced by

China. http://www.efchina.org/Attachments/Report/reports-efchina-20050608-en/7_Climate_change.pdf [Accessed 27 Jul. 2019].

Jinnan, W., Dong, C., Zhizhong, Z., Hanli, C., Shuting, G., Yuantang, L. and Chazhong, G. 2004. China national energy strategy and policy 2020 Subtitle 6: Energy, Environment and Its Public Health Impact. http://kigeit.org.pl/FTP/PRCIP/Literatura/050_China_Policy_2020_Energy_Environment_and_Its_Public_Health_Impact%20.pdf [Accessed 24 Oct. 2019].

Lee, M. and Zhang, N. 2012. Technical efficiency, shadow price of carbon dioxide emissions, and substitutability for energy in the chinese manufacturing industries. *Energy Economics*, 34(5), 1492–1497.

Li, H., Zhao, X., Yu, Y., Wu, T. and Qi, Y. 2016. China's numerical management system for reducing national energy intensity. *Energy Policy*, 94, 64–76.

Liu, J. 2019. China's renewable energy law and policy: A critical review. *Renewable and Sustainable Energy Reviews*, 99, 212–219.

Marketos, T. N. 2010. China's energy geopolitics: The shanghai cooperation organization and central Asia, Routledge, London and New York.

Meidan, M. 2016. The structure of china's oil industry: Past trends and future prospects, University of Oxford, Oxford Institute for Energy Studies.

NDRC (National Development and Reform Commission). 2016. Energy production and consumption reform strategy (2016–2030), http://www.ndrc.gov.cn/zcfb/zcfbtz/201704/t20170425_845284.html. [Accessed 27 Mar. 2020].

Qi, S., Peng, H., and Zhang, Y. 2019. Energy intensity convergence in Belt and Road Initiative (BRI) Countries: What Role Does China-BRI Trade Play? *Journal of Cleaner Production*, 239, 118022.

Sahu, B.K. 2018. Wind energy developments and policies in china: A short review. *Renewable and Sustainable Energy Reviews*, 81, 1393–1405.

Schuman, S. and Lin, A. 2012. China's renewable energy law and its impact on renewable power in china: Progress, challenges and recommendations for improving implementation. *Energy Policy*, 51, 89–109.

Shen, W. 2017. Who Drives China's Renewable Energy Policies? Understanding the role of industrial corporations. *Environmental Development*, 21, 87–97.

Si, S., Lyu, M., Lin Lawell, C. -Y. C. and Chen, S. 2018. The effects of energy-related policies on energy consumption in china. *Energy Economics*, 76, 202–227.

Sinton, J. E., Stem, R. E., Aden, N. T., Levine, M. D., Dillavou, T. J., Fridley, D., Huang, Y. J., Lewis, J. I., Lin, J., McKane, A. T., Price, L. K., Wiser, R. H., Zhou, N. and Ku, J. Y. 2005. Evaluation of China's energy strategy options, lawrence berkeley national laboratory. *National Renewable Energy Laboratory*. https://eta.lbl.gov/publications/evaluation-chinas-energy-strategy. [Accessed 25 Sep. 2019].

Song, Y., Zhang, M. and Sun, R. 2019. Using a new aggregated indicator to evaluate china's energy security. *Energy Policy*, 132, 167–174.

Tianjie, M. 2016. China's 5 Year plan for energy, The Diplomat, 6 August 2016, https://thediplomat.com/2016/08/chinas-5-year-plan-for-energy/. [Accessed 09 Feb. 2020].

UNDP China 2012. Climate change and development in China: 3 Decades of UNDP Support, *United Nations Development Programme China.*

Wallerstein, I. 2010. Northeast Asia in the multipolar world-system. *Asian Perspective*, 34(4), 191–205.

Wang, J., Feng, L., and Tverberg, G. E. 2014. An analysis of China's coal supply and its impact on China's future economic growth. *Energy Policy*, 57, 542–551.

Wang, X. and Zhang, S. 2017. Exploring linkages among China's 2030 climate targets. *Climate Policy*, 17(4), 458–469.

Yatsui, T. 2017. China's energy policy and related issues towards 2020, Mitsui global strategic studies institute monthly report, April 2017, 1–4.

Zhang, P. and Wu, J. 2018. Performance-based or politic-related decomposition of environmental targets: A multilevel analysis in China. *Sustainability*, 10(10), 1–16.

Zhang, P., Wang, X., Zhang, N. and Wang, Y. 2019. China's energy intensity target allocation needs improvement! Lessons from the convergence analysis of energy intensity across Chinese provinces. *Journal of Cleaner Production*, 223, 610–619.

Zhao, Z., Zhang, S., Hubbard, B. and Yao, X. 2013. The emergence of the solar photovoltaic power industry in China. *Renewable and Sustainable Energy Reviews*, 21, 229–236.

Zhen, W., Mingming, L. and Haitao, G. 2017. A strategic path for the goal of clean and low-carbon energy in China. *Natural Gas Industry B*, 3, 305–311.

https://doi.org/10.1142/9781786349224_bmatter

Index

F

X

Y

Z

www.ingramcontent.com/pod-product-compliance
Lightning Source LLC
LaVergne TN
LVHW022306150926
848178LV00004B/74
* 9 7 8 1 7 8 6 3 4 9 2 1 7 *